15 MONTHS IN SOG

A Warrior's Tour

Thom Nicholson

PRESIDIO PRESS

BALLANTINE BOOKS • NEW YORK

A Presidio Press Book
Published by The Random House Publishing Group
Copyright © 1999 by Thomas P. Nicholson

Published in the United States by Presidio Press, an imprint of The Random House Publishing Group, a division of Random House, Inc., New York, and simultaneously in Canada by Random House of Canada Limited, Toronto.

Presidio Press and colophon are trademarks of Random House, Inc.

www.presidiopress.com

Library of Congress Catalog Card Number: 99-90094

ISBN 0-8041-1872-8

Manufactured in the United States of America

First Edition: July 1999

We didn't see or hear anything that seemed suspicious until we came to a wide stream, maybe a thousand yards from the little hill where the old fort was located. As the point squad started across, a single automatic weapon clattered a red stream of death at us. If the enemy gunner had been only a little more patient, he could have greased the whole bunch of us in the middle of the water. As it was, he killed one of the strikers and wounded another very slightly in the hand.

In an instant, nearly everyone on our side dropped to the ground and opened up. The VC over there must have been scared half to death, or shot to hell, or both; when we cautiously crossed the stream, the night remained quiet. By that time, the light from the star shells helped illuminate the ground in front of us, but the flickering light made every bush come alive, every tree seem a threatening, half-visible menace. Detailing a couple of men to carry the KIA, we moved as quickly as possible, using the trees and brush for cover, toward the hill. But it sounded as if the shooting had lost some of its previous intensity. . . .

To my dearest wife, Sandra,
without whose love, support, encouragement, and assistance,
it would never have happened

To my son, Tim, now serving in the army,
following in my footsteps, of whom I am very proud

To my old Marine buddy, Dan Guenther,
who said I should do it in case someone might be interested

Most of all, to those brave men who we lost there,
who will remain forever young in my memory

Contents

Map 1. Republic of Vietnam

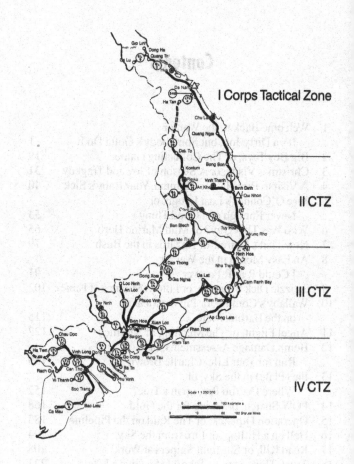

I Corps Tactical Zone

II CTZ

III CTZ

IV CTZ

Scale 1:1,250,000

0   40   80   100 kilometers

0   40   80   100 Statute Miles

Map 2. I Corps Detail

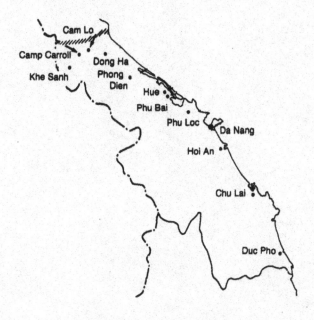

1

Welcome Back to the War
or
It's a Dirty Job, but Somebody's Gotta Do It

The air was sticky—humid and hot, just as I remembered—as I stepped off the big silver bird chartered from Pan Am. There was the same old familiar smell; rotted vegetation, sewage, and burned jet exhaust, all fighting for nauseous supremacy. "Hell," I grumbled to myself, "what'd you expect? This is Vietnam, you ain't been gone that long, trooper."

My thoughts returned to the scene at the airport in St. Louis. My young wife, our two little ones in her arms, all sobbing as I climbed on the plane that was to carry me away from all I loved. I doubt if the boys understood what was going on, they were so young, but the tears being shed by their mother had both of the youngsters wailing away. The sight is etched in my memory forever, all three of my loved ones' faces contorted with grief and streaked with tears. I thought my heart was going to break as well. I sat down next to a grandmotherly woman, who wisely looked away while I wiped the tears from my eyes and attempted to compose myself.

"Going off to Vietnam, son?" she finally asked. The polite question gave me a chance to talk, if I wanted to.

I didn't. So I just nodded and turned my face to the window, staring at the white clouds floating beneath the plane. She never said another word to me the rest of the trip to San Francisco. Bless her kind heart.

After a time, as the miles between my family and me increased, the lump in my throat diminished enough to allow me to suppress the almost physical pain of leaving. I was to spend the next fifteen months endeavoring to hold back the persistent nausea of separation. Any time I let it surface, the hurt was back, sharp and heart-wrenching as the day I left.

I inhaled again the distinctive odor of Vietnam. To this day, I can recall the smell; it has soaked into my memory like sewage on a sponge. I squinted in the harsh sunlight around the concrete apron of the massive air base at Cam Ranh Bay, Republic of South Vietnam. I was a young captain in the U.S. Army arriving for my second tour of duty. I was lean and mean, the product of a refresher course at the Jungle School in Panama, the Canal Zone, and anxious to find out what I would be doing the second time around. I had served the first tour as executive officer in a Special Forces A-team in the Central Highlands of South Vietnam. I had seen the elephant (been under enemy fire), as the old army saying went, and was ready to boss some men in combat, the most challenging assignment to which an army captain could aspire.

A continuous relay of F-4 Phantom fighter planes streaked off the hot concrete runway and into the harsh, blue sky, the jet engines' roar drowning out any hope of conversation, their sooty, black exhaust drifting away with the slight breeze. The 230 men with me, and a single female soldier, shuffled toward a concrete-block building with a red sign over the door: 2023D PORT AUTHORITY, WELCOME TO SOUTH VIETNAM. Underneath a smaller sign read: NEW ARRIVALS FOLLOW THE ARROWS TO CENTRAL PROCESSING.

Sweating in the fierce sun, my group of new arrivals obeyed like mindless automatons and entered a large room at the corner of the building. An air force sergeant, his nose red from sun or booze or both, stood beside a long, wooden table, and, as soon as the door shut behind the last man, launched into a droning monologue about in-processing, how to conduct yourself, etc., etc. I don't remember another word he said and doubt if he could have five minutes after he finished.

I glanced around at my fellow travelers, all innocent, new

fresh meat for the war. Just then, somewhere else within the building, two hundred plus lucky survivors were hearing their final out-briefing, probably given by another bored sergeant, before loading aboard the plane I'd just exited. They were about to depart for a long-awaited return to the real world, the land of the big PX, the good ole U.S.A. "Oh well," I consoled myself, "only 450 days to go, and counting."

I had decided to extend my tour an extra three months in country. That way, I could go directly to Fort Benning, Georgia, upon my return and enter the Infantry Officers Career Course (IOCC). If I got home too early, I might be sent elsewhere for a year of troop duty, and I wanted to get IOCC behind me before I was assigned to a permanent duty station. I hoped the extra three months would be safe and quiet. My wife threatened to kill me if I got greased away during my extension. Her tongue could be sharper than my Ranger knife. I figured I'd hear it in my grave if I made the mistake of dying in Vietnam.

Suddenly, the bored NCO's voice cut through my musings. "All air force personnel to Room A, army to Room B, and navy-Marines to Room D. Any others to Room C. There, you will be picked up by your respective replacement battalions and taken to temporary billets while awaiting in-country assignment."

I grabbed my duffel bag, stuffed to the brim with the essentials I needed, like socks, shorts, and a nifty Browning, 13-shot, 9mm pistol I was sneaking in country against regulations. I also had a custom-made hunting vest with extra pockets, my old jungle boots from the first tour, several sets of civvies for relaxing when away from the jungle, and a little ditty bag filled with toilet articles.

A couple of first-timers behind me were complaining to no one in particular that they already had orders assigning them to a unit.

"Don't believe it," I counseled, the weight of experience giving me authority to put in my two cents' worth. "Army Command at Saigon can reassign you to anyplace you may be needed, once you arrive in country. Your orders don't mean squat."

Inside Room B, a sweating sergeant first class (E-7) waited for our arrival, along with several pencil-pushing clerks from the replacement depot. We handed over our orders and were herded to army-green buses outside the door. At the repple depot, located at the far end of the runway, I wasted little time getting under a long, cool shower and into the cot assigned me, with its draped mosquito netting and clean sheets. If I ended up in the 4th Infantry Division, as my orders stated, I'd see little of either for a long time.

I reported to Officer Assignments early the next morning. To my delight, the personnel major in charge of infantry officers asked me if I wanted to go back to the 5th Special Forces Group. "They've had a few unforeseen casualties and are asking for SF-qualified officers."

"Yes, sir!" I was so elated, I nearly shouted. I had hoped to be able to transfer after six months with the 4th Division, but this was better yet. I felt I belonged in Special Forces; the 4th Infantry Division was for grunts, mud-pounders, jungle-humpers. I was Airborne Special Forces, a cut above such a mundane assignment. Besides, we got to wear the nifty green beret instead of the standard, army-issue, green baseball cap.

The next morning, well before sunrise, I was on the shuttle plane to Nha Trang, the headquarters of the 5th Special Forces Group, anxious to get my duty assignment for the coming year.

Was I ever disappointed. "S-5 with C Company, Pleiku," the gray-haired older major who was the personnel officer (assistant S-1) at group headquarters told me, as he passed me my assignment orders.

I left his office numb with disbelief. S-5 meant Civil Affairs (CA). Assignment to the C-team meant higher head-quarters. I'd be involved in building dispensaries and rice warehouses for villages of the local area of operations (AO) for C Company, the control headquarters for A-teams in the

Central Highlands. I would be a staff puke, as far from the guns as any "Saigon cowboy," the derogatory term we field soldiers used for the support people way to the rear. To my mind, Civil Affairs was a nothing job that involved the handling of a lot of Vietnamese money, dealing with local contractors, bribing the various district chiefs to ensure their cooperation, sending out action teams to survey potential CA projects. I wanted a combat assignment, damn it, as long as I was going to be in Vietnam. My first tour had been in a rather quiet district of central Vietnam. I had been the executive officer (XO) of the A-team assigned there, and the action had been sporadic. It made for a long and rather boring year. I wasn't back in Vietnam to pass out tongue depressors; I wanted to shoot it out with the bad guys.

I knew the executive officer of the 5th SF Group, Lt. Col. Dan Schungel; I'd served under him at Fort Carson, Colorado, in the 5th Mechanized Division, during 1963 and '64. Then, I'd been a gung-ho lieutenant commanding the heavy mortar platoon of his battalion, the 2/10th Mechanized Infantry. I'd worked hard for him, and I hoped he would remember that.

Screwing up my courage, I went to his office. He was happy to see me, and we made small talk for a few minutes. Finally, I made the plunge. "Sir, please help me get another assignment. I don't want anything to do with S-5 work. There must be something else available." I was hoping he would give me my own A-team to command, for old times' sake.

Lieutenant Colonel Schungel's eyes narrowed, and his displeasure was obvious. An assignment was an assignment, and a person was expected to fulfill it, to the very best of his ability. He looked over my shoulder, silent, thinking. Finally, old loyalties got the better of him, I guess. He jotted a note down on a slip of paper. "CCN called and asked for another captain just a few minutes ago. Tell the S-1 that you'll be going to them."

I grabbed the slip of paper. "I don't think I know what unit that is," I remarked. I did not remember hearing of a "CCN" the last time I was in country.

"MAC-SOG," Lieutenant Colonel Schungel grunted. "CCN is their northernmost operation, up at Da Nang. Stands for Command and Control North, which is a cover name. You'll get briefed about what the job is when you get there." He turned back to the stack of papers on his desk. "Good luck, Tiger." He smiled at me with his recruiting poster–perfect senior-officer look. "You'll need it."

I fairly waltzed out of the room. "MAC-SOG," as we called it, the Military Assistance Command's Studies and Observations Group. Super spook, black death dealers. I was going to the cream of the crop. Only the best of the SF got assigned to SOG. I couldn't have been more pleased with myself if I had just picked the winning trifecta at Churchill Downs.

The S-1 was nursing a sunburn on his high forehead, rubbing some white grease on it when I returned. He did not like me going over him to get reassigned. Screw him, the desk puck. What did I care?

"I'll book you out first thing tomorrow," he grumbled. "The CIA has a daily flight from Nha Trang to various places up north. We hitch rides with them all the time." He studied me with a slightly mystified expression the staff types reserve for a warrior, sort of a "What rock did you get raised under?" or "What happy dust you been sniffing lately?"

"Sir," I asked suddenly, "where is CCN anyway?" Of course, to me, it really didn't matter if the unit was stationed in hell.

The look he gave me now was one of abject scorn and maybe just a little pity. He must have thought I was out of my head from the heat. Volunteering for an assignment with a spook outfit and not having the faintest idea what it was all about.

"Da Nang, up in I Corps, Marble Mountain." He pronounced it "Eye Corps" in the standard military way. "CCN's just a cover name, so MAC-SOG isn't mentioned." I knew that, but didn't say anything. You could see his barely repressed shudder at the mere sound of the names. He was the epitome of the professional staff officer. Happy to be as far away from the guns as possible, immersed in his paperwork, and intrigued by the psychology of anyone who thought war meant combat rather than shuffling papers.

The flight from Nha Trang to Da Nang was as smooth as silk. We touched down on another ten-thousand-foot runway built by one of the numerous American construction firms brought over from the States. I briefly wondered how the government of South Vietnam would utilize what we were going to leave behind when the war was over. Little did I know.

Four other SF troopers and I walked through the airport building toward a rickety, old, half-size school bus that had seen better days. CCN was painted in foot-high, white letters on its side. The old bus was painted jet black and had a bullet hole in the left front windshield. The silver cracks radiating from the hole completely criss-crossed the window. Facing oncoming headlights, it would be a bitch to drive at night.

I couldn't believe my eyes. The escort officer that jumped off to meet us was Paul Potter, a wisecracking lieutenant I'd been friends with back in Fort Bragg, North Carolina, during the SF officers' course. We had a fast, backslapping reunion and piled on the bus with the others. He was short, stocky, and cocky.

"What are you doing here, you little hillbilly pissant?" I quizzed my friend, punching him on the shoulder.

"Not much lately, you rednecked peckerwood, sir," Paul replied, to show he respected my new rank. "I'm due to rotate back to Bragg in a week. For the past month, I've been doing gofer work for the XO back at CCN. You know, go fer this, go fer that. Before that, I was a launch officer at Forward Operational Base 2 (FOB2) up at Camp Eagle, where the 101st Airborne has an aviation brigade located."

"What do you launch?" I asked quite innocently.

"Jesus, Nick," he responded. "Don't you know what you've got yourself in for?"

"Nope," I replied. "All I know is that it was CCN or a staff job at C Company, Pleiku. I volunteered, sight unseen."

Paul gave me a look one would save for a slightly demented cousin. "CCN works across the border, in northeast Laos, north Cambodia, and some in southern North Vietnam. We monitor and interdict the Ho Chi Minh trail. Either with six-man recon teams or with larger strike force units, up to company-size in strength when the target justifies it. It's a top secret operation. You can't even tell your wife or family what you're up to. Our base camp is as secure as a bank vault, but we hang our ass out on a very short limb when we cross the border: no ID and it's kiss yourself good-bye if Charlie gets ahold of you."

"Do tell," I airily replied. "How did a loud-mouthed beer-head like you ever keep from spilling the beans?"

"No shit, Nick," he answered grimly, a stern expression on his round, cheery face. "It's hard time at the penal barracks at Fort Leavenworth if you talk out of turn. From the moment you get on the bus, you're under top secret security regulations. Don't say nuttin' to nobody if you want to stay out of trouble."

I shut up and contemplated Paul's words while we made the long drive on a well-worn macadam blacktop road that deteriorated into a well-rutted dirt road as soon as we got out of town, headed toward my new home for the next few months. Heavy, green-painted army and Marine trucks zipping past made the trip exciting by itself, not to mention my anticipation at getting to my new assignment.

We headed south out of Da Nang, following the curve of the bay. We drove past a Marine airfield and a navy evacuation hospital. Both seemed plenty busy. Then, we passed an immense scrapyard filled with destroyed tanks, wrecked trucks, and jeeps, as well as stripped-down shells of helicopters, which were stacked up like cordwood. I was fascinated by the debris of war piled up in the barbed wire–enclosed yard. Just before we reached a dark upthrust of rock, which had to be the Marble Mountain I had heard about in Nha Trang, we turned into another compound enclosed in barbed wire. Rolls of coiled razor wire and tangle-foot barbed wire were piled six feet high and just as deep. A sharp-looking SF sergeant and a stern-looking Vietnamese soldier checked our orders and then waved us through the front gate.

I smiled. In a big arch, from one side of the entrance gate to the other, in two-foot-high letters, was a sign: WE KILL FOR PEACE. Underneath was the camp symbol, painted on a blood-red shield: a white skull suspended below an open parachute, a green snake, tail protruding from one eye, head from the other, glared at the visitor. From the four corners of the shield, lightening bolts arced toward the skull. What a macho, grab-your-balls welcome sign, I thought to myself. My adrenaline got to flowing even faster.

The main camp of CCN was a four hundred- by six hundred-foot rectangular compound, surrounded by barbed wire, with twenty-foot-tall guard towers at each corner. There were only two exits, one to the road I'd just arrived on, and another to the beach of Da Nang Bay, behind the camp. Inside the compound, orderly rows of Quonset huts lined the rear half of the camp, and cavernous buildings made of corrugated metal and concrete the front. Paul said that the camp had room for 250 SF soldiers and 400 Montagnard mercenaries, whom we used as our strike troopers. An imposing concrete building smack in the center of the compound caught my eye.

"What's that?" I asked. I pointed to the big concrete structure as we pulled up to a prefabricated building with corrugated siding. A sign proclaiming the prefab HEADQUARTERS, CCN was fastened alongside the door.

"That's the TOC," Paul replied. "It's nearly impregnable. The walls are three-feet-thick concrete. Only one entrance, and that's always guarded."

The TOC (tactical operations center) was the hub of business for the camp. From inside its concrete protection, plans were made, teams dispatched, messages received, and operations orders given. Everything that happened started and ended there, first as a plan, then as an operation order, then as a briefing, and, after the operation, as an after-action report that went down to Saigon to MAC-SOG headquarters.

CCN was situated along the beach of Da Nang Bay. A person could walk out of the back gate right onto the sand of the beach, only twenty yards from the polluted waters of the bay. To swim in it was to risk mysterious diseases since the city of Da Nang, with its population of over 500,000, dumped its sewage directly into the blue-gray waters. Still, I swam there every chance I got and never was sick. Angels watch over fools and SF soldiers, I guess.

Paul dropped us off at the HQ building, and I reported in. The S-1 turned me over to the XO. Skinny, sported a big nose and pale eyes too close together, with a sallow complexion that accentuated his sunburned face and arms. He was additionally cursed with a pronounced receding chin. He had shifty eyes, as if he was trying to catch me staring at his nonexistent chin. He flipped through my record folder and turned me over to the camp commander, Lt. Col. Jack Warren, a hard-core soldier if there ever was one.

Lieutenant Colonel Warren was the toughest and most intimidating combat commander I ever served under. He lived to kill the bad guys, and worked hard at it. He also made sure we all kept pace with him. He could roast a young captain's ass pink with a few, well-chosen words if he did not have his ducks lined up properly. Colonel Warren was shorter than average, lean and wiry, but looked like he could win a triathlon. His flashing dark eyes bored right into you when he asked a question. He was no-nonsense and truly a professional soldier whose intensity made me a bit nervous, right from the get-go.

My new boss gave me a quick rundown about CCN and its

assigned mission. "I run a taut ship, Captain. Do your job, and do it right the first time. Then we'll get along. Fuck up, and you're gone, period. I need an assistant S-3, operations officer, for a while. When Captain Jones rotates end of February, I'll consider you as his replacement in command of my raider company."

My heart beat a little faster. Command of a raider company. That was hot stuff. I almost missed the rest of Lieutenant Colonel Warren's monologue.

"You'll be involved in distributing Italian Green, a secret project sent up from SOG HQ. You'll find out more about it at the S-3 briefing Major Toomey will give you. I'll send for him right now and get you started to work."

I was hoping for time to get some chow at the mess hall, but I decided to shut up, and saluted my way out of his office. I wanted to earn that company command.

Maj. Samuel Kanniu Toomey was a half-breed Hawaiian and looked more Indian than Caucasian. His hair was coal black, and his skin was darkened by the sun. Although stocky, there was a fluid grace to his every movement. He took me over to the tactical operations center, briefed me on my duties, and quickly put me to work writing operation orders and planning Italian Green (IG) inserts for coming recon missions.

"Italian Green" was a code name for booby-trapped munitions and supplies. We would find a supply cache somewhere along the Ho Chi Minh trail and, in the name of lowering enemy morale, sneak into it booby-trapped ammo that would explode on use. Somebody figured it would shorten the war if the Viet Cong lost confidence in his supplies. It was a dangerous operation, and I'm doubtful that it was very effective, but faithful to our orders, we did it.

I settled in and was soon deeply involved with my duties. On Friday morning, Major Toomey called me into his office. "We're having a going-away party this Saturday night, for all the guys rotating Stateside. I want to go for a while, so you'll have to stay here as duty officer. If I don't get too drunk, I'll relieve you before it breaks up and you can have a drink or two with everyone."

"Thanks, sir," I answered. "Lieutenant Potter is a friend of mine. I'd like a chance to hoist a few with him before he leaves."

Paul had gotten me assigned a room in his hootch, as we called the Quonset huts where we slept. "You're lucky," he told me. "The end room was just vacated last week. You'll have two walls with windows, and better ventilation than the other rooms. You'll be right next to me, you lucky shit. Just call if you have a good lookin' gal to share." I remembered from our last duty together that the little ell-tee had a king-size yearn for the females.

The officers' quarters—formally Bachelor Officers' Quarters or BOQ—were situated along the east fence of the compound. A drainage ditch ran between the company-grade building (for lieutenants and captains) and the field-grade quarters (for majors, the commanding officer, and VIPs). A narrow foot bridge had been built to cross over between the two buildings. Each hootch was a Quonset hut, built of corrugated steel to resemble a massive toilet paper tube cut in half lengthwise and dropped on a concrete slab. Each was about sixty feet long, with a center hallway and individual rooms, smaller ones for the company grade, larger ones for the field grade. Every room had a solid-wood door and heavy screens on the windows. The doors had a hasp lock which could only be secured from the inside. "Be sure to lock it at night when you turn in," Potter said. "Just in case any bad guys come around and try and fuck up your dreams." I nodded absently. The place was too well guarded.

Saturday night, I reported to the TOC and spent a quiet evening with the dozen other soldiers unlucky enough to have duty while the party was going on, a slam-banger, with booze flowing like rivers and the lucky departees being toasted again and again. True to his word, Major Toomey showed up about midnight, three-quarters looped, but able to navigate.

By the time I reached the officers' club, it was well after midnight, and a new moon did little to drive away the darkness. The party was too far along for me to catch up, so I spent a few minutes laughing at the antics of the mostly inebriated revelers and playing "Remember so-and-so?" with Paul. He was barely able to keep his head up, and, at the rate he was slugging down boilermakers, was due for a miserable morning, his last day before leaving to out-process at Nha Trang.

"Come on, Whiskey Puss," I said as I finally helped him to his feet. "Time for you to go in to deep defilade and get some rest." Only with my support did the singing and shouting short-timer walk out of the club and back to the BOQ. I steered my laughing, happy-go-lucky friend to his bunk and dumped him on it, clothes and all. I hadn't reached the hall before he was snoring like a buzz saw. Never giving a thought to waking him and telling him to lock it behind me, I quietly shut the door.

My room was next to his, so it wasn't long before I, too, was sound asleep, dreaming of happier days with my friends and family.

I jerked awake at the sound of an explosion and immediately pulled on my pants and boots. I thought a VC rocket had hit inside the compound. Then I heard running feet, and doors opening, followed by the distinctive *krump!* of Chinese Communist grenades exploding and the sounds of rifle fire. I backed up against the rear wall, crouching behind my small desk, and peered out of my corner window. What the hell was going on? I heard Paul's door slam open, the metallic bump of the grenade hitting the concrete floor, and the massive *krump!* of its exploding. Hot shrapnel tore through the wall and hit my bunk and desk, but I was shielded and remained unhurt. The handle to my door turned, and I held my breath.

Fortunately, the hasp lock held firm. The movement ceased, and a dark form darted out the front door toward the field-grade BOQ, across the little bridge.

Without thinking, I shot the running man in the back, and the slender body flopped down into the ditch between the two buildings. A second enemy darted out and made it to the door of the next building before I could shake the shock of the first kill from my muscles. I fired just as he entered the doorway and sensed I'd hit him but didn't see him fall. If he was hit, it was only a wound.

That sapper must have dropped his bag of grenades inside the hallway then continued out the far end, because there was a terrific explosion, and the back end of the building started burning. I had just bent over to drag my web belt and extra ammo magazines out from under the bed, so any shrapnel that flew through the open window missed me. The outside wall of the BOQ was shielded to window height by sandbags, so nothing penetrated lower than the sill. Peeking out, I saw no sign of movement, although bullets were flying in all directions. The guards on the other walls and men inside the compound had started to fight back against the attackers.

I crawled out of my window, the shredded wire screen no longer a barrier, and hid in the ditch. Sticking my head up and looking around, I saw movement and fired at it, until it faded into the shadows of the officers' latrine.

We officers couldn't, of course, share a potty with the enlisted soldiers. I never was really sure why, unless the army didn't want the ordinary soldier to know just how full of it most officers were. I watched, but nothing happened, so I assumed the VC had hidden behind the flimsy wooden building or run on, out of my sight. A couple of shaken officers peeked out the door of the junior BOQ and saw me.

"What the hell is happening?" one whispered. His face was white in the glow of the burning building across the ditch. By then, several buildings were on fire, adding to the visibility.

"Sappers inside the wire," I whispered back. "Get your ass down here before it gets shot off." I made room for them by pushing my kill to the side, a boy, surely less than eighteen, his eyes half open, a look of shock or pain evident in the firelight. Blood trickled out of his mouth, between clenched teeth. I never even noticed if he was dead, or merely dying. A fine, misting rain began, then steadily grew heavier, falling on my bare shoulders. We crouched in the ditch, water running past our ankles, and waited to see what would happen next.

A terrific volume of fire came from the direction of the front gate, and I wondered if we were under assault from that direction as well. In a few minutes, it grew quiet. The rain continued, and the sizzle of the dying fire and the shouting of American voices were all I could hear. What the two other soldiers and I said, if anything, I don't remember. I was shaking like a leaf; the initial rush of adrenaline had passed. The dim twilight of morning arrived before I even considered leaving the cover of my ditch or the company of my two companions.

The VC attackers had swept through the camp like a deadly whirlwind. Only ten of them were killed inside the walls. The front-gate guards shot twenty more as they tried to wiggle under the wire and cross the road to the safety of the rice fields beyond. During the next few hours, a dozen more died in the reaction sweeps by local Marines. We probably got most of the attackers, but they had killed twenty-eight Americans and forty-one of our Montagnard mercenaries. One of the dead Americans was Paul Potter, still in his bed, his blood soaking the thin, army-issue mattress. He had not awakened at the sound of the grenade landing beside his bed. It had been easy for the VC. His door had been unlocked, in part, thanks to me.

Hot tears of anger and frustration coursing down my cheeks, I stood beside my friend. If only I'd awakened him, I thought to myself. It's not fair. He spent a year here, and now with less than a week to go, he's dead. "Goddamn those VC bastards," I said. "I'll kill every motherfucking slope bastard I see, so help me God."

Lieutenant Mahorn came in the room with a camp medic. The young officer had spent the entire fight gathering wounded and taking them to the dispensary. Although covered with blood, it was all someone else's. His face was grimy and streaked with sweat or rain, or both. He'd been shot at by both sides and had pressed on, doing his best to save the injured. It was an act of supreme bravery. I found out later that his recommendation for an award had been turned down because of insufficient eyewitness accounts of his action, or some such crap. "Get out of here, sir. We'll take care of things now."

I wandered outside and leaned against the sandbagged wall of my hootch. One of the captains who worked in the S-2 shop rushed up. "There's somebody in the crapper," he breathlessly announced. He looked more scared than I was, and I didn't think that was possible.

"Jesus, Floyd," I snarled back at him. "Don't be shy. Just do your business and get on with it."

"No, that's not what I mean," he replied, looking with an ashen face at the bloodsoaked body of my friend being carried out on a bloody stretcher. "There're some gooks in the crapper. I heard 'em when I went over to use it. I got Sergeant Calloway to watch 'em while I went for help."

I grabbed my M-16. "Come on, let's smoke the bastards out. Now's our chance to get a POW and find out what the hell is going on."

We ran toward the wooden latrine where I'd seen the movement earlier. Just before we got there, gunfire broke out. Sergeant Calloway had gathered some of the men running around the camp, and they had opened up on the hidden VC.

"Stop firing. Cease fire," I screamed as we ran toward the men. A half dozen men were standing in a big semicircle around the latrine, firing through the wooden walls as fast as their M-16s could cycle.

Raggedly, the firing stopped, and we moved cautiously to the shattered door which had been punctured by dozens of bullet holes. I looked inside, my heart racing like a trip-hammer. What if one was still alive and blew my dumb head clean off? Too late. In the steel fifty-five-gallon barrels, placed under the holes cut in the wooden seat of the latrine, two dead VC lay huddled, shot to pieces, adding their blood and guts to the knee-deep filth in each barrel.

I looked down dispassionately at the disgusting sight in the latrine. "Damn. What a way to start my tour."

"Welcome back to the war, Captain," one of the NCOs said, spitting on the bloody, shit-covered kills lying in the foul-smelling barrels at his feet. "Now, I've gotta take them turds outta there and put 'em with the rest of the KIAs."

He looked up at me, a resigned grin on his sweaty and dirty face, his white teeth accentuating the grime. "It's a dirty job, but somebody's gotta do it."

We eventually pieced together what had happened. A half mile down the bay was the sleepy little Vietnamese fishing village of Xom Son Tui. For the previous three days, Viet Cong soldiers, well-trained combat sappers (specialists who handled explosives), and assault commandos had been infil-trating into the tiny village, a couple at a time. Threatening death to any resisters, they moved into the locals' homes.

Around midnight on that Saturday, they gathered at the edge of the bay, then stripped to shorts or tight breechcloths. Carrying only rifles, ammo, and high explosives, the nearly naked men entered the warm, dark waters of Da Nang Bay. The bay's shallow slope allowed them to wade fifty yards off the beach, invisible to anyone watching from land.

It took a couple of hours for the thirty-five to forty men to reach a spot opposite the CCN's barriers along the beach. They had targeted the slumbering compound for a long time.

At the signal, the infiltrators in the camp security company disposed of the loyal guards along the back fence. We found three the next day with their throats cut. Then the traitors opened the back gate for the invading enemy. The raiders fanned out along the back wall, from the north to the south. Upon command, they moved to their preassigned targets, silent and deadly.

Nobody knows for sure who fired the first shot, but it may have been the VC killing the guard in front of the TOC, where the door was locked as usual, but that didn't matter. Two sappers pushed in an air conditioner from its mount in an exhaust hole cut in the concrete wall of the windowless TOC then threw in a ten-pound charge of Russian plastic explosive. The resulting blast killed ten of the fifteen men inside and knocked out the rest.

Other sappers and commandos had then run through barracks, shooting and throwing grenades at the sleeping occupants. Some opened up on the revelers still at the party, pinning them inside, and keeping them out of the fight for the camp. The officer's club had a strict rule prohibiting weapons where drinking was allowed. If the VC had known that, they could have waltzed in and killed a couple of dozen more men.

2
Big Boy Toys
or
The Collecting Game

For the next few days, we worked furiously upgrading our defenses, halfway expecting the VC to hit us again. The frenzy of activity helped me get through the shock and pain of Paul's death. I spent every working minute getting settled into my new job as well as working on the new camp defenses laid out by Lieutenant Colonel Warren. The busy days passed, and Charlie didn't reappear, so we slowly reverted back into a more routine life in a war zone.

Everyone had lost friends during the attack, and our morale was low. The destroyed buildings were quickly replaced, and the torn scrap that was once home to somebody was taken down the road to the dump, the pain of our losses subsided, and life went on. Several investigators came up from MAC-SOG headquarters in Saigon, and I thought for sure our commander would be relieved, but nothing happened. Nobody said much about the celebration or the fact that so many of us were potted before and during the assault. In truth, it probably didn't have much impact on the outcome of the action; the cluster of men at the party took only two casualties, which was probably a lot fewer than would have been the case if everyone had been in bed. Most of the men who were killed by the raiders had been asleep in their rooms when they died.

We cleaned out the ranks of the security company, firing anyone hired in the last three months. Several of the guard company soldiers were already gone. They had slipped away with the escaping VC or deserted to avoid being arrested and questioned. I know I wouldn't have wanted to be in their shoes, the way those of us who survived the attack felt about traitors in our midst.

The Wednesday after the raid, the 5th Group chaplain came up from Nha Trang and held a memorial service. I was still pretty shook-up over the loss of Paul, and it was a sad, melancholy day. The army has a standard setup for memorial services. Empty boots, a pair for each lost soldier, are lined up in front of a white linen–covered table, upon which, on this day, lay twenty-eight green berets. God, it was a gut-wrenching occasion. More than once, I had to drop my head to inconspicuously wipe away tears. I didn't want to appear soft in front of the others at the service, but I couldn't keep the tears from spilling out.

I regret to this day that I didn't ask to go back to the States as the army escort officer with Paul's body, but the idea never entered my mind until it was too late.

Everyone stayed as busy as possible, training new replacements, practicing defensive measures in case of another raid, doing weapons qualifications, and so on. Personally, I doubted if we'd ever be hit again; the VC didn't go where they were expected. But we sure as hell were ready for them from then on. Actually, we and the Marines from a nearby unit, the 3d Amtrac Battalion, had killed almost all of those involved. The mud Marines went after those who made it out of the camp and hunted them down in the brush for the next couple of weeks.

My grief for my friend lost its intensity in training and guard duty, which were added to my normal responsibilities as the assistant S-3. The CO found out I had an engineering degree from college and ordered me to design and supervise the construction of a sandbagged guard post on top of the TOC, where guards could survive any ground attack. We placed a double row of razor wire completely around the building. Now, the only way inside was a path from the gate in the wire to the steel door. Too late, we had learned how dangerous it was to be trapped in the windowless building. We also bolted the air conditioner to its frame to prevent anyone from pushing it in.

Protected by the walls of his office, Major Toomey had suffered little from the sapper bomb that almost destroyed the building. Only his hearing was temporarily damaged, even though he'd been knocked unconscious by the explosion. He was tough and soon was back at work, running the TOC and planning operations.

Besides the wounded and the dead, we had one other loss, our XO. Incredible as it seems, he had slept through the attack. He had taken on a snootful of booze at the party and had passed out on his bunk at the far end of the field-grade BOQ. If he'd lived at the east end of the building, he would have burned to death in the fire that consumed half of the building.

I didn't see it, but I heard that he staggered out of his room the next morning, hungover, shirtless, and barefoot, gaping in amazement. The story got out that he bitterly complained that he had not been awakened by anyone during the commotion of the fight. All day, he ran around, giving orders and trying desperately to be useful and noticed by everyone. Before long, he was hearing whispers and laughter behind his back everywhere he went.

His paranoia grew more pronounced. He seemed determined to sneak up on a person, to catch the unfortunate fellow laughing at him. His job performance deteriorated, and before long, he was gone, officially a victim of "combat fatigue." To this day, he probably wishes he had died in the attack rather than live with the embarrassing truth he has had to carry as part of his personal baggage.

Major Toomey called me into his office early the next week. "You graduated from SF scuba school, didn't you, Nick?"

"Yes, sir," I replied. "Took my A-team through just last year. That was a bitchin' three weeks, but I'm qualified."

Major Toomey nodded. "Good, 'cause we've been tasked by XXIV Corps to recover some stiffs from a chopper that went down yesterday in the bay." XXIV Corps was the highest army command in I Corps of South Vietnam, sharing the fighting in South Vietnam's northernmost region with the III Marine Amphibious Force.

Major Toomey continued. "Seems a unit up north was flying a couple of jeep-wreck victims back to the morgue when their Huey lost hydraulics and splashed into the bay. Pilot and crew escaped, but they want us to get the bodies out and attach a line to the chopper for salvage if possible. See if you can find a couple of others who're scuba qualified and take the boat out to the navy lighter anchored over the crash site." Major Toomey pointed on a map opened on his desk. The spot was about two miles out in the bay.

"No problem, sir." I was elated at the prospect of diving again. I had not expected to get a chance to do it while in Vietnam. "Where do I get some gear?"

"We've got the latest stuff in supply," he replied. "Ask Sergeant White to fix you up. I told him you'd be needin' it."

Sgt. Rosco White's skin was as black as obsidian, and his smile as warm as the hot Georgia sunshine of his youth. He was a large man and probably had trouble keeping his weight within the standards. I'd already met him and been charmed by his down-home personality. He was a fine human being and one hell of a Scrabble player. In fact, he was the best I ever saw. He loved to get into a game with officers, who undoubtedly thought they could easily handle a dirt-poor son of north Georgia, then beat the pants off them while lightening their wallets. Honest to God, he used to spend his free time reading the dictionary. I had learned an expensive lesson the hard way a couple of weeks earlier and thereafter would play him only for fun. I did my best, though, to get on and stay on his good side. I'd learned a long time before that a friendly supply sergeant was a valuable asset for a young officer. I showed up at the supply shed with the two NCOs who volunteered to dive with me.

"Sergeant White," I hollered from the counter at the entrance to his cavernous "house of plenty."

"Back here. Whatcha want?"

"I need to use the scuba gear. I'm going diving for Major Toomey. Can you fix us up?" White was busy ordering the stock of exotic and mundane items we needed. One of the supply sheds had burned during the raid, and much was lost in the fire. He came out of his little office and jerked his chin at the pile of diving gear sitting in the corner.

"All ready for you, Captain. Just sign right here." He gave me the supply requisition sheet which showed I had taken responsibility for the gear.

I hoisted the heavy yellow tank of air on my back and breathed through the rubber mouthpiece, checking the air.

"Don't worry, Cap'n," White remarked. "I just filled 'em. I wouldn't want any off'zer who can play Scrabble as good as you to run out fifty feet down."

"I guess it's nice to know you think I'm good for something, Rosco."

White smiled at me mischievously. "The S-3 said you'd be needin' the boat as well. Well, here're the keys fer it. Now y'all be careful, and don't damage my baby."

"Don't sweat it, Sarge," I drawled. "I'll take good care of your baby."

Sergeant White had scrounged the boat from some Harbor Command swabbies, and it was his pride and joy. I happened to look over in the corner, at a pile of Russian AK-47s found after the raid. "Better let me have a couple of the AKs for trade bait. We're headed out to a navy salvage ship. The sailors may be in a souvenir mood."

"Here." White reached under his counter. "Take a couple of VC flags I had made. They always bring top dollar with the navy."

"What's this stuff?"

"Chicken blood. Makes the flag worth more if it has VC blood all over it."

"Hell, Sergeant, nobody's gonna fall for that."

"Take my word fer it. They wanta believe. Just be serious when you explain the tragic cost of getting this symbol from the desperate enemy hordes."

Before noon, sergeants Jones and Wiznowski and myself were alongside the navy barge. My volunteer assistants were both young NCOs from opposite sides of the U.S.A., yet they could have been brothers: brown hair, brown eyes, well-built, walking advertisements for the American way of life. We climbed on board the navy barge and met the CO, a baby-faced navy lieutenant, a friendly swabbie, what we army types call navy folks. He gave us a quick rundown of the situation. I suppose because we were different from most of the military types he came in contact with, he went out of his way to be pleasant. Just about all the other service members liked Special Forces. Whether it was our green berets, our dynamic personalities, or our unquestioned good looks, I don't know.

"The best we can determine," he said, "the chopper went down right around here. I suggest you let one of my men tow you in your boat while you three fan out and search for the wreckage."

Soon, the three of us were in the warm water, holding to fifty-foot towropes while the navy slowly cruised a simple up-and-down search pattern. It wasn't long before Sergeant Jones spotted the wreckage by a bluff of silt-covered coral. It was down about forty feet, the boom broken off from the body of the aircraft. Several small sharks were swimming around, perhaps drawn by the smell of the bodies. The sharks pulled back as we moved in, circling just at the limit of our vision. I kept a wary eye for their bigger brothers.

We anchored the motor boat and dove down to the wreckage. The cargo doors were open, revealing the two dark rubber body bags strapped down in the passenger compartment. We unstrapped them carefully. The occupants inside were limp and difficult to maneuver since rigor mortis had passed. I sent Jones and Sergeant Wizzer up with one body between them. While they were gone, I swam into the front cockpit.

There, hanging on the back of his seat, was the pilot's web gear and, strapped on the belt, a chrome-plated, two-inch-barrel Smith & Wesson .38 revolver gleamed in the filtered sunlight. It was beautiful. "Finders keepers, losers weepers," I mumbled to myself. In a flash, I had it in my swimsuit, and as soon as the two NCOs came back for the second cadaver, I hooked up the towline and swam up to the boat above me.

Stashing the pistol in my gear, I took one of the AK-47 rifles and climbed back on the barge. Showing the much-in-demand trophy, I asked the navy lieutenant, "Got a nice AK-47 here. What'll you give me for it?"

Boy oh boy, did his eyes bug out. You could see the naked desire for the souvenir gleaming in his eyes; I suppose all his dumpy boat did was chug around Da Nang Bay, policing up trash, or something. His eyes swept around the deck. He was thinking furiously. "How about ten gallons of ice cream?"

"Nope, not enough."

"How about the ice cream and the latest six copies of *Playboy* magazine?"

"Well, we're gettin' there. What else?"

"What else you want?"

I looked around. "I'll take that portable generator," I said, pointing at the little two-and-a-half-horsepower, gasoline-powered unit sitting on the fantail. Portable generators were wonderful backups to the big truck-mounted ones used to serve the camp's electrical needs. The TOC would welcome a portable unit if the big boy went out during a critical phase of a cross-border operation. "And, those binoculars." I pointed at the weather-worn case holding a pair of 10x50 navy binoculars hanging from a hook by the bridge door. I could use those myself, if and when I got into the field.

The boat driver was a little reluctant, but when I added the blood-spattered Viet Cong flag, which I swore was taken at great cost in a suicide attack, he quickly agreed to the deal. Swiftly, we transferred the goodies to our little boat and departed, in case our navy friends came down with a case of buyer's remorse. The boat skipper could always get the equipment replaced; in the whole of South Vietnam, the magic phrase was "combat loss." No matter how badly you screwed up and lost something, if you could classify it as combat loss, the supply system made it up. I imagine the report on the lieutenant's binocs and the generator simply read, "Combat loss while on patrol in the Bay of Da Nang."

Sergeant White's eyes danced with a true scrounger's appreciation when I showed him the generator. He was aware of the myriad uses for a portable, gas-powered generator. Then I flashed the pistol, now shining in the afternoon sun.

"Oh, *Dai Uy* (Vietnamese for captain, pronounced Die We), I gotta have that pistol. Whata' ya want fer it?"

"Well," I said, a little reluctantly, since I hadn't planned on giving it up. "Make me an offer."

White went into his supply room and came out with a brand new M-16A3 rifle, with the short barrel and collapsing stock. The weapon was little more than half as long as a regular M-16 rifle. To a gunslinger, it was a thing of beauty. He lay it on the countertop and waited for my response.

I wanted that rifle, but tried not to show it. "What else you got?" I asked, not wanting to appear too easy.

"How 'bout these here test grenades?" White went back, deeper, into his inner sanctum and emerged with a small wooden crate. He carefully opened the box and set it on the counter. Inside were the new, golf ball–size M-44 fragmentation grenades. They were nifty. A person could carry a dozen or more on patrol, as opposed to only four of the regular-size M-2 or M-26 grenades. "Gettin' close," I countered. "How about the scuba gear I used today?"

"Deal," White fairly shouted. He grabbed the pistol and

rubbed its shiny barrel on his sleeve, grinning in satisfaction. He'd had a warehouse burn down in the midnight raid, so he was wheeling and dealing all over, writing everything off as combat loss. It had to be the best time in his supply sergeant's life.

The trip to the underwater grave of the chopper turned out to be extremely profitable for me and left my supply sergeant friend happy as well. All in all, a good day's work. And the NCOs had fresh ice cream for supper. I was making friends and influencing folks right and left.

I had brought with me from the States a beautifully made Buck Company bowie knife. It was already strapped upside down on the left side of my web gear suspender, ready for quick use. I added the navy binocs to my gear and hung my new minirifle above my bunk. My toys were beginning to add up.

Thanksgiving Day rolled around, and, wouldn't you know it, my name came up on the Italian Green duty roster. If any recon teams ran across a cache of North Vietnamese ammunition on that day, I would be the officer in charge of a team that would fly out to the site and surreptitiously insert the booby-trapped munitions into the enemy cache. I crossed my fingers that no sites would be found; I was looking forward to the turkey dinner planned at the mess hall.

I wasn't too keen on the Italian Green idea from the first. I can admit it would be detrimental to the enemy's morale to be shooting rockets or mortar rounds at the Yankees and have one go off in his face. The thing that bothered me was that we didn't destroy the other ammo at the cache site, allowing who knows how many thousands of rounds of good ammo to continue down the Ho Chi Minh trail. If the shell fired just before the one that was bobby-trapped hit some unlucky soldier on his head, blowing him to smithereens, he wouldn't give a shit for the morale factor caused by the Italian Green round that was going to blow away the VC gunner with the next shot.

However, the orders had come up from HQ in Saigon, so

every time we found an unmanned cache, we slipped in a few IG rounds. We would chopper out to the site, sneak up, slip the stuff in, and chopper out as fast as we could. It was dangerous work, since, usually, where there were caches, North Vietnamese Army (NVA) soldiers were close by.

About three, just before the mess hall was due to open, wouldn't you know it, Recon Team Sidewinder called in a spot report. They'd run across an NVA cache just across the Laotian border, about fifty miles from Da Nang. An SVN-SOG chopper was called in and, grumbling at my bad luck, I started to put my gear on.

"What's the matter, Nick?" Major Toomey walked out of his office.

"I've gotta run an IG insert, dammit. I'll miss Thanksgiving chow, sure as shootin'."

"Hell," Major Toomey responded after a moment's thought. "I don't like turkey all that much, anyway." He rubbed his big hands together. "I'll make the run, and you get some grub. I haven't gone out on an IG insert yet. It should be fun."

"You certain?" I asked. I hated to crap out on the S-3. After all, it was my job, not his. I sure did want some of that turkey though.

"No problem." He smiled conspiratorially. "Just don't say anything to the CO. I'll be back inside an hour." He turned back to his office, and came out momentarily, putting on his web gear. "Here," he said to me, handing me his nifty 7.65mm Beretta automatic. "Hold this for me until I return. I don't want to leave it in my office, and I'm not going to take it to the BOQ, so the old man doesn't see me and nix my going."

The burly major ran out to the chopper pad where a black H-34 Kingbee chopper flown by an SVN pilot assigned to the SOG program was waiting, its big, three-blade rotor slowly spinning. I could see the other six members of the insert team loading the boxes of sabotaged 82mm mortar ammunition into the ship. Major Toomey jumped on board, and the Vietnamese crew chief slammed the door shut.

With a mighty roar of its engine, the twenty-year-old helicopter left the pad and soon was out of sight, flying west toward the border. I clipped Major Toomey's little pistol on my belt and walked over to the mess hall.

I was just finishing the pumpkin pie when one of the tactical operation center duty NCOs ran into the mess hall and whispered in the CO's ear. He quickly pushed aside his plate and got up, motioning me to follow him. "What's up, sir?" I asked as we hurried toward the TOC.

Lieutenant Colonel Warren tersely answered: "The IG insert chopper was shot down en route to the target. Just got the word. Everything's on fire, and the escort choppers don't see any sign of survivors. Who's the team leader?"

With a heavy heart, I told him. His glance would have melted snow, and he started to ream my butt for letting the S-3 go out, but after I explained that Major Toomey had asked to go, he quieted down. I explained what had happened, and he mellowed a little.

"You're one lucky boy, son. Just be grateful you weren't killed instead of Sam Toomey."

I've lived for years with the knowledge that because of my desire for turkey, another man died. It's a grim burden, and one I'll never shake.

I treasured Major Toomey's nifty little pistol, safeguarding it as the major requested. But we never were able to get into the crash site because of the high concentration of antiaircraft guns in the area. Major Toomey and the team were carried as missing in action for years afterward.

One night about a week later, while getting ready to go on guard duty, one of the young sergeants just arrived from the States saw me with my new rifle, new binoculars, new knife, packet of golf-ball grenades clipped to my belt, little automatic pistol, and the 9mm Browning automatic that I'd brought from home. That gave me a big pistol at my belt and a little one under my arm.

"Boy, *Dai Uy*," he remarked enviously. "You sure do have a lot of nice toys."

"Yeah," I answered with only partially veiled sarcasm, as I knew what the true price in lives and misery had been. "Didn't cost me hardly a thing, either."

3

Christmas Visits
or
A Season of Joy and Tragedy

Time passed, everyday activities consumed our thoughts, new things happened, memories were gradually softened by daily reality, and suddenly, it was December. I stayed pretty busy. For one thing, I had to assume the S-3 duties until a new major arrived from the replacement pool in Nha Trang. That suited me just fine: It was good experience, and I did not want to stray too far from my desk inside the TOC just then. It was probably just my imagination, but I had sensed an unspoken rebuke from Lieutenant Colonel Warren when I explained why Major Toomey was on the downed chopper instead of me.

The Old Man couldn't come right out and say, "Why weren't you killed instead of my operations officer?" But the belief that he thought it nagged at me. It was unfair to the Old Man, but I couldn't shake the tension whenever I was around him. To the day he left the unit, I tried to avoid being alone with him any more than my duty made absolutely necessary.

Our new S-3, Major Skelton, flew in from Nha Trang a couple of weeks before Christmas. He was an old-time Special Forces officer, his weather-beaten face lean and bronzed with the years of outdoor activities any good SF soldier longs to live. He had been working over in Thailand with the 46th Company, and was elated to be back in the action. I spent the next few days bringing him up to speed on TOC operations. He caught on fast and soon had the TOC humming productively. The month was going by quickly, and operations across the border continued at a heavy pace. We lost a Montagnard, or Yard, soldier now and then, but American losses for the month were zero. Maybe the gods of war were giving us a breather from the shocks of August through November.

The middle of the month, my brother Bill, a platoon leader in the 1st Air Cavalry Division, got a five-day in-country R & R (rest and recuperation). He wrote that he was flying up from Saigon, where his unit was stationed, to pay me a visit.

On the day of his arrival, I proudly drove my new jeep to the Da Nang airfield to pick him up. I'd just won it in a poker game from a reckless captain in the recon company who had tried to bluff into my full house, aces high. The jeep had originally belonged to some Army Advisory Command NCO, who had sold it to an officer in CCN when he rotated back to the States. The officer had in turn sold it to my card-playing friend when he rotated. Now, it was mine. The jeep had been repainted and renumbered by one of the easily bribed maintenance soldiers over at the vehicle depot. It had new papers, and wouldn't be confiscated unless I was involved in some traffic accident, when the serial number on the frame would be checked and found to be different than the one on the papers I carried. So I drove more carefully in Vietnam than I do in the States; I dared not be stopped for any traffic violations.

In terms of support equipment, CCN was a lean organization. The TO&E (Table of Organization and Equipment) called for six jeeps, a couple of $2^1/2$-ton trucks for the S-4 shop, and a single $3/4$-ton for the S-2 and S-3 to share. Just those vehicles for a camp that was home for two hundred of the most resourceful and larcenous Special Forces soldiers ever assembled in one place.

The last time I counted, there were over a hundred personal-use jeeps, stolen, without prejudice, from every branch of the service, the Vietnamese, the Koreans, the Germans, civilian contractors, the Red Cross, and any other organization that had vehicles. We also had four $2^1/2$-ton trucks, a half dozen $3/4$-tons, the old school bus that we used to pick up replacements, and a staff car for the CO that had been stolen from an air force motor park in Saigon then smuggled up to Da Nang, over five hundred miles to the north. The story was that we had used the air force to ship the stolen car to us. It made us all very proud to be so devilishly clever.

All the vehicles were painted flat black rather than the standard army olive drab. When everyone was in camp, our parking lots were a wondrous thing to behold. Whenever big brass was due in to attend briefings or such, the stream of vehicles headed out the gate to preselected hiding spots created traffic that looked like quitting time on an LA freeway.

Bill was a sight for homesick eyes to see. He had been in country six months by then, stationed with the 1st Air Cavalry Division outside Saigon. He was lean as rawhide and brown as a berry. We looked like brothers, except that I had dark hair, and he had fair; the hot Vietnamese sun had bleached his blond hair even lighter. Since we were both average height, and built like the former football players we were, we stood out in the crowd of newly arriving Marines and Vietnamese soldiers deplaning with him. At least I thought so. As we walked out of the terminal together, I couldn't help but think there wasn't a better looking pair of studs outside Hollywood. He showed a strained nonchalance when he saw my jeep. "I'm in the field so much I don't need one," he casually informed me. Still, he was envious, I just knew it. Besides, I still had lots more goodies to impress him with back at camp.

Bill's eyes really bugged out when he saw my home. He had come out of the brush, where a hot beer was a treat. I had a single room, clean linen, and a hootch gal to clean my room, wash and iron my jungle fatigues, and polish my boots. The mess hall was air-conditioned, and movies were shown there every night. My office in the TOC was cooled as well. On a normal day, the hottest I got was walking from the TOC to the mess hall for chow.

I still had to work my twelve-hour shift that day while Bill slept late in the VIP room I got for him, next door to my hootch. After weeks in the brush with his unit, the soft bed and clean sheets must have been a welcome luxury. Every day, he'd eat and swim at the beach until I got off duty. Then, I took him around Da Nang and to the numerous officers' clubs, where he downed many a cool brew and ogled the nurses. I almost had to hog-tie and throw him on the plane when it was time for him to return to his unit. He was definitely ready to become a CCN volunteer. I watched his plane rise off the hot concrete and disappear into the deepening dusk of early evening. The dark thought that we might not see each other again, back home at the end of our tours, flitted across my mind. Shaking the unwelcome image away like a pesky fly, I drove back alone, deep in rumination.

As it happened, Bill arrived back at 1st Air Cavalry too late at night to be choppered out to his unit, so he stayed over at division HQ. Early the next morning, an NVA rocket hit the bunker where some of his unit were sleeping, and a dozen men were killed or wounded. If it hadn't been for his visit to me, he might have been with them. It made the guilt I was carrying over Major Toomey's death a little more tolerable.

The Christmas season was fast approaching. Following custom, we anticipated that the idiots running the war would order a holiday stand-down, and we'd be restricted from operations for a few days. That would give the NVA and the VC a chance to rest and refit so they would be harder to handle afterward. But the cease-fire made good headlines back home for the politicians.

I tempered my natural loneliness during that special season with the memories of happier times surrounded by my family at other Christmas celebrations.

Just before I had left the States, my wife, sons, and I visited my folks. The last night, while we were out seeing friends, my mom and dad put up a Christmas tree and decorated their home just as if it were Christmas. We walked in to songs of the season and presents all around.

"We'll just celebrate a little earlier this year," my mother said, tears glistening in her warm, brown eyes. It was so sad, but so thoughtful and loving. I knew that reliving that joyous evening would help me get through the difficult time away from home and family. Most of the presents they gave me were for use after I returned, not to take with me to Vietnam. It was meant to be that way, a good omen, and was their way of giving me confidence that I would survive the tour.

My time overseas was immensely more bearable because of the love and concern of my family. It made the hard times easier and the lonely times bearable. I pity those who faced the agonizing separation and loneliness of the war without the love of a family to sustain them. My wife wrote me nearly every day, and the rest of my extended family wrote regularly. Except for the insignificant bit of time involved in trying to answer all the letters, it was a great morale booster.

The day before Christmas, the S-1 stood up in the morning briefing and asked for volunteers to guard church services for the local Vietnamese at midnight Mass. I was quick to add my hand to the many going up. The VC had put out the word not to have services in the village church, or it would be attacked. The old priest, a crusty Vietnamese named Father Hoa, wasn't having any of that crap. He was plowing ahead full steam with his plans. All he wanted from us was enough armed men to keep the bad guys away. One of the things I hated most about the VC was their cruelty to their own people. It was bad enough that we Americans were killing Vietnamese; after all, that was what we were there for, to bomb them in groups or to shoot them one at a time. But it sure frosted my ass that they did it to each other in the name of freedom, Communist style.

Christmas Eve, I was posted just outside the door of the simple church, along with a bunch of my buddies, armed to the teeth, just hoping some overzealous VC would show his face. The opinionated old priest wouldn't let any of us inside if we were armed, but from where I was, I had an unobstructed view of the services.

I'll never forget the sweet little girls, dressed in their best clothing, usually white *ao dais* (a combination of long pants worn beneath a long shirt, slit to the waist) singing "Silent Night" in Vietnamese as they marched into the church. The candles held by the adults cast a warm, yellow glow on their smiling, innocent faces. They hadn't been corrupted yet by the war, and I hoped that they hadn't experienced too much horror and filth so early in their lives. My thoughts returned to my family and my little boys, and the familiar old lump worked its way back up into my throat.

The service went off without a hitch, and while we kept a close watch on the old priest and his church, we never saw any attempt to mess with him by the VC. Good thing, too; he was a very popular man.

Lt. Col. Martha Raye, the movie star, showed up right after Christmas. Colonel Maggie, as we called her, was touring Vietnam for the USO, and stopped by the compound while she was in the area. Maggie Raye was as wonderful, brave, and compassionate a human being as I've ever met. She was down-home, a square shooter, in spite of being a famous Hollywood comedienne. She was also a qualified nurse and pitched in more than once when visiting a unit that had casualties. The Special Forces had fallen in love with her and her way of showing up at the out-of-the-way places where SF troopers worked. We never were hesitant about showering her with affection, and Colonel Maggie returned our good feeling in kind with every bit of her great big heart. She actually was a reserve lieutenant colonel in the Army Nurse Corps. But she had the heart of a four-star general.

Maggie always knew several of us from earlier USO tours or from visits to her home in LA because she had extended an open invitation to SF guys passing through the West Coast to stay awhile. So we rolled out the red carpet and welcomed her as an old friend to visit with us. She was supposed to visit for just a couple of days, but as circumstances would have it, she stayed even longer.

Colonel Maggie drank vodka straight, and by gosh, could she do it right. She drank many a big rugged SF trooper under the table and called out in her raucous and hearty voice for the next victim to step up. Her presence made the upcoming New Year's celebration one to anticipate.

The day before New Year's, we were tasked by HQ MAC-SOG to put out a reaction force at a key intersection of the Ho Chi Minh trail to be ready to strike in case the NVA started moving supplies the minute the holiday cease-fire ended. B Company, the reaction standby unit, packed up and was choppered out by noon.

They were back by four, shot to hell and back. I debriefed the senior surviving American, Lt. Will Turin. "They were all over us as soon as we landed," he said as he struggled to maintain his composure. "Captain Jones was hit almost as soon as he dropped off the chopper. Lieutenant Jefferson and Sergeant Proudlock dragged him to a pile of brush next to the LZ (landing zone). The NVA had the LZ completely covered by fire."

Lieutenant Turin paused to take a deep breath. He was streaked with sweat, and he kept licking his dry lips. His young face was drained of blood and pinched tight in nervous reaction to the events he'd just experienced. His hands twitched, and his voice was higher pitched than usual. "My chopper touched down only long enough to pick up three of the men from the first lift. There's six still out there. Captain Jones, Jefferson, Proudlock, and Lieutenant Nham of the VNSF, and two Yards."

He paused and wiped the sweat from his camouflaged brow, smearing the black and green grease all over his hand. "We circled and called for twenty minutes, but never got a reply. Finally, we ran low on fuel and returned to base." He looked up with anguish all over his face. "Jesus, Captain, we've got to go back. They may still be alive. We've gotta get 'em."

"Don't worry, Will. The CO is sending out a scout team

right now. They'll drop in a few klicks (kilometers) from the LZ and work their way in close. If they find anything, we'll send in a strike force ASAP."

Just before dark, the word came over the radio. The relief team had sneaked up to the hot LZ. No sign of NVA, but the six dead CCN troopers were still where they fell. The NVA hadn't yet stripped or mutilated the bodies, which was really weird. Their usual tactic was to behead dead SF soldiers so they could show the grisly trophies to local villagers. They also took anything of value from the bodies. I suppose the constant air cover over the ambush site had scared them off. The team brought the dead soldiers back with them on the extraction chopper.

Colonel Warren had the entire command out at the tarmac when the Huey arrived. Two hundred saddened American soldiers stood at solemn attention as the six limp bodies were lifted off the chopper, which then hammered aloft and, dipping its nose into the wind like a bow of respect, roared away. For a moment, the living stood in silence. Colonel Warren gave an impassioned speech about danger, bravery, and sacrifice, and we then slowly filed by our dead comrades and returned to our duties, soberly reflecting on what we saw. The still faces and sightless eyes of our dead comrades watched us as we filed past. They were beyond our understanding now, taking one last look at the living before going into the dark confines of their metal caskets for the long trip home and the final, sad good-bye from their loves ones.

Captain Jones and Sergeant Proudlock had been very popular with everyone. They had a lot of friends mourning them that evening. Colonel Maggie stayed an extra day, being there to talk, drinking with those who wanted company, consoling saddened friends. She was just great. I am privileged to have had her for a friend.

That night, I sat at my desk, writing a letter home to my wife. I was as sorrowful as any of the others, but I also was carefully containing excited feelings. The CO had given me command of the late Captain Jones's company. I was now the commanding officer of B Company, the raider company for CCN. The tragedy brought with it a gift for me. The command of a combat unit in the best and fightin'est organization that crummy war had. I would gratefully give it up to have Jones and the others back, but we were at war, and such things happened. As foolish and, yes, as callous as it may seem, I felt a rush of excitement as I viewed the coming new year.

4

A Visit to Bon Hai
or
Momma, Your Baby's Sick

Happy New Year, 1969. Now that I was a company commander, rather than just an assistant staff officer, I sensed a subtle change in the CO's attitude toward me. Perhaps I was back in the good graces of Colonel Warren. So, wouldn't you know it? He got transferred. A new boss, Lieutenant Colonel Isler, came on board. We discovered we shared a love of football, and while I wasn't down-home comfortable with him, at least I wasn't crossing the street to avoid him. "The Iceman" was a big fan of the New York Jets and Joe Namath, and offered to bet any amount they would beat the NFL in the Super Bowl. He ended up making a pile of money from diehards like me, who swore the new league's champion team couldn't whip the Baltimore Colts on their best day.

I put many hours in January 1969 running B Company through general training exercises to upgrade their basic skills and to give me a chance to evaluate my command and the company's level of training, the quality of the officers and NCOs in charge, and the quality of the Montagnard soldiers.

B Company was 188 men strong at full strength, with four platoons of 45 soldiers and a headquarters section of 8 men. The Montagnard soldiers were from the Bru tribe, which came originally from Northern Laos. CCN had nearly three hundred Bru under contract. I also had five young American lieutenants to boss around, four platoon leaders and an executive officer, whom everyone had started to call ell-tees. I was fortunate to have a top-notch company first sergeant named

Sam Fischer, who was a seasoned, professional soldier. He was short and rapidly heading to baldness, with a friendly, weather-seamed face, browned by the sun. He was crisp and sure of himself, with a strong military bearing. He had been a Special Forces NCO for many years and knew how to guide me in the direction he wanted me to take without ever giving offense. As long as I listened to him, I stayed out of trouble.

My XO was a medium-height, dark-haired, husky youngster from Ohio named Peter McMurray, all full of piss and vinegar and the exuberance of youth. Of course, everyone called him Mac, so I called him Pete. He was great to work with, and we became close friends. His infectious laugh and devil-may-care attitude were just the tonic I needed to keep me loose.

Pete had been with the company for a few months and knew what it took to make the unit run efficiently. His support was essential in my transition of command. The unit slowly recovered from the shock of Captain Jones's and the others' deaths. First Sergeant Fischer and I kept the men busy training, which helped to keep their minds occupied. It showed just how fleeting personal emotions among soldiers were. Once gone, quickly forgotten, until the quiet times, when dark memories slipped back into consciousness, uninvited.

I spent my days inspecting the men and their training, just to get them used to seeing me, and to help if I could. I had my choice of a new lieutenant to replace Jefferson, and chose 2d Lt. Ray Lawrence, who had just come up from Nha Trang as a replacement. He was a tall, gangly redhead, born and raised in South Carolina. Ray was perfect in temperament for command of a Montagnard platoon. I never saw him angry or impatient with his troops, who could do things that would drive a teetotaler to drink.

The eager, young Montagnard soldiers were anxious to please me and tried their best to do what I asked of them. Most could understand pidgin English, or even more, unless I tried to fuss at one of them for messing up. Then it was, "So solly, please, no understand English." Compared to Americans, they were little fellows. Most were well under five feet six inches, and dark brown from all the years in the bright Southeast Asia sun. Many were seasoned troops who had survived the Lang Vei fight in February of '68. Prior to that, they had been run out of their traditional home in Northern Laos by the NVA. They were very brave and tried hard to be good soldiers when Americans led them. They didn't like the Vietnamese and wouldn't fight for the ARVN (Army of the Republic of Vietnam) Special Forces officers assigned to our unit. That suited me fine as I wanted to command them personally.

I made it a point to find a tall Yard to be my radio operator, since I'd learn the hard way in my first tour that the VC liked to start an ambush by shooting at the taller targets, who were usually Americans. I considered that a most unfair way to start any fight, but if they insisted on being so determined to shoot me, I did my best to make it hard for them to find me.

To my satisfaction, one of the soldiers in the company was nearly six feet tall. If I hunched down, we would present two similar targets instead of one to an eagle-eyed VC rifleman. The tall Yard's name was Pham Tuc, and he had the usual baby face and dark, chocolate-colored skin of the Montagnard. He was thin, wiry, and tough, and stronger than a person would ever imagine from looking at him. Pham was proud as could be to be chosen for the honor of carrying the *Dai Uy's* radio. I never went to the field without him. He was barely seventeen, and come to find out, the son of the headman in his home village. Pham was a brave and loyal soldier, and I sort of unofficially adopted him like an older son. His karma and mine all interwoven, we grew to be very fond of one another.

Colonel Isler sent for me toward the end of the month. Briefly, we discussed my company and how I evaluated their skills at soldiering. "Nick, I want you to fly up to Bon Hai with the body of the striker killed Thursday in the grenade accident."

A Montagnard soldier from recon team Coral had been

setting up an ambush during training exercises. Apparently, he'd pulled the pin on a hand grenade prior to setting a booby trap, and the grenade exploded in his hands. Since he was a member of my company, I had been waiting at the dispensary when they brought in the body. Pham had been with me because he claimed the dead striker was a cousin from his village.

The M-26 grenade is a deadly efficient antipersonnel weapon in which notched piano wire is wrapped around an explosive charge. When the charge blows, the wrapped wire breaks and fans out in a thousand little shards of hot death. Hold a grenade in your hands when it explodes, and it makes quite a mess. The dead striker was shredded meat, no hands or face, and most of his insides, outside. Pham was white faced, but otherwise took the tragedy well because the Yards believed in reincarnation, that death was only the first step in a new start, hopefully in better circumstances.

Colonel Isler continued. "The dead striker came from the Montagnard settlement up at Bon Hai, and we need to recruit some more men to replace the losses of the last two months. Take a couple of your officers and an escort of local Yards. Major Khai (who was our Army of South Vietnam counterpart) is giving the dead man a VN award for heroism during his last recon mission. Present it to the dead man's family."

The Iceman paused and lit one of his thin cigars. "Try to recruit a dozen new men if you can. See Captain Lopez, and get some piasters (Vietnamese currency) for bonus money for the village chief. Lopez'll tell you what the going rate for a death benefit is. I'll order a chopper to pick you up tomorrow morning. Get back by dark tomorrow night. Oh, yeah, tell Lopez to get you a couple of cows, too. The Yards will want to have a feast in honor of your visit and for the funeral. They make quite a party out of their funerals."

Isler smiled at me with a wicked gleam in his eyes. "Watch out for the drinks. The stuff they serve will cut varnish."

I saluted and left the Old Man's office. Back in the company area, I sent for First Sergeant Fischer. As soon as he settled down in the other chair in my little office, I told him about the escort duty and our recruiting assignment. "Who should I take with me?"

The old NCO didn't hesitate a second. "Me and Ell-tee McMurray. The Yards all love Lieutenant Mac, and he'll fit in real good. I'll lay on some troops for the escort. Most of them are from Bon Hai, and will welcome a chance to visit their families."

"Make Pham the NCOIC," I said. "He's a cousin to the dead man and besides, he can translate for us."

"Hell, sir, all these Yards are kin. Just ask 'em." The old NCO laughed.

We were all waiting on the macadam tarmac heliport at ten o'clock the next morning. The casket containing our dead striker was covered with the yellow-and-red-striped flag of South Vietnam. Pinned to it was a small medal dangling from a bright red ribbon. I remember thinking the little piece of metal wasn't much of a trade for the dead man inside. For just an instant, I saw myself returning to my family the same way, but I swiftly pushed the morbid vision away. Death was the one thing you never wanted to dwell on around there. You simply trusted to fate and tried to do your job. What happened, happened.

The sacrificial cows were securely caged in their transport pens, mournfully mooing their displeasure at the tight confines. After we lifted off the tarmac, the pen would be slung beneath the chopper, and the doomed animals would ride the whole way like caged birds on a string. It would be uncomfortable, but a lot better than what was in store for them when they touched earth again.

I heard the *wop, wop, wop* of the Huey helicopter long before I saw it crossing the river from the Da Nang airfield. As we squinted against the sand kicked up by its whirling blades, the casket was loaded in, and we scrambled on board.

In a few seconds, the chopper lifted off, and tilting the nose to pick up speed, we zipped over the junkyard across the road from camp and climbed into the warm air, our dinner dangling below.

The flight over the war-torn country was visually intriguing. The greens and browns of the low mountains seemed serene from where we were, yet I knew that down below, men were hunting other men. Their throats dry, their palms sweaty with fear and tension, they must envy us so remote above them. I loved flying up there, cool and safe, like an omnipotent overseer.

I envied the flyboys in the war; they flew above the dust and sweat of the ground, zooming along in their magnificent flying machines. But I also felt some disdain. Up there, they were beyond the ground pounder's ever-present fear of meeting a bad guy around the next bend of the trail and the gut-wrenching sound of bullets cracking past your ear. Of course, I'm sure the flyboys would give me a passionate argument about the hazards they faced.

McMurray was laughing and talking to one of the Yard soldiers, who probably didn't understand a word he was saying. Fischer was asleep, resting up for the coming party, I figured. I remained quiet and watched the passing countryside, reveling in the view. That whole part of South Vietnam was covered by rice paddies cut out of the jungle, criss-crossed by trails and dirt roads. Countless bomb craters filled with rainwater reflected the sun's rays as we flew over them. The ground below would be red someday as the steel shrapnel rusted back into the earth.

The village came into view, and the pilot banked the chopper as he lined up for his landing. It was a typical Yard village, eighty to a hundred grass huts built in a circle around an open, central area. The construction was standard design. Every hut had grass-covered sides and roof and was raised about four feet off the ground. Underneath were pens for chickens and pigs. The slash-and-burn fields adjoining the village had been planted in corn and sugarcane. More an orange-red clay then dark brown dirt, the ground didn't look very rich. Several scruffy dogs began to bark excitedly at our approach. The pilot banked over the village, and the local residents quickly congregated, awaiting whatever the flying machine was bringing them.

The pilot skillfully grounded the caged cows then slipped a few yards to the side before settling down and cutting his engine. As the turbine whine died, Pham jumped out and ran to an older man. He respectfully spoke to the old Montagnard, who wore a faded blue shirt, a loincloth, and flip-flop sandals. His headband was made from numerous bright strings woven into a sort of rope. He was short and worn down by time and his hard life. His mouth lacked most of the usual number of teeth. His lips were the deep red of a longtime betel nut chewer. The dark colored skin on the old man's face was wrinkled and creased.

As Pham talked, I saw the old eyes look into the side door of the chopper at the flag-draped casket. The old man turned back to the assembled people, and Pham ran back to where I and the others were standing by the dark shape of the helicopter. The metal popped and cracked as it cooled, but the silence after the noise of the trip was intense. I led the other Americans with me to where the old man waited. He bowed politely and spoke to me in the Bru dialect. I motioned for Pham to translate.

Pham spoke to us. "My father says you are welcome. He says you are to wait at his house while he takes the body of my cousin to the house of his brother." Pham led the way, and I followed with Pete and Sergeant Fischer.

The houses were all very similar, about twenty-by-forty, and off the ground far enough for the pigpens and chicken coops to fit under them. The doorway was reached by a notched log used as a stairway from the ground. A brightly colored cloth was the doorway's only barrier to the elements and that was tied back, allowing easy access to people, dogs, and flies. Although it was already quite warm, every hut had a small fire going, the smoke of which had to filter through the grass roof, but it kept most of the bugs out. It also saved on matches when supper time arrived.

The ever-present smoky fire in the confined space of the huts gave Montagnards a distinctive odor, especially when they were sweating. It reminded me of a barbecue odor from summer nights long ago, back home in Arkansas, when my dad was cooking steaks on the grill. I loved the smell of the Yards and never grew tired of it. The body odor you might have expected of an unwashed "savage" just wasn't there.

We stopped at the central hut of the village where the chief lived, and paused while the coffin was carried past. The pall-bearers were followed by several sobbing women and many villagers. On impulse, I ordered the hand salute so that we could honor the fallen soldier on his last journey and, incidentally, improve our stature in the eyes of the grieving villagers.

After the crowd passed by, we climbed up the log steps. I asked Pham, "Is your father chief of the village?"

With a shy bob of his head, Pham indicated yes. He then told us how the tribe had arrived there. "We once lived many miles over there." He pointed to the mountains in the west, in northern Laos. "My village chose to fight with the Americans from many years ago. Before you ever came to South Vietnam. When your soldiers left, my father moved across the border to the Special Forces camp at Lang Vei. We fought there when it was overrun last year. Then we move here to Bon Hai, and I join Special Forces army, and now fight for you, *Dai Uy* Nicholson."

Sergeant Fischer had told me the story. When the camp at Lang Vei fell to a determined assault by North Vietnamese soldiers in February of '68, what was left of the villagers had moved on to Khe Sanh. Then, the NVA attacked the Marines there, and the villagers were forced on to this place. Now, the remnants of the once-proud people were trying to stay alive by growing what little would flourish in the poor soil and taking handouts from U.S. AID (Agency for International Development) workers. They made what money they could by renting their sons to the American Special Forces as mercenaries.

Pham and the other Yard soldiers soon had their pants and shoes off, replacing them with loincloths and flip-flops, like the rest of the men in the village. When the old chief got back, Pham introduced us to him, his mother, his two younger sisters, and a small brother. The females had all put on blouses, which none were wearing when we arrived. I suppose they had experienced the reaction of Americans to bare breasts. Only a few very old women stayed in custom and left their breasts bare.

Every woman over sixteen had her two front teeth filed off flush with their gums, making them look, to me at least, like aborigine vampires. Everyone, man and woman, chewed betel nut, which colored their teeth jet black and made their lips and tongues crimson red. Their feet were as wide as they were long, with splayed toes and horny soles; more than likely none had ever worn shoes. Still, the women had a natural beauty and grace and were delighted to see Pham and welcome us to their home.

Pham quickly presented loincloths to me and my comrades, which we reluctantly put on. Our white legs caused many a giggle among the brown-skinned locals, but we endured the embarrassment out of respect for their culture and in the cause of good relationships, just as our training back in the States had emphasized.

With Pham's help, I made my pitch for new recruits, and the old chief promised ten. At Pham's nod, I passed over the VN bounty, about fifty thousand Vietnamese piasters. The official exchange rate made the transaction worth about fifty dollars in U.S. money. It certainly didn't seem like much for their sons, but times were hard and lives cheap in South Vietnam in those days. The chief promised to have the "volunteers" ready for pickup when we left, and we concluded our business.

"Now village will sacrifice cow and have big feast," Pham announced with a grin. The tall Montagnard boy led us to the village square, for want of a better term, where one of the cows we delivered was staked out, stoically awaiting its fate. The entire village, save for the home in mourning, was there. The people surrounded the cow, the men closest, then the women and children intermixed. By the time everyone had assembled, it made quite a crowd.

The old chief stepped out and made a welcoming speech to us and had all of us Americans led to small stools next to where he would sit. Several men carried out huge clay pots, a green banana leaf tied over the top of each one. These were set around the circle formed by the assembled villagers.

"What's that?" I whispered to Sergeant Fischer. I watched uneasily as the top covers were removed and buckets of cool spring water poured into the wide mouths of the jugs. A profusion of black bugs scurried out.

"Just the Vietnam equivalent of cockroaches, *Dai Uy,*" Fischer chuckled. "Don't worry, they left plenty for us."

"Plenty of what?" I grumbled, as the men produced slender, five-foot-long bamboo shoots which had been converted into straws. The men rammed the straws down through the oily-looking water. With much gusto, they sucked long swallows from the bottoms of the pots and pronounced the stuff fit to drink.

Belching in appreciation, the old man passed me his straw. With bravado overcoming my apprehension, I took a hard pull on the bamboo tube. A foul-tasting, highly alcoholic concoction burned its way down my throat and exploded into a fiery ball in my stomach. "Wow," I finally managed to gasp. "That stuff sure packs a wallop."

Sergeant Fischer laughed and reached for my straw. "Beats anything you can buy in the NCO club, for a fact." He sucked mightily and passed the straw on to the next man in line. Across the way, I saw Lieutenant McMurray happily tapping another pot and resigned myself to the inevitable. It was going to be a drunken afternoon. Just that once, I'd bend my vow to lay off the hard stuff forever. I sure hoped Paul Potter would understand my breaking my vow to him.

After a couple of passes around the circle of thirsty men, the jug was nearly empty. I had high hopes that I'd seen the last of the local "white lightning." Unfortunately, that wasn't the case. The last man to drink just poured in some more water, and presto, another round was ready. My head was getting light as a helium-filled balloon. I missed the first part of the chief's speech, although Pham was translating it into my ear. His voice just added to the buzzing in my head from the potent brew I was sucking down.

The old chief brought out the new volunteers for my unit, and introduced them to me one by one. They were just kids, most likely fifteen to seventeen years old. They all smiled and bowed politely, pride and a manly determination visible on their young faces. I shakily got to my feet and welcomed them to the American Army. "The Bru are strong fighters," I intoned, Pham rapidly translating at my side. "Together, we will kill many VC." My translator must have jazzed up my little speech, because the crowd let out a mighty yell when I finished. It wasn't until much later that I realized that most of these boys would be dead before I finished my tour. I doubt if half of them ever returned to the village in one piece. Most likely, their only way home was just like the one for the boy I'd brought with me, in a wooden box, with a gaudy little trinket for his grieving family to mark his passing.

The village medicine man now got up and led the cow into the circle of villagers. One of his assistants skillfully slit the animal's throat and another put a big metal pot underneath the dying animal's neck to catch the gushing blood. After a mournful "moo," the unfortunate animal keeled over. That resulted in a robust cheer from the onlookers. The pot of blood was passed around, and everyone took a sip. The taste of the warm fluid should have sickened me, but I guess the effects of the home brew numbed my senses enough to overcome it. I smiled a bloody grin at Sergeant Fischer as he carefully took a tiny swallow and passed the pot on to the next man.

"Guess we're honorary members of the clan now," I told him as I reached for another swallow of the wine. Fischer just smiled and nodded, sucking mightily on his reed straw. I had moved up a tiny notch in his opinion.

Village women stacked piles of brush around the dead cow and set it ablaze. For a while we all drank and watched the fire burn. My body was numb, my tongue thick, and my head spinning. Surprisingly, I was also famished. I made small talk with the village men, using Pham as my translator, occasionally speaking in the pidgin English and Vietnamese they might possess. I flirted outrageously with Pham's older sister, who looked better and better the more wine I drank. Each time, my dashing smile was returned in full by black teeth, filed gap visible, before she shyly covered her face with her hands and giggled helplessly.

If I hadn't imbibed so much of their hooch that I was incapable of moving, much less procreating, there might have been a half-breed Montagnard in my family tree. I found out later that, in their eyes, it would have been impolite to turn me down if I had insisted on her hand for a one-night marriage. Lucky girl, saved from a fate worse than death. Lucky me, for that matter.

Finally, the women allowed the fire to burn down, by which time the poor cow was very scorched, on the outside at least. The ladies moved in with sharp knives, and set to carving up dinner. Nearly raw hunks of meat and organs were swiftly passed around, men first, and we all set to feasting, much like early man did, I suppose.

The hot meat was juicy and tasty, and I ate my share and more. The cow's smoking skull was split and the gray-red brains were put on small skewers and roasted over the remnants of the fire. The last of the blood was used as a dip or a sauce. A person would have to have been drunk to enjoy the afternoon, and I really enjoyed myself. The carcass was reduced to skin and bones by dusk.

Sergeant Fischer and my equally sloshed lieutenant poured me onto the chopper when it arrived and held me in as it swooped into the air while I waved good-bye to my new family and friends. I believed myself to have been the life of the party, laughing, flirting with the gals, and telling scandalous lies to everyone who would listen. I guess Pham's translation raised my stories to even more outrageous heights.

I didn't start getting really nauseated until we hit some turbulence halfway home to Da Nang. Then, I set a modern-day record for puking out one's guts at three thousand feet. Any VC below us were subjected to an intense and disgusting bombardment of my stomach's contents.

I was sick the rest of the month.

5

Jose O'Connor's Last Laugh
or
Never Enough of a Good Thing

The recovery period for my hangover set a modern-day record for misery. Once again, I renewed the famous and familiar vow, "No more of the hard stuff." I promised the god Bacchus that if ever I recovered, I'd never get that sloshed again. A pledge I'm proud to report that I've kept for the past thirty years.

Experienced SF soldiers, who knew about the effects of the Montagnard home brew, gave me plenty of good-natured ribbing as I slowly and painfully returned to being a normal human being. Even Colonel Isler flashed me a bemused grin the first time I saw him after I emerged from my sick bed. My poor, wasted body was cleaned out, top to bottom. What a way to lose weight fast. If I could have brought it back to the States, I could have made a million bucks. And the weight would have stayed off; nobody would ever have wanted to use that method twice, believe me.

As I've said, our camp sat on the beach of Da Nang Bay. The bay was set in a big valley, with high mountains rising to the west and north, encircling a flat expanse of rice paddies nearly ten miles across. It sort of resembled a soup bowl, half buried in the sand. Inside the perimeter of the high mountains was the city of Da Nang, swelled to overflowing with war refugees. Add to the mix about twenty thousand American military men, and you get the picture.

Driving south, away from the city, was the big Da Nang airfield, which was constantly active with jets and cargo planes roaring off the concrete runways or coasting in for a landing. Helicopters buzzed around like angry wasps, darting here and there on the business of war. There was also a large navy contingent stationed at Da Nang harbor, and ships were stacked up out in the bay, awaiting their turn at the many unloading piers, which were just across the Da Nang River from the airfield.

Farther down the beach to the south was the headquarters of Company C, 5th Special Forces, which commanded all the regular Special Forces camps located in the northern region of I Corps. Next door to C Company was the 3d Marine Air Base, which supported the Marine units working in the northern provinces. Next was the navy field hospital, an oil tank farm, and a small POW compound. Across the road was the massive junkyard I mentioned earlier. It was filled to overflowing with destroyed tanks, trucks, jeeps, armored personnel carriers (APCs), Marine amphibious tractors (amtracs) which looked like an army's APC on steroids, and the rest of the refuse of the war. The junkyard was a treasure chest of spare parts and "goodies" to those of us with the inclination to deal with its keepers. Fresh serial numbers for our jeeps, rebuilt carburetors, tires, generators, firing pins for rifles, desks, typewriters, the list of goodies to be found there was endless. The soldiers who were assigned to the junkyard had one of the most profitable assignments in all of South Vietnam, since we paid whatever was asked for the things they sold.

The reason was simple. In the midst of plenty, relative to supplies to prosecute the war, there was always something we were short of. Once we asked for five hundred sets of fatigues for the supply shed. We got ten thousand sets delivered, yet a simple carburetor for an old M-35 jeep was not to be found, except at the junkyard. The lucky soldiers assigned to man the junkyards grew rich, I'm certain. Cash, enemy souvenirs, a sister's honor, whatever they wanted, they got, or we walked, and a good SF trooper never walked anywhere if he could ride.

Just to the south of our compound was the forbidding up-thrust of rock called Marble Mountain. Beyond the rocky barrier of Marble Mountain was the 3d Marine Amtrac Battalion and the village of Xom Som Tui, from where the NVA sappers had launched the attack on us in August. From our back fence, we could see the despised cluster of grass huts, and many a scheme to repay the villains responsible was hatched and reluctantly discarded over cool beers at the club.

Actually, those poor villagers would certainly have had their throats slit if they had informed us of their unwanted guests. Of course, even that knowledge didn't temper our hatred for the village and those unfortunate people caught between the two warring parties, both uninvited, in their land.

Beyond the village and the Marine base lay only swamp, rice paddies, heavy jungle, and the South Vietnamese fighting against us, or Viet Cong, who we usually called Charlie, or VC, if not something worse. Lately, we were seeing more and more North Vietnamese Army (NVA) regular troops, hiding up in the mountains that defined the rest of northern South Vietnam; the Tet offensive of January 1968 had resulted in the death of most of the VC in I Corps and elsewhere in South Vietnam.

The Marines had a small defensive outpost located at an old French fort right at the base of the high ground to the far west end of the valley. They had the unenviable assignment of patrolling the exits from the west, which was "Charlie Land," and of providing early warning of incursion into the local Da Nang AO (area of operations). The Marines knew their business, as was proven by the high number of KIAs they counted in the hunt for our attackers in the fall. Except for the sad truth that we army types were handsome dudes and the Marines were all ugly grunts, happier in the dirt and weeds than in civilization, you couldn't have told us apart.

In every war, one is going to meet a number of unforgettable characters. Some brave, some cowardly, strong or weak, smart or dumb, sane or crazy. The list of descriptors would fill a page. I met my share of them. One of the most amusing I met was Sgt. Jose O'Connor.

One of my best recon team leaders, Sergeant O'Connor was a half-Mexican, half-Irish, blue-eyed, tanned, Latino cavalier, and a ladies' man from the top of his jet-black hair to the tips of his toes. He was husky and dark, with a devil-may-care buoyancy about him that made everyone he met like him instantly, especially women. When he smiled, which was often, his pearly-white teeth would almost blind you.

Jose bragged that he had slipped across the Rio Grande from Mexico and joined the army before the INS was able to catch and deport him. Once he was in the service, it was too late to ship him back. He'd been assigned to Special Forces ever since, spending a good deal of time stationed in South America, where his Spanish increased his value to the army. The rest of his enlistment time, he alternated between Fort Bragg, North Carolina, where Special Forces HQ was located, and Fort Bliss, Texas, where he could visit his relatives south of the border.

He had been in Vietnam about a year when I took over B Company, and had just extended for an additional six months. He had command of recon team Cobra, where he was famous for his ability to take his team in and out of tight spots without ever taking casualties.

Early in February, after a hard night of drinking with the regulars at the NCO Club, where the troops had spent time complaining about the lack of revenge against the offending village across the water, O'Connor decided to take action on his own. Originally, everyone had demanded we burn the place to the ground for harboring the VC who'd attacked us. Everyone agreed. Something was called for, something big.

I was officer of the day that night—how about that for a contradiction in terms? Thus, I had a front seat to the whole saga.

About two o'clock in the morning, Jose and a truckload of drunken troopers pulled up to the front gate. I stopped them and climbed up on the running board so I could see the driver up close and smell his breath. He was sober, although he was a minority of one. He grinned sheepishly at me, and shrugged his shoulders as if to say, "What can I do?"

"Where you taking these bums?" I asked. The driver was the junior member of O'Connor's recon team, so new to CCN that he was still pissing Stateside water. Of course he was eager to be one of the guys. Jose was sitting next to him in the cab, so sloshed that I doubt he could have staggered across the road without falling flat on his face. The men in back were singing at the top of their voices one of the favorite songs of the airborne trooper, "Blood on the Risers."

"Special mission, Cap'n Nick," Jose slurred. "Don't worry, I've got everything under control."

"Hell, O'Connor," I replied, "every man in this truck, except maybe Spivy here, is so piss-potted that he doesn't even know what his name is. Where the hell are you going?"

"It's secret, honest, Captain. We'll be back in a minute. Jus' going down the road a ways to pick up somethin' we need to pay back the dinks over in the vil' there." He jerked his thumb toward the offensive Xom Son Tui.

"All right," I answered. "Just stay away from the MP checkpoint at the bridge. And Spivy," I admonished the young driver, "don't let anyone else drive this truck. You understand?" Spivy nodded. I noticed the buzz cut of his hair was so short I couldn't tell if he was blond or dark-haired. Then he noisily shifted gears, and the truck lurched out of the gate and turned east toward Da Nang. Shaking my head at the spectacle and hoping I hadn't turned a whirlwind of destruction loose on the world, I watched the truck disappear in the darkness. I could hear the singing voices long after the noise of the vehicle was gone.

About an hour later, the truck came back, with Spivy its only occupant. "Jesus Christ, Spivy," I screamed at him.

"Didn't I tell you not to lose those drunken bastards? Where the hell did you lose them?"

"Sir," the young sergeant answered, trying hard not to grin. "Sergeant O'Connor respectfully requests that you make a tour of the perimeter and don't come back to the front gate for thirty minutes." He looked anxiously down the dark road.

I thought I could hear the sound of a tracked vehicle approaching the camp. "Now who in hell would be driving a tank down the road in the middle of the night?"

"Don't ask, sir. Just make your rounds. Please, sir. Right now." The young sergeant was fairly hopping up and down in excitement.

Hestitantly, I nodded. "Okay, Spivy, I'll make my rounds, but you'd better not be setting me up for an ass-chewing from the XO." He grinned in relief, and hurried me on my way. I took plenty of time, even going inside the TOC, which was almost soundproof.

When I returned to the front gate, the Montagnard guards were all smiles at the joke, whatever it was, but they wouldn't let me in on it. All I could get from them was "O'Connor funny, *Dai Uy.*"

The rest of the night passed uneventfully, and I breathed a sigh of relief when the sun came up. Whatever O'Connor was up to, it hadn't happened on my watch. I should have walked the fence again, but decided it was better if I didn't, in case there was something I shouldn't see.

As I ate breakfast, I sensed a mood of jocular anticipation sweeping the men in the mess hall. Clusters of them would whisper together and then dash for the door, giggling like kids with a secret. Spotting O'Connor over at one of the tables, drinking coffee and looking bleary-eyed at his surroundings, I eased up beside him and sat down. "What the hell's going on, O'Connor?"

"No so loud, *Dai Uy,*" he moaned in misery. "My head's 'bout to bust wide open." He slurped some more of the coffee. Looking up at me with eyes nearly bleeding red, he flashed his big smile and whispered, "Take a look over beside number four guard tower."

Following the flow of gazers headed that way, I walked to the southwest corner of the compound, where a twenty-foot-tall tower marked the corner of the defensive perimeter of the camp. There, just outside the wire, half-buried in the sand, was a massive, M-110 self-propelled howitzer, its mighty eight-inch gun pointing like a dark, menacing finger of accusation right at our offending village across the bay.

Troops were laughing in glee as they came up and inspected the gun, while across the open expanse of water, the cowed village was quiet as a mouse in a bed of sleeping cats. I must have invented a dozen new ways to cuss a man as I hot-footed it back to the mess hall. "O'Connor, you crazy, pea-brained wetback," I snarled as quietly as my enraged blood would let me. "Where on earth did you get that cannon, and what are we gonna tell the XO when he finds out who put it there, and who let it into the compound?"

Casually, O'Connor brushed aside my anger. "Relax, *Dai Uy*. How long do you think its been since the XO walked the perimeter of the camp? Nobody will tell him or the CO, and in a week there'll be no way anyone can prove who did it or when. Relax, man. It's cool."

Damned if he wasn't right.

For the next two weeks, countless MPs and a certain Marine artillery unit were looking all over I Corps for their stolen self-propelled gun. It seems whoever took it had swept the road of any tracks, and the twenty-ton monster was not to be found anywhere. I heard the Marines were tearing their hair out at the idea that anyone could steal something so big and noisy right out from under their noses. Of course, to any rational man who knew Marines, there was an easy answer. The army did!

Some time later, some big-shot Marine was flying his chopper over the camp and spotted the missing gun. The chopper landed right on the beach, and a very steamed Marine colonel was all over our colonel, wanting to know just how that gun got where it was. Colonel Isler soon had every officer in camp giving statements, but I could honestly say that I didn't see a thing on my guard shift. Everyone swore that the gun arrived on a different day, and even the investigators from CID (Criminal Investigation Division) couldn't pin the rap on anyone. There were a lot of dark looks invested on innocent-faced young officers and NCOs, but nobody spilled the beans, and the mystery remained unsolved.

O'Connor's laugh was the loudest of all whenever another phase of the investigation was launched. The village across the bay remained extremely quiet for two weeks, while the cowed villagers waited, in sleepless dread we hoped, for us to fire the cannon pointed directly at them.

Poor Colonel Isler suffered through the numerous queries from the furious Marines and I Corps army officers who had to placate our Marine comrades. It was one of the best coups counted by our camp in a long time, and it was a topic of gleeful conversation for many weeks thereafter.

Not long after the gun caper, the military command in Saigon pulled a currency switch on everyone in country. On switch day, the camp was sealed up while everyone exchanged all the military scrip we used in country for a new issue. Paymasters were dispatched to every location in the entire country at the same time, and until the currency switch was completed, every camp was closed, and nobody was supposed to go into town. That was to insure that all the whores and black marketeers would end up with old, inactive scrip, which would certainly cause financial pain for those people, but satisfied the bluenoses in HQ that we were doing our best to put the hard-working Vietnamese entrepreneurs out of business. My hootch girl, who cleaned the room where I stayed, came crying to me. She would lose the money she had made selling the sewing she hawked on the side of the road on her days off. I felt sorry for her, but what could I do?

O'Connor burst into my office a short time later. "*Dai Uy*, I'm taking my hootch girl into town. She's sick and needs to get to a doctor fast."

I sighed, "Jose, you know I can't sign you out without a TS pass signed by the colonel. Everything's closed up tighter than a drum." The TS pass was supposed to be used for "top-secret" travel only, and would get O'Connor past the MP checkpoint at the bridge leading into town. The MPs couldn't even ask what the bearer was going to do. The MPs and White Mice (Vietnamese MPs) had been ordered to let anyone showing such a pass through, no questions asked.

Somehow, O'Connor had found out that the camp was about to get closed, and had rushed over to HQ and gotten the Old Man's signature on a TS pass. I knew O'Connor had several girlfriends working at the various bars and whorehouses in town where he spent his off-duty time. "Okay, Sergeant," I agreed. "But don't ask me to help you convert all the money you're gonna bring back. If you get caught, it's your ass."

"*Dai Uy*," he answered with his happy laugh, "you don't need to worry about this Irish chili pepper. I never get caught." He was right again. He came back a couple of hours later, and soon had every man in camp turning in money for him. The scrip he bought from the girls downtown for fifty cents on the dollar, he converted at face value. He must have made a fortune, as well as earned the undying appreciation of all those whores. That was one debt I'm sure liquidated in full as fast as he could recover from the previous repayment.

On the last day of the month, Team Cobra was alerted for a quick-reaction insert into the 905 Base Area, almost due west of Da Nang just across the Vietnam-Laos border. I escorted Jose and the rest of his team to the chopper pad. The three Americans and four Yards were all loaded down with ammo, water, and food. Their faces were blackened, and green tape covered the metal parts of their gear.

"Take care, you little jumping bean," I said earnestly. "Nine-oh-five is a hot spot, so keep your head down."

"Don't worry about me, *Dai Uy*." He laughed. "I'm gonna run recon forever." He waved good-bye as the chopper hammered its way off the ground.

Team Cobra ran into trouble from the start. According to the after-action report given by his one-one, Sergeant Spivy, who was the only American survivor, trail watchers got on them almost immediately upon insertion. As night fell, O'Connor led the team on a big loop, trying to cut behind his trackers, but stumbled onto a large unit tracking them. The initial firefight killed the third American—a new kid on his first insertion—and two of the Yard soldiers.

Spivy reported that O'Connor was hit early on in the ensuing battle. The little Mexican NCO had crawled to a fallen tree and propped himself up so he was facing the main force of enemy, and ordered Spivy and the two remaining Yards to move down a creek to some high ground. Then they were to lay low until morning. Spivy was crying when he finished telling me. He had argued to stay with O'Connor, but reluctantly obeyed his wounded sergeant's last orders.

The last they saw, O'Connor was firing down the trail and tossing grenades. After a while they made the high ground and crawled under some bushes. Soon it became all quiet except for the shouting of NVA soldiers looking for them. The three survivors remained hidden where they were all night without being discovered.

In the morning they sneaked back to the spot where they left O'Connor, but no one was there. Often, the NVA took American bodies back with them to show off to locals. The three men looked around for signs of the two Americans and the Yard striker without success. Finally, they gave up and called in an emergency extraction helicopter. Jose O'Connor had made his last recon.

The camp was devastated when we found out the extent of the losses incurred by Team Cobra in their fight with the NVA. We held a solemn memorial for the fallen troopers and got on with the business of the war. We sure missed the little chili pepper. He had left a bunch of grieving friends, anxious to avenge him.

A week or so later, the CO called me in and told me to write O'Connor's wife a letter explaining what I could and conveying the unit's deep condolences at his becoming an MIA. I carefully wrote as much as possible of the circumstances surrounding his MIA status and how much we all liked the little rascal. Taking his wife's address from the unit record, I sent it off to her in Fayetteville, North Carolina, the nearest city to Fort Bragg, home of Special Forces.

I resumed my daily routine, letting the fallen O'Connor and the grief of his loss slip away to the dark place where I stored all my unpleasant memories.

About three weeks later, I received a summons to go see the Old Man. "Nick, didn't I tell you to write Sergeant O'Connor's widow and to convey our condolences?"

"Yes sir," I replied. "I did it right away. She should have had it a couple of weeks ago. I don't mind saying that it was a tough one to write."

"Well, I just got a letter from her today, saying that some army friends told her about his being MIA, but she hadn't heard anything from the army. She's asking me what's going on. Write her again, telling her what you can, and directing her to get in touch with the nearest army base for assistance."

He passed me the letter. I looked at the return address. "Here's the reason," I explained. "Mrs. O'Connor is in Fort Bliss, Texas. She must be visiting relatives. I wrote her at Fort Bragg. I'll get on it right away." I took her address and quickly wrote a letter similar to the earlier one. I put it in the mail sack and got back to other business.

A short time later, I received another summons to the Iceman's office. "Captain Nicholson, what the hell's going on? I told you to write O'Connor's widow, not once, but twice. Now I get another letter from her, saying she's heard from some of his family that he's been killed, and what should she do?"

"Honest, Colonel, I did write. Let me see the letter." I looked at the envelope. It was addressed from someplace in Mexico. I quickly scanned the ragged handwriting. "My God," I gulped. "This name is different. This isn't the same name as the name on the other letter. What the hell is going on?"

The Iceman grabbed the page and looked at it, a frown on his face. "Time to get somebody higher up than us on it. Thanks, Nick. I'll take care of it from here on."

I saluted and got out of the office. I voiced my suspicions to First Sergeant Fischer as soon as I got back to my company HQ. "I think the little bastard had two wives, that's what I think." Fischer just shook his head. We had other things to get done, and my words were soon forgotten.

As usual, I was wrong. The crazy little chili bean had three. One in Fort Bragg, one in Fort Bliss, and one in Mexico. That way, no matter where he was, he had a warm bedmate to snuggle next to. Like all good gossip, the word soon got out about O'Connor's trio of wives, and many a glass was raised to the memory of our horny little Latino friend.

Somewhere in the Valhalla for fallen warriors, I'll bet Jose O'Connor is still laughing his last laugh, the loudest of all.

6

Who Was That Guy?
or
Mud Marine Hero

By early February, it was the middle of the rainy season for us in I Corps; the northern section of South Vietnam had a spring wetting, while the southern half had fall monsoon. Every time we had a lull and the weather abated a little, our VC friends got more active in our AO. They used the bad weather as a time to refit and rest up for the hard work ahead.

Since the logistic requirements for cross-border operations were so much more involved for a larger-size unit like mine than for the small reconnaissance teams, CCN had not inserted my men on an operation over the unmarked border into Laos or North Vietnam for some time. I was anxious to get my feet wet leading my company out in the bush. The only question was when and where.

During the first part of the month, CCN recon teams had several close scrapes with the enemy because, since the choppers were not all-weather aircraft, bad weather made it difficult to get the recon teams out. Add to that the additional negative of not having air force fighter-bombers to work over the scene of the action, and some bad-weather operations became pretty scary. The one sure way we had to break contact with the enemy was to call the fly-fly boys on them. The average NVA soldier had a real aversion to a five-hundred-pound bomb being planted right next to him. Without air support, the contacts with Mister Charlie on his home turf got a good deal hairier.

I was anxious to get my new command into the bush for

some field training. I wanted to test them in the woods to see if all the training they had received had sunk in before we went out for real, on a cross-border operation. As the wet days followed one another with monotonous regularity, I became desperate. I asked the Iceman to let me take the whole company to the field in the local area for a week of training in patrolling, ambush techniques, and reconnoitering. He okayed my request, but sent me to see the Marines, to request an area close to CCN. "I want to use our own trucks for logistical support instead of depending on air assets."

Operational control of the entire Da Nang valley belonged to the Marines, as part of their assigned mission to protect the city and its important airfield and shipyards. Early the next day, I drove over to III MAF HQ in Da Nang to coordinate the operation with their staff pukes. The Marines were concerned we would stumble on their local patrolling and interdicting operations for the Da Nang defense region. I swear, staff officers are the same no matter which branch of service they're in. All huff and puff, and they'll never make a decision without a conference to concur and to cover their asses.

After reviewing my training plan with what seemed to be the tenth identical staff officer, I finally got the okay to go to the woods. I would have to remain at the far southwest end of the Da Nang valley, next to the mountains, but that was acceptable to me, since the terrain was rugged there, with lots of realistic training areas available. To add spice to the stew, it was also Charlie's land once the sun went down. That meant we might get to train for real with booby traps and snipers to liven up the lessons.

At night, we would have to set out real ambushes and, who knows, maybe get into a real firefight with a small patrol of bad guys. The local VC were certainly active enough to stumble upon us, or vice versa. I couldn't wait, and drove my subordinates hard to get the men ready. The young fire-eaters I had assigned to B Company didn't need much encouragement. They were as anxious as I to get in the woods and savor the excitement of some real contact with Charlie.

We moved out at dawn, almost two hundred strong. The exercise began with a forced road march of some ten miles, right to the very edge of our assigned training area. The little Yards, all loaded down with ammo, field gear, food, and water, stayed up with me and the other Americans, even though they had taken two steps to our one. I insisted that everyone carry all the ammo they could, just in case the weather prevented us from getting resupplied. My first tour, I was in a protracted firefight with a VC company near Pleiku, when we ran out of ammo. I'll never forget the sinking feeling in my gut when that happened, the fear that the VC would find out, and stroll in and take my head for a souvenir. Fortunately, just before dark, an extrabrave chopper pilot dropped off enough bullets to carry us through the night.

I was more than a little uncomfortable with the chopper support CCN had assigned to support field operations. The powers that be in I Corps HQ had decided the SVN Air Force would become our primary source of helicopter support instead of the 101st Division Aviation Battalion at Camp Eagle, about fifty klicks north of Da Nang. Our support would be closer, but not nearly as dependable, nor as well trained. To make the situation worse, the ARVN Air Force only flew the H-34 Choctaw choppers, which were nearly twenty years old and slow, instead of the newer and faster Huey choppers of the 101st. Painted in the black colors of CCN, the old choppers were an awfully inviting target to any hotshot NVA ackack gunner.

The uncomfortable reality of the H-34's age and condition, apparent to the passengers, who sat right under the massive transmission of the bird and were usually bombarded with hot drops of leaking oil or hydraulic fluid, didn't improve our disposition. Any crash impact would certainly drop the hot engine right in our laps.

The gung ho SVN pilots who flew the lumbering, old warbirds were top notch, so that offset some of the negatives. Unfortunately, I believed none were as good as the fine, young American warrant officers who flew for the 101st; I trusted them above any others. They were famous for coming in for their pickups, no matter how hot the LZ was. I hoped we'd get the 101st if the going got really rough. Only later, when the poop hit the fan one day, did I learn the VN aviators were, in truth, the better choice when things got *really* hot.

B Company worked hard the rest of the day, training and practicing combat maneuvers until sundown. As soon as it was dark enough to hide our movements, we left the spot where we had eaten cold, long-range reconnaissance patrol rations (called LURPs) and moved to our first RON (remain overnight) site. LURPs are dehydrated glop, but filling and, I suppose, nourishing. I had chosen a great spot, I thought, to RON. It was at an intersection of two trails headed directly for Da Nang in the distant northeast. From our position, we could see the fiery red cones of exhaust as jets took off for night missions from the always busy Da Nang airfield, many miles to the east.

A rumble of thunder warned of approaching rain. It didn't take long to reach us. We endured a vicious thunderstorm, with flashes of lightning and pelting rain. It was over by midnight but left everyone soaked to the skin and very uncomfortable. The night was cool and damp as we huddled in our ponchos and waited for the dawn.

Around two A.M., I had finally dried out enough to think of getting a couple of hours of sleep before the sunrise stand-to. I figured the storm had discouraged any Viet Cong from walking down the trail we were hidden beside, at least on this night.

I might have known that uninterrupted sleep was too much to hope for on my first night in the brush. We had called in our RON coordinates to the area fire control center immediately upon reaching the site. The AFCC radio operator repeated the numbers I had read him in the daily one-time cipher. Foolishly, I just supposed that made everything all right. Around three-thirty, the world came down on our heads, scaring several year's growth out of every man on the mission, including me.

It seemed that the Marine cannon units that provided long-range fire support to the Da Nang defenders never received the message that B Company, CCN, would be bivouacking at such-and-such trail crossing. They had scheduled some H & I (harassment and interdiction) fire on said intersection for 0330, just in case some nasty Charlies were walking along at that spot at that exact moment. Just think what the odds were on catching someone at some spot on a map at the very moment we fired. But, we Americans had lots of ammo, and H & I kept the gun crews busy, so they repeated it nearly every night.

Down came about twelve 155mm rounds, all at the same instant. This was the standard artillery plan with the ominous name of TOT (time on target) fire. Luckily for us, the Marines were good shots, and all the rounds hit the intersection. Since we were thirty yards or more off the road, none landed in our midst. More importantly to our survival, the heavy rains had softened the sandy soil enough that most of the explosive impact was absorbed by the ground. However, listening to red-hot shrapnel whizzing overhead at zero-dark-thirty in the morning is not the best way to start a day.

With the roar of an oncoming train and then the breath-stopping *krrump!* as the first impacts blasted the night, I damn near had a heart attack. It sounded like the world had come to an end, right next to my foxhole. I squatted down, getting my butt good and muddy, hoping none of the rounds landed short. Then, after the ground quit shaking, I got on the radio to the area fire control center screaming numerous insults about the radio operator's ancestry, and giving him, in the clear, exactly where we were on the map. Lieutenant McMurray cautioned, "Sir, if any Charlies are monitoring our radio freqs, they'll know where we are."

"Hell, Pete," I snarled, "Better that than letting the G-d'ed Marines blow us to hell in a handbasket. They're on our side, for Christ's sake. I don't need any friendly-fire casualties to explain to the CO."

Fortunately, my message was quickly relayed to the offending artillery units, and the second salvo was directed somewhere else. With what dignity I had left, I cleaned myself up and took stock of the chaos resulting from the close call.

Men were shouting and moving around, and several flashlights blinked on, destroying any hope that our location would remain a secret to nearby VC. "Okay," I muttered to myself, "if this is the best you can do, we'll train some more on night security procedures."

"Mac, send the platoon leaders to me right now," I called over the company radio to the XO. My lieutenants hurried to my hole, all as shocked by the artillery barrage as I was. Explaining what had happened, I chewed their butts good for losing control of their people. "We'll start out in ten minutes, night movement down the trail *there*. Maybe that'll help the strikers to see the wisdom of staying quiet in an ambush site."

Since old Charlie put ambushes on trails and roads, just as we did, the silence exhibited by the young soldiers as they cautiously went deeper into the "badlands" was gratifying. By morning's first light, I think they understood that I put a lot of emphasis on the need for light and noise discipline at an ambush site.

Fortunately, we didn't encounter any bad guys, so the lesson was learned without cost. The little soldiers quickly understood that I meant business in the brush. It was okay to be a little slack in camp, but out where the game was for real, I didn't want any screwing around. I had two sons to raise, and I meant to get home to them.

The next few days passed routinely, with a lot accomplished in training, and on the last evening we moved into our nightly RON without having seen a single VC or having suffered any training casualties. Since we were two hundred men armed with automatic rifles and with M-26 hand grenades hanging from every place possible on our web gear (called LBE, for load-bearing equipment), that was saying a lot.

On the last night of the exercise, after making sure the outposts were in place and every man had constructed some kind of hasty fighting position, I settled into the scooped-out depression I called a hasty foxhole. I could hear Pham settling down close by me in the pitch blackness of the night. I quickly fell asleep, dog-tired from the strain of commanding men in the field for a week.

First Sergeant Fischer woke me about two A.M. "Sir, there's a hell of a firefight going on up yonder. Must be the old French fort under attack." The top sergeant pointed me in the right direction as I rubbed the sleep from my eyes and put on my glasses.

Sure enough, in the foothills about three miles away, star shells were slowly drifting down out of the low-hanging, gray clouds, illuminating the wet land and black sky. The faint sounds of gunfire cracked and popped, and trees came alive in the flickering chemical light. Not two minutes later, a chopper roared overhead, headed toward the outpost. I whispered to Sergeant Fischer, "Get on the horn (radio), Top, and let air force combat control know where we are. I don't want any gunships to take us for the bad guys."

I knew some of the night choppers had infrared scopes on their gunsights, and my two hundred unwashed men would surely send out a bright signal to any trigger-happy gunship driver. In fact, the army was said to have little boxes with body lice in them that could smell a man at five hundred feet, and stamp their feet or something to alert a tracker. So, I didn't want to take any chances so close to heavy fighting.

As we sat there and watched the show, Pham eased beside me. "Radio, *Dai Uy*," he whispered. I took the handset and leaned back against the side of my shallow hole.

The call was relayed by the AFCC from the HQ, 3d Marines: Proceed with your unit toward coordinates AX blah, blah, blah, with all possible haste. Relieve besieged outpost defenders and hold until reinforcements arrive at first light. Do you copy?

"Affirm, Tango Zulu out," I replied. "All right, Top," I whispered to First Sergeant Fischer. "They want us to get up there and give 'em a hand. Get the company ready to move out."

"Shit, Captain," Fischer answered. "The VC'll have the road covered tight as a tick on a coon dawg's butt, as long as it's dark. If we go bustin' up there like the 7th Cavalry to the rescue, they'll shoot our nuts off."

Since I had no desire to sing tenor the rest of my life and still had ideas about a basketball team–size family, I nodded at the wisdom of his counsel. "Good point, Top. We'll head out cross-country. Get the XO up to me quick. And send for Sergeant Garrett and the VN sergeant—Trung, isn't it? Their squad will be on point."

I called the AFCC and told them of my plan while the company was loading up. The men were quiet, and I didn't see a single night security violation. AFCC wasn't happy and told me the Marines at the fort were in desperate straits, but I flat out refused to go up the road in the dark. "You'll have to get the CO of CCN to order me before I'll do it," I insisted. "Meanwhile, we're wasting time arguing. I'm departing RON now and estimate arrival at the outpost at 0430."

The two NCOs I had sent for arrived. Sergeant Garrett was a first-rate soldier, a slow-talking cracker from Georgia with the scarred face of a man whose teenage years had been plagued by superzits. He had joined the army to get away from poverty and was a gung ho career man. Like many southern boys in the service, he was lean and rawboned, able to withstand the rigors of army life in the field without a thought of complaint.

Giving Sergeant Garrett orders to stay off the road but to

go as fast as he could cross-country, I moved the company out. Movement was slow, and Americans were fighting a desperate battle ahead of me, but we couldn't do any good getting the shit shot out of us before we even got to the old fort. The wet brush quickly soaked our clothing, increasing our discomfort. The drip of raindrops muffled the tread of our boots on the wet ground. Besides, I consoled myself as I panted through the darkness, "They're only Marines."

My estimate of the net worth of a handful of Marines was about to take a giant leap forward. Live and learn. Those Marines were about to show me some real heroism.

We didn't see or hear anything that seemed suspicious until we came to a wide stream, maybe a thousand yards from the little hill where the old fort was located. As the point squad started across, a single automatic weapon clattered a red stream of death at us. If the enemy gunner had been only a little more patient, he could have greased the whole bunch of us in the middle of the water. As it was, he killed one of the strikers and wounded another very slightly in the hand.

In an instant, nearly everyone on our side dropped to the ground and opened up. The VC over there must have been scared half to death, or shot to hell, or both; when we cautiously crossed the stream, the night remained quiet. By that time, the light from the star shells helped illuminate the ground in front of us, but the flickering light made every bush come alive, every tree seem a threatening, half-visible menace. Detailing a couple of men to carry the KIA, we moved as quickly as possible, using the trees and brush for cover, toward the hill. But it sounded as if the shooting had lost some of its previous intensity.

Of course, choppers and planes were overhead, blasting the hell out of anything that even looked like a target. VC and NVA soldiers were tough, but nobody could take the massed fire of helicopter gunships very long without backing off. The enemy soldier was well able to face fire from an opponent on the ground, but when the airplanes zipped past, dealing death

with startling, overwhelming, high-volume efficiency, his re-
solve quickly faded.

Sergeant Garrett sent word back that he saw activity to his
front. I really didn't want to go into an attack formation so far
from the objective, but we couldn't walk up single file, right
to the door. One of the most hazardous undertakings is an assault directly into the face of the enemy, so reluctantly, I
spread the word for the unit to go on line, and off we went,
three platoons abreast, and my little HQ section behind the
middle of the formation.

The line of men stretched about a quarter of a mile, and I
couldn't see either end from my position. It was definitely
pucker time for everyone; not a man of the two hundred, slowly
advancing with me toward the sound of the guns, could have
squeezed out a fart louder than a gnat's whisper.

My mouth was dry and my palms were sweating profusely.
Oddly, I couldn't seem to get a full measure of air in my
lungs; every breath was more like a gasp. Out of the darkness,
far off on the right flank, heavy gunfire shattered the calm.
Lieutenant Cable's platoon had run into an ambush. The ser-
pentine line of men went to ground like a poleaxed mule.
After a second of swallowing the heart lodged in my throat, I
whispered to First Sergeant Fischer. "Stay here while I see
what's happening. If I call, start the 3d Platoon on a sweep
toward the gunfire. Come on, Pham."

The Montagnard radio operator and I started in a hunched-
over trot toward the fighting, trying to keep some cover between us and the shooting enemy. The red tracers zipping
through the branches and leaves overhead didn't do much for
my sense of well-being. The crack of passing bullets was
mixed with the snap of the branches they hit. I figured that
was exactly what my bones would sound like if one hit me.
Afraid to go back, afraid to go ahead, I pushed on.

Just as we came up to the men of 1st Platoon, lying on the
ground or kneeling behind trees, the firing stopped, and a
disquieting silence greeted me. "Lieutenant Cable," I whis-

pered to the platoon leader, who was peering around a large tree trunk, "what's happening?"

"Don't know for sure, Captain. They started firing at the point squad, and we just started to work our way around 'em when they took off. Must have been a security team. I don't think we got any of 'em."

"Okay," I answered. "Pham, get Fischer on the horn." I took the handset and spoke softly. "Fischer, it must have been a VC security team with a machine gun. All quiet now. Get 'em up and started forward. I'm on my way back to your location."

"Wilco," the raspy voice on the radio answered. I could see the men in front cautiously move forward as I headed back to the center of the formation. In a few minutes, I was again behind the center platoon. We continued moving toward the hill and the beleaguered Marines. The gunfire over there was clearly diminishing in intensity, so I pushed the men as hard as I dared.

"Pham, give me the radio." I grabbed the offered handset and called for Lieutenant Cable. "Sneaky One-Six, this is Sneaky Six. What's your situation? Any casualties?"

"One dead and two MIA, from the point squad. I didn't stop to look for them," Cable answered.

"Roger," I said. "We'll police them up after daylight. Keep moving. Sneaky Six out." I had adopted Sneaky Six as my radio call sign and I was supposed to use it every time I identified myself on the air, but I often forgot when things got hot.

We hadn't gone more than another hundred yards when the left flank erupted in fire. Again, the entire line stopped, and again, by the time I got there the enemy had boogied, having accomplished their mission: to delay and harass us as we closed on the old fort.

That time there were no losses, and the enemy fire faded away quickly. Pushing on, we finally made it to the edge of the cleared ground in front of the old fort. It was as quiet as it had been noisy only moments earlier. Either we had scared the attacking VC off or, by design, the bad guys had gone before we could hurt them. I moved to the front door of the fort and met a sweat-streaked Marine NCO with a bloody bandage around his left arm.

"Gunnery Sergeant Fowler, Captain. Mighty glad to see you. It was getting a little sticky around here for a while." The old Marine NCO was sucking on an unlit cigar, stopping every once in a while to spit. He stuck out a grimy paw and gave me a hearty handshake. Things must have been tight before we arrived.

"We'll get out security and make a sweep, as soon as it's daylight," I replied. "Where's your CO?"

"The ell-tee's wounded. The corpsman's working on him now. You want to speak to him?"

"Naw." I turned to give orders to my platoon leaders, who had gathered around, waiting for their instructions. "I'll catch up with him later, after I get things organized." I moved my men out and set up a security ring around the old compound. The air force was still dropping flares, and the choppers were buzzing about like angry hornets, but all was quiet on the ground.

It didn't seem long until the pink sky in the east announced morning. As the light increased, I looked around the area. There were lots of signs on the muddy earth, and here and there a body lay crumpled, but not many. The VC had the annoying habit of dragging off their dead so we couldn't get a good count of their casualties. A few blood trails led back into the brush, and the junk scattered about showed that a battle had been fought. The first good rain would wash it all away, and the land would once again look as it had for millennia.

Now that we could see, choppers began to land with frantic regularity in the courtyard of the fort. Fresh Marines jumped off, their rifles ready, and formed up to go into the brush after the attackers. Wounded men were loaded on the empty ships and carted off to the navy evac hospital, only ten minutes away by air.

I reported in to the no-nonsense Marine battalion commander, who was in charge of the reinforcements. He thanked me for our help and said we were relieved of any responsibility once the final choppers carrying his battalion had landed. By eight o'clock in the morning, our job was done. I had my soldiers stand down beside the dirt road, and I ordered the 3d Platoon out to gather up their casualties from the first ambush at the river. As the Marines started off into the bush after the survivors of the attacking force, I wandered back inside the compound to get the story of the fight.

The dozen or so Marines still alive and unwounded from the original force were eating C rations and drinking warm beer that had been brought in on one of the relief choppers.

I asked for the story of the fight, and the same NCO whom I'd talked with earlier filled me in between bites. The understrength Marine platoon had taken on a good-size force of VC or NVA attackers. Only by shifting from wall to wall as the attack intensified did the Marines beat off the determined attack.

The gunny took me outside and showed me his defensive points and the flow of the battle. The walls had been blasted open from RPG (rocket-propelled grenade) rounds in several places. Hasty barricades of sandbags, debris, and lumber showed how the Marines had repaired each breach. As I walked around the compound, I saw a round, bloody spot about every five feet, going here or there.

I watched my XO, Lieutenant McMurray, coming up the path from the road back to town. The company was all formed up along the road, as I'd been instructed to road march in from the fort back to CCN. My curiosity got the better of me.

"Sergeant, what the hell is that spot I keep seeing all over the place? That round one there." I pointed at the bloody mark on the ground.

"Oh, that," the Marine spoke with an obvious pride in his voice. "The ell-tee got hit early on in the fight, nearly blew off his foot. He ran around on the bloody stump until it was over, and then he fainted from loss of blood. They took him out on the first chopper." The crusty NCO shook his head and gave a wry laugh. "One of them hotshot college boys. Didn't have the sense to stay inside, where he'd be safe."

The look he gave me of pride, comradeship, courage, Semper Fi, all wrapped in one proud glance, said it all. "Damn," I muttered, "I sure wish I had gotten to meet him." We stood there, silent, savoring the calm and a soft, morning breeze, our appreciation all the more intense because of what had preceded it. Lieutenant McMurray reached us and reported the company ready to march. I made my farewells with the brave old Marine and headed off with my soldiers. I thought about the heroic defense of the fort all the way back to CCN.

I never did find out the Marine lieutenant's name, and always wished I had. He was some Marine hero. Just one of the many unfinished stories in Vietnam, 1969.

7

Now That's Scared
or
Hazards in the Bush

My officers and I grabbed seats in the TOC briefing room.
The air in the concrete-enclosed operations center crackled
with excitement. Recon team Asp had found a new road
being cut through the jungle of Base Area 910, west and north
of the A Shau Valley. The route led straight across the border
from Laos to the site of the old Special Forces A-team camp
in the valley that had been overrun by the VC in 1966. One of
my buddies received the Distinguished Service Cross from
that fight. Finally, B Company was getting a cross-border
mission. We were gonna put my company down on the new
road and kick some butt. I was as excited as a kid contem-
plating summer vacation.

Since 1966, the enemy pretty much had the A Shau Valley
to himself. The 101st Airborne had gone in for a while in
early '68 and kicked ass, but as soon as they withdrew, ol'
Charlie was back in business as usual. The intelligence types
figured he was building up his supplies in the base area as a
prelude to an attack on Da Nang, just fifty miles due east.

What never made sense to any of us grunts fighting the war
was why we would go in and take an area, paying in sweat and
blood and tears, and then pull out, giving back to the enemy
what we had won so hard and dearly. It was another example
of the muddled thinking of the brilliant minds in charge, both
in country and across the big pond in Washington, D.C.

Enemy activity in the vicinity of Base Area 910 had increased steadily since the monsoons abated. After hearing the

recon report about the new road, the camp commander decided to insert my company. Our mission was to land by helicopter across the border near the new road and then patrol to the west, looking for supply dumps, truck parks, or enemy camps.

The idea of finding and destroying a big supply dump or a truck park was exciting because it meant a tangible result for all the patrolling as opposed to our just shooting at unseen soldiers in the brush. To blow up a truck, now, that would be something. We had standing rewards, like R & R leaves, cash, chrome-plated pistols, and presentation knives for outstanding accomplishments in the field. I was anxious to get my unit into a situation where we could earn some of these goodies.

We hadn't received much recognition for the fight at the old fort. Although my company did not arrive until the attackers had already broken off their assault, I believed our approach had hastened their departure. Despite my opinion, the fact that I had taken three casualties without any significant body count had generated a mild reproach from the bean counters at higher HQ. I resolved in the future to be more creative on counting dead enemy bodies even if I was not sure there were any to count. Absurd as it seems, almost no matter how screwed up an operation, if you claimed a large body count, the big brass ended up happy.

I discussed the pending operation with Major Skelton. We decided to send in two platoons, with the rest of the company on standby at the launch site as reinforcement in case the men on the ground ran into anything big. I would go in with the first group, and let Lieutenant McMurray command the rest of the company at the launch site. That would allow me a chance to wet my feet as commander, and be on top of any situation that arose. It was my first chance to become involved in a cross-border mission, and I wasn't about to spend it at the backup site.

We launched just before dark from Camp Eagle, where the

101st had their helicopter brigade. We had to use the Vietnamese Air Force special operations choppers for transport, flying the whole company up from Da Nang a platoon at a time. The plan was to insert the 1st and 2d Platoons, and then go back to Da Nang, remain overnight and the next morning fly the rest of the company to Camp Eagle. Those of us in the first launch would be on our own until the rest of the company arrived at Eagle and could come to our support.

The mission was planned for five days, so I packed accordingly. My load was similar to that carried by all the Americans in the unit. What the Yards carried wasn't too different, although we Americans usually carried a bit more of everything because we were bigger.

I wore the standard tiger suit of green and black stripes that was designed to make the wearer less visible in the jungle. My face was covered in black greasepaint to hide the pale skin. I hated the stuff. It seemed to hatch a crop of zits whenever I wore it for any length of time. I envied the darker skinned members of my unit, with their natural camouflage. Even the black Americans had to wear some of the oil-based camouflage, usually a loam or green color, to break the outline of their face. Everybody hated the stuff.

My combat pack was filled with dehydrated LURP rations, a poncho for rain protection, a liner for the cool mornings, batteries for my flashlight, a half-gallon of water in a plastic canteen, an extra pair of socks, a 1:50,000 map of the area, a small hammock made from parachute silk, and a medic kit that I filled with the supplies I thought might come in handy if I or someone else got shot.

On my web gear, I had attached a quart canteen, a compass, my flashlight, a yellow smoke grenade, a Willy Peter (white phosphorus) grenade, and a small pouch holding twelve of those special golf ball–size M-26A1 minigrenades. I also had my big pistol, a Browning Hi-Power 9mm, and my bowie knife. I carried my prized M-16A2 assault rifle, with collapsing stock and twelve-inch barrel, and 240 rounds of ammo, loaded in twelve magazines. In each of my leg pockets, I stuffed six 40mm M-79 grenade-launcher rounds for the sawed-off "thumper," my pet name for the standard M-79, 40mm grenade launcher, which I had modified by cutting off the barrel and stock until it looked like an oversize pistol. The M-79 had an effective range of three hundred yards, and the exploding grenade had a lethal radius of ten meters. The little weapon was a great persuader when confronting bad guys in bunkers or to discourage them from getting too close while chasing you in the bush. The *krump!* of an M-79 round going off was a common occurrence in a firefight since every squad had at least one M-79 assigned to it.

I had VC sandals to wear if we got on the road. That way anyone who spotted our tracks might mistake our sign for VC and not American troops. Taped to one ankle was a five-shot .32 automatic, a last-resort weapon, and on the other was a six-inch throwing knife. In one pocket was a leather-covered lead sap that might come in handy if we had to subdue an NVA prisoner. In another pocket, I stuffed candy, gum, and toilet paper. Finally, I had those navy binoculars hung around my neck.

In one shirt pocket, I carried the SOI (signal operating instructions) so I could send messages in the correct code and answer any radio challenges with the correct response. Otherwise, they might think we were VC trying to send a false message. I also carried several small packets of powdered coffee that came in the standard-issue C rations. Used like smokeless tobacco, stuffed between lip and gum, the impact of the coffee's caffeine being absorbed into the bloodstream jarred you awake, no matter how tired you happened to be. There were times you just could not sleep, not if you wanted to see the sun rise.

Finally, each man was required to carry a small can of serum albumin taped to the top of his web gear, right behind the neck. That way, it could always be found in the dark. Serum albumin was used to expand the volume of blood in the veins of wounded soldiers as a defense against the shock caused by rapid loss of blood that usually accompanied a gunshot wound. As many men died from going into shock as from the physical damage of the bullet. We were trained to inject the serum into our own veins if nobody was around to help. The container was about the size of a soup can and, taped to the back of the web gear, it made a passable pillow during rest stops.

As I stepped onto the landing pad, the setting sun blazed a rusty red, thanks to the dust kicked up by the flashing rotors of the waiting choppers. Loaded as I was, I weighed in at about three hundred pounds. Needless to say, I waddled rather than gracefully sprinted to the doorway of the first chopper in line. I wanted to turn and wave at McMurray, watching from the edge of the landing pad, much in the spirit of John Wayne, but that would have required too much effort.

Thanks to a helping pull by the crew chief, an oily, grimy little ARVN buck sergeant, I clambered onto the big, black CH-34 chopper and collapsed on the first seat. The aluminum frame and canvas seat groaned, but held me. The helmeted head of the pilot nodded down at me as the final man scrambled on board, and the silvery Plexiglas visor reflected my image back at me. I assumed he was looking for the "go" sign, so I gave him the thumbs-up. In a moment, we were airborne, *whapp*ing through the muggy evening air toward Laos and the setting sun.

My tension and excitement continued to build as the dark green hills grew closer. In no time, we flew beyond the flat, water-covered rice paddies, with the setting sun reflecting a thousand shards of light from the surface, and crossed over the first of the tree-covered mountains.

Without warning, the pilot made a great swoop and started to descend toward a small hill, the top blasted bare of trees from some long-ago bomb strike. Before I could gather my thoughts, the pilot skillfully flared the old bird on the landing zone, and out we went. I waddled toward the tree line and directed my men to fan out in a hasty defensive perimeter. I shucked my pack and web gear next to Pham and turned back toward the LZ.

It was my intention to return to the center of the LZ and direct the remaining troops to different sectors of the hilltop. But I stepped on a ground-hornets' nest, and was immediately in trouble. I screamed like I'd been shot as several of the little airborne killers stung my lower legs. Fortunately, the noise of the arriving chopper drowned me out. One of the little devils got into my pants leg and lanced me a couple of more times before I trapped him between my bare skin and the fabric. I squashed the little bugger into a greasy smear and jerked down my pants to rub ointment on the burning lesions. The incoming soldiers were treated to the sight of their fearless commander giving them a moon shot, right in the middle of the war zone.

By the time I treated myself for the hornet stings, everyone had landed, and the Kingbees roared off to fake a landing on another hill some distance away. That was supposed to deceive the bad guys as to our true location. It was standard procedure for insertions, but I often wondered if it was worth the effort.

In the darkening silence, I rounded everyone up. We moved off the hill in the direction of the road, which I had spotted from the air just before we landed. The jungle was thick and darned near impenetrable, so we progressed slowly. My leg was burning from the hornet's assault, but I attempted to shrug off the pain, while soundly cursing the "Viet Cong hornets."

The darkness settled in quickly in the heavy brush. We went into a cold RON. No fires or noise. The night passed slowly. Thanks to the pain of my "wounds," I stayed awake most of the time.

As soon as the first pink blush of dawn made things visible, we moved out, still headed toward the road. So far, we had seen no sign of the bad guys, and we did not appear to have any trackers on our trail. Maybe the fake landings had confused the enemy as to our true location after all.

The going was rough, and progress was slow. The steamy jungle restricted our movement toward the target, which wasn't all that far away, at least as the crow flies. Fighting the heat, sticker bushes called wait-a-minute bushes, and nasty little stinging flies all the way, it was nearly noon before the lead squad whispered back that the road was just ahead.

It was an eerie feeling, coming upon the freshly cut roadway, right smack in the middle of the dense, uninhabitable jungle. The damp foliage was menacingly dark as I spread the platoon out on either side of the freshly slashed roadway, and we started moving north toward the source of all our troubles, North Vietnam.

Surprisingly, we found nothing nor saw anything of interest, even though we cautiously followed the road all day. Every place that even suggested it might be a likely place to put a truck park or supply area, I stopped and investigated. It was as if the NVA had built the road and then abandoned it. Not even a tire track was found. We did spot a couple of footprints, which heightened our tension, but we never saw a single sign of vehicle traffic.

We continued until nearly dark, when I set up another ambush along the road. We settled in for another cold RON. I got on the radio to the relay plane and reported the lack of contact. Every operation across the border had a Covey, a high-flying radio-relay aircraft, on station during daylight hours. The returning orders from Covey said to march on the next day, following the road, and to keep our eyes open for any sign of use by the enemy.

The next day was a repeat. We moved slowly, ever deeper into the jungle, away from the border without seeing any indication of activity or use. We had covered fifteen miles or better by then, and I was convinced the road was intended for use sometime in the future even if we hadn't seen any concrete sign that it had ever been used. Everyone was frustrated by the hard going without contact.

That night, we could faintly hear the sound of engines way off to the west, over a ridge from where we were positioned. At the morning check-in, I reported the noise and requested permission to leave the road and move cross-country toward the source. I was convinced the road we were following was a dead end. The road was well constructed and expertly camouflaged, but not yet being used. Small trees had been bent over any bare spots left in the jungle where big trees had been chopped down. In a few weeks, the rapid jungle growth would completely cover the roadway from the air. But already, the canopy of trees and brush was so dense that we rarely saw the sky from the ground.

Covey relayed the approval of my request to move toward the sounds we had heard during the night. "There's bad weather on the way in from the South China Sea," the radio operator added. "Be prepared to extract at 1900 hours tonight, unless you find something hot."

I acknowledged and moved the platoons out, straight west, through the jungle. "We're jerking the string on this operation tonight," I told Turin and Cable, my platoon leaders. "If we don't find anything by five o'clock, we'll find us a good LZ and call in the birds to take us home." Neither soldier argued the call. We were all tired and discouraged by the lack of success. The short, dark Turin and his taller blond friend Cable headed back to their platoons.

After a hot, tiring day of hacking our way west, I called it quits. We didn't find any sign of another road, and the harsh up-and-down terrain, combined with the heavy jungle growth, slowed our progress to a crawl.

"Okay," I panted at the five o'clock rest stop. "Head for this hill," I pointed on the map to the chosen spot. "I'll call in the pickup choppers while we get an LZ cut."

As we turned in the direction of the pickup point, I alerted Covey that we were headed for the LZ site and gave him the grid coordinates from the map. He rogered and promised to alert the pickup choppers to stand by.

One of the point squad soldiers came back and directed me to the front of the platoon. Sergeant Bledsoe was there. He was sweating like a stuck pig in a barbecue pit. "Sir, there's a trail headed the way we're goin'. You wanta follow it?" He pointed at a rather wide path worn or cut through the brush.

We hadn't seen hide nor hair of any bad guys, and everyone was just about bushed. I okayed the request, even though it was a risk to walk down any trail in the jungle. "Don't get careless," I warned the point squad sergeant, unnecessarily. He had more to lose than I did, if he got careless. Bledsoe was one of my younger platoon sergeants, but an experienced Special Forces NCO. He just nodded and headed his men out, and I fell in at the end of the first platoon, with Pham, my ever-faithful radio operator, still beside me.

The day was ending as we moved down the trail toward the hill I had chosen to use as the LZ. I started off walking along the edge of the trail, as per SOP (standard operating procedure). Before long, I was right in the center of the trail, where the walking was easiest. I started forward to tell Bledsoe that we would be leaving the trail in a moment, to head uphill. I was coming up behind him at the front of the unit when it happened.

Why they were there, neither I nor probably they had the faintest idea. But the NVA outpost was at a bend in the trail and no more aware that we were strolling around the neighborhood than we were about them. The fellow sitting on top of the dirt-and-log bunker must have been stunned at the sight of Americans walking right toward him as if out on a Sunday stroll. He froze for so long that I was completely exposed to him before he sprang into action.

The thought that he had a tall American right in his sights must have made him flinch as he pulled the trigger on his

AK-47. The first I knew about him, he was spraying bullets all around me, and the rest of the platoon was diving into the brush left and right of the trail. For what seemed like an awfully long time, I gaped at the presumptuous little NVA soldier, who wore a wide grin as he filled the air around me full of screaming lead. A bullet that passes close to your ear makes a most discouraging *snap!* as it goes by. The best I can describe it is like someone cracking a bullwhip in your face. I'll be damned if I can figure out how he could miss me, as close as I was to him, but he did. I should be grateful he slept through marksmanship class in basic training.

Without knowing quite how I did it, I leaped about twenty feet into the brush from a standing start, sprawling beside my men, who had prudently headed there at the first shot. Screaming at the troops on the other side to fire against the bunker, I got the men on my side of the trail moving around to the right, planning to envelop the enemy position. The three enemy in the bunker were shooting in our general direction as fast as they could squeeze the triggers on their weapons. The trees were taking all the punishment, and we scrambled as fast as possible away from the enemy's fire.

There was high ground to the right, and the ten or so men with me were soon above and beside the bunker, even though we couldn't see it for all the brush in the way. Cautiously, we eased down toward the sound of the hammering guns.

"There it is, *Dai Uy.*" Pham had spotted the bunker, dug into the ground and well camouflaged. I could see the flash of red fire from the muzzles of their rifles as the doomed men inside fired down the road at where we had disappeared. "Thumpers," I whispered to the men carrying M-79s like mine, "fire on my command. The rest of you assault as soon as the grenades go off." Three of us aimed the deadly little 40mm grenade launchers at the bunker. "Fire, fire," I screamed. *Thump! Thump! Thump!* and then *Krump! Krump! Krump!* The noise of the 40mm grenades drowned out the shouts of the assaulting soldiers, following me right at the dust and smoke that enveloped the bunker.

A single man staggered out the back of the bunker and started to hotfoot it down the trail. A dozen M-16 bullets knocked him flopping to the ground. The other two NVA soldiers never emerged from the bunker. One of the Yards threw a grenade into the front firing hole and the resulting *ker-rump* collapsed the structure in a billow of dust and wood chips.

We were in deep shit, and headed south; any NVA within two miles would be hustling our way to see what was going on. Without my urging, which I was doing plenty of, we scrambled up the hill where we planned to make the LZ. The men immediately moved into a defensive perimeter around the top, and Sergeant Bledsoe started to clear an LZ for helicopter landings. A couple of grenades at the base of the smaller trees dropped them out of the way, and the bigger ones fell to the blocks of C-4 explosives some of the men carried for just such a purpose.

I called for an emergency extract, and we settled down to wait for the choppers. Since they had only fifty miles to come, we would be gone in thirty minutes. My right leg was hurting like hell warmed over. I supposed one of the hornet stings was acting up. I sat down on a blasted tree stump and pulled up my pants leg. There was blood all over my right calf. The NVA had come closer to me than I thought. A piece of copper casing had spun off a bullet that must have hit at my feet, and cut into the muscle, slicing a deep gouge out of the flesh. It was bloody and it hurt, but it was only a minor injury, considering what might have been.

Even though it took only thirty minutes for the choppers to arrive, we were under sniper fire before we all got out. As I peered out the door of the last extraction chopper, I could see a large number of green-clad enemy moving through the brush toward our little hill. It had been a close call. CCN looked awfully good as we pulled in, just as the sun set over the mountains from which we had just departed.

After debriefing, I limped over to the dispensary and had my leg cleaned and bandaged. "Hell, Captain," the SF medic chuckled. "You won't even have a scar from this one to show your grandkids." He carefully wrapped the white bandage around my tanned calf, several red whelps from the hornet's attack clearly visible on my leg. The gray-haired, black NCO whom we called "Big Momma" was as good a doctor as most full-fledged medical doctors, especially on gunshot wounds. He was probably on his third or fourth tour, as medics were in short supply.

My only response was a weak, "Doesn't break my heart. Besides, it didn't even hurt. Especially when compared to those damned hornet stings."

He just smiled, and continued to bandage my wound. "Were you scared when the VC blazed away at you?"

"Hell, not really," I replied. "Talk about frightened. When those VC hornets got after me, I damned near crapped in my pants. Now that was scared."

8

An Easy Month in the War
or
I Could R & R Forever

Colonel Isler called me to his office a couple of days later. "How you feelin', Captain Nick? The leg okay?" He puffed on one of the smelly, little cigars he was so fond of. It did keep the bugs away, I supposed, so it had some merit.

"Fine, sir, it was just a scratch." I was grateful I hadn't lost any men from making too hasty a decision about walking down a trail in the middle of enemy country. I knew better, and the slight discomfort from my healing leg was a sharp reminder to think twice before doing something so foolish again.

"Well, the medics say you're no good in the bush for a couple of weeks, so I'm gonna send you to Thailand on TDY (temporary duty)". He smiled at the absurdity of his next question. "That all right with you?"

"Great, sir," I answered, fighting to suppress a grin. "What'll I be doing?" Thailand was the most favored R & R spot in Southeast Asia for SF troops. America had had an SF presence in that serene country for many years by then. The list of "cool" spots was a well-known secret to the proud wearers of the Green Berets. I was more than happy to be going there on business. It stood to reason that fun would follow.

Iceman leaned back in his chair and looked at a big map of Southeast Asia decorating his wall. "The air force wants a couple of liaison officers to fly as Prairie Fire control in their airborne radio relay and control ship out of Udorn."

Prairie Fire was the general code name for our cross-border operations conducted in northern Laos and southern North Vietnam. We called in for air support to a big C-130 radio-relay aircraft through air force radio operators on the Covey plane. The Prairie Fire relay then vectored fighters and B-52 bombers for us to use on targets discovered during reconnaissance operations.

The Old Man continued. "They want to try using SF people as the radio link to inserted recon teams, to see if the communication between the flyboys and troops on the ground is any better. Anyway, that's what I was told by our HQ in Saigon. Since you're on light duty for two weeks, you're elected. Go on over and ride around the sky all day." Colonel Isler smiled. "We want to keep our flyboy brethren happy. If the air force decides to make it a permanent arrangement, then Nha Trang (Special Forces HQ) will have to make an officer assignment slot available. You be back here in two weeks. Clear?"

"Yes, sir." I paused. "You know I'm due for R and R the last week of the month? I'll be out of the loop for better than three weeks. That all right?"

"Well, you're not fit to go in the bush as it is." Colonel Isler scratched his arm and thought for a minute. "Go on. We'll get it all over with at one time."

"Yes, sir." I saluted and scooted out of his office before he could change his mind. I whistled as I hurried to pack my civvies. I didn't waste a minute getting away, and was out the gate and on the way to the airfield faster than Superman could change in a phone booth. What a lucky break! It was worth the minor inconvenience of a sore leg. Thailand for two whole weeks, and it didn't even count against my R & R time coming up right behind it.

I arrived at the air force base outside of Bangkok before dark on one of the many transport planes that flew throughout Vietnam and the surrounding countries. Those MAC (Military Airlift Command) pilots sure saw a lot of country, lucky devils. Of course, both the air force fighter jocks and those of us who used them, looked down on them as flying truck drivers. To paraphrase a lament I heard from more than one air force officer, "If you ain't a fighter pilot, you ain't shit."

The major in charge of the reception station glanced at my orders temporarily assigning me to Udorn and looked at a blackboard on the wall. He was air force, filling a plush slot in a soft billet. He looked it with the baggy eyes and red nose of a man who was probably hitting the sauce too hard every night. Listed on the blackboard were the flight schedules to all the different air bases in Thailand. There were a bunch of them. There were so many airplanes in the Thai sky, in fact, that it was rumored the birds had moved out until the war was over. They probably figured the old neighborhood was ruined anyway.

"Nothing going up country until Sunday, so you may as well come back at 1600 hours then. I'll have you on the passenger manifest for Udorn. Relax, enjoy the weekend in Bangkok. Check-in is two hours before takeoff. See you then." He turned away to other duties, and I left the place, happy at the layover.

Could life be any better? Not only was I away from Vietnam for two whole weeks, but I now had a weekend in Bangkok. I was outta there and on my way to the restaurants and bars of the city before the generous major had even focused on his next piece of paperwork. I had been in Bangkok before and wanted to see if the New York Massage Parlor still stocked the best looking masseuses in the Orient. As you entered the opulent interior of the place, a glassed-in amphitheater holding fifty numbered seats was on the right. In the seats sat forty or fifty beautiful Thai girls, waiting for you to pick them to be your "special lady" for the time you were there. It was like being a kid in a candy store. Half the fun was just making the decision which sweetie pie you wanted walking up and down on your back. Those little Thai gals gave a massage that would turn Superman's muscles into Jell-O.

The old place hadn't changed a lick from my last visit two years earlier. I exited in a most relaxed frame of mind. A good meal, more visits to the places on my list, and safe, relaxing sleep for the next two nights. I was rejuvenated to the maximum.

Properly refreshed, I showed up for my hop up country just in time to catch the shuttle run to the big air base in the center of Thailand. The flight was a milk run, and those of us aboard took advantage of the droning roar of the engines to catch up on our sleep.

Udorn was filled with planes of all descriptions: F-111 attack-bombers, F-4 Phantoms, U-2 recon planes, C-130 transports, C-47 Spookys (aerial gunships), and F-105 "Thuds," the workhorse fighter-bombers of the war. The noise and the smell of burnt kerosene were very nearly overpowering, even worse than Cam Ranh Bay in South Vietnam. Planes were taking off and landing in a constant stream of controlled tumult.

I checked in with the unit I was temporarily assigned to, the 425th Air Command and Control Squadron. They issued me a bed in a clean, air-conditioned hootch, which was what I expected from the air force. The next morning, at 0500, I reported to the flight line for my first ride on the Prairie Fire air-control plane.

It was a big, four-engine C-130, with a trailerlike commo module in its cavernous interior. The trailer was chock-full of radio gear and electronic gizmos for doing heaven only knows what. It all seemed very mysterious and awesome to a simple ground-pounder like me. Inside the trailer was a full bull (0-6 colonel, as opposed to 0-5 lieutenant colonel) air force colonel and twenty other officers and airmen of various ranks. Every plane that flew into the combat-zone airspace of northern Laos and the juncture of the two Vietnams would be controlled from that plane. The colonel's job was to make the hard decisions on priorities if a conflict arose between simultaneous requesters.

At 0530, just as the sun peeked over the green canopy of

the Thai jungle, we were airborne. In thirty minutes, the droning plane and its inhabitants were on station, five miles above the dark green jungle at the panhandle of northern Laos. We were close enough to talk to men on the ground or in the air, but far enough away from any potential enemy AA (anti-aircraft fire) to be reasonably secure. One of the air force radio operators showed me how to operate the radio unit I was to monitor and gave me the SSI/SOI book that had the code words for the day.

For the next twelve hours, the pilots bored a fifty-mile circle in the sky while the two dozen men inside the CCC (command, control, communications) trailer talked with men and planes busily engaged in the never-ending task of blowing little brown-skinned men into littler pieces. I had several conversations with recon teams operating on the ground, and if any needed air support, I passed them over to the air controllers on board. When my radio was quiet, I looked out of the little round windows of the plane at the fluffy white clouds or at the dark ground far below.

Promptly at 1800 hours, the pilot came over the intercom saying that we had just been relieved by the night crew (in an identical plane), and were on our way back to base. We were on the ground thirty minutes later, and not long after that, I was headed out the gate of the air base, civvies on and looking for excitement as it says in the song. The army had sent three officers for the liaison trial, so I was off duty for the next twenty-four hours. I was determined to spend the time wisely, getting lots to eat, and relaxing, as much as my money and imagination would allow.

On the recommendation of one of the officers I'd met in the plane, I headed for the nicest restaurant/bar in the town. Udorn was a Thai boomtown, filled with bars and every other sort of establishment to separate the American soldier from his money. From booze to babes to black-market shops to legitimate Thai retailers, the town was wide open and ready to provide whatever was wanted, for a price. I wasn't particularly looking to meet anybody, since I was due to meet my wife in just three weeks. So right off I met the sweetest young thing imaginable. Her name was Kim, or so she told me, between licks on my ear with her soft, tickly tongue. She sat down beside me before I'd even ordered my meal, and introduced herself. She informed me that she was mine for the night for only five hundred *baht*, about twelve U.S. dollars. Kim was young (I was afraid to ask just how young), beautiful, and had been working as a bar girl only three months. That meant she had learned all the things Yankee soldiers liked to do, and yet hadn't been completely jaded by the life of a whore. I was sorely tempted, and shall refrain from commenting further as to my strength of will. She was enthusiastic and fun, and we had a great time together. I bought her contract for a week and let her show me another side of Thailand.

I had not meant to stray from the path of celibacy, yet looking back, it seems that I fell off the wagon awfully easily. You have to put yourself in my shoes. From the minute I arrived in Vietnam, I had decided I would not worry about tomorrow. That just made the war that much worse. I was given a gun, and told, within limits, to kill at will. So, I was full of the power I had. I was almost a god, myself. I know that when any firefight was over, my first thoughts were always erotic. I sort of understood that, feeling death so close, I wanted the soothing power of sex to remind me that I was still alive. And, of course, there was the very real possibility that I would die in Vietnam. I know I never would have strayed if I was away on a business trip back in the States, and I would have been deeply hurt if I found out my wife was doing the same to me while I was in Southeast Asia. But I was there, Kim was next to me, available without effort, and I yielded. I'll answer for it later.

While Kim wasn't educated, she was no dummy, and we got into many an interesting discussion as to the merits of Thailand's helping the United States in the war. During the next two weeks, whenever I was off duty, we were together. She helped me buy gifts for my family from the many merchants, and haggled the prices down from their original quotes with a flurry of rapid Thai. I saved enough on my gifts to pay her fee, and didn't worry since I would have spent more just to have the pleasure of her company.

One afternoon, Kim took me to visit her folks in their small village about an hour away from the base. Their home was grass and logs, built right over the rolling brown waters of some river. We could jump in off the back porch, and did, accompanied by several smaller brothers and sisters, who seemed fascinated by the white-skinned Yankee soldier their older sister had brought home. She took me to ancient Buddhist temples, the kind of thing one would see at Angkor Wat, in Cambodia. It was a memorable day.

I enjoyed my visit with the Thai family and showered them with gifts purchased under the direction of Kim. Her folks were dirt poor, or they would never have allowed their oldest girl to go into prostitution. I had taken her into the base PX (post exchange) with me at Udorn, and her eyes nearly bugged out at the treasures available. I know she thought I was a rich man, the way I spent money on her, but then to her, all Americans were filthy rich. What we had together was just an interlude in time, apart from the demands of the war and life itself.

My days and nights were busy, but in different directions. I enjoyed working with the flyboys, but considered myself a cut above most of them. They had it made; only a small number strapped themselves into a plane and went out where the bad guys were. And even they mostly just zipped by high up and dropped their big bombs on some poor unfortunate's head before heading back to the barn for a cool one and a hard night's partying. The unlucky ones, who ran into the telephone pole–size SAMs (surface-to-air missiles) that turned their planes into aluminium confetti, deserved my respect. Those pilots got to see the elephant up close, the way my men did when the bullets started flying. Only then did the flyboys' bravery and willingness to sacrifice impress me. Another bunch of air force folks I really respected were the SAR (search and rescue) fliers. Those fellows had more guts than I ever thought about having. I had a chance to observe them in action later in my tour.

The majority of the air force guys stayed back at the way-to-the-rear airfields, in a gentle country like Thailand with its gentle, beautiful women, and enjoyed the war from a distance. Of course, they worked hard and did what was asked of them, but still, to live in Udorn and get paid combat wages and never hear a gun fired at your ear . . . I guess that's why I envied them so much.

Only once did anything happen on my shift in the sky that I remember thirty years later. One afternoon, just before we were due to be relieved, I got a call from a CIA operative deep in northern Laos on a recon mission with some local Laotian soldiers. Contrary to what was said by the politicians, we were using Laotians against the NVA in a big way. The CIA advised them, using old SF retirees, or even men assigned to temporary duty with the agency. It was bad duty, since everything was secret, a backdoor operation, not out in the open like in Vietnam. The talk among us SF types was that if you got deep in the shit, the CIA would just write you off then recruit another fool to take your place.

This particular CIA officer had just gone into his RON for the night when he came on the air, talking real soft. "Prairie Fire control, this is Eagle Three-three. Can you hear me? Over."

"Eagle Three-three, this is Sneaky on Prairie Fire Control. I hear you. Over."

"This is Eagle Three-three. A battalion of NVA are stopping almost on top of me." He gave me the coordinates, which I logged in the activity book. "They're all over the place. I'm shutting down for the night. Don't call me until I check in tomorrow morning."

"This is Sneaky. Understand. You're going on radio silence until daylight. Do you want an air strike on your position?"

"Neg, Sneaky. It would grease me with them. I'll follow 'em tomorrow and give you coordinates for an air strike when I can. I'm shutting down now. They're getting too close to talk anymore. Eagle Three-three out."

I passed on the information to my relief at the end of my shift and crossed my fingers for the brave American stuck in the middle of all those bad guys. For the next two days, we called for Eagle, but static-laced silence was the only reply. Another nameless hero added to the roster of the dead. If I try real hard, I can still hear his whisper in my ears. "Eagle Three-three calling Prairie Fire. Over."

It turned out to be a great two weeks, and I hated to leave, but all good things do come to an end. Almost before I knew it, I was saying good-bye to Kim, and her soft, brown eyes were overflowing. At the gate leading to my plane, I held her while she softly whispered her farewell, then I kissed her for the last time. I turned away, an ache in my heart. My eyes were misting over, and I nearly bumped into some new airmen arriving on the shuttle I was to leave on.

I turned for one last wave, but Kim didn't see me. She was giggling and talking to one of the new arrivals, trying to talk and stick her tongue in his ear at the same time. So much for love when it's time to make some money.

That gave me something to think about as I flew back to South Vietnam. There's a time and place for everything, and just then, it was time for her to make hay while the sun was shining. If we hadn't flooded her country with big-spending GIs like me, who had more money than good sense, she probably would be married to some young rice farmer, raising little Thai babies. Way to go, America!

I got back to Vietnam just in time to make a report to the big shots and pack for R & R in Hawaii, where my wife was waiting for me. She'd left our little grunts with her folks and headed over to the sun-caressed islands to soothe me and reward my sacrifice with six grand nights of passion. Wisely, I said nothing about where I had just been, or with whom.

My wife, so tall and darkly attractive, with her blue eyes and sweet breath, was a welcome sight after the shorter Vietnamese women who always smelled of *nuoc mam* sauce. Made from fermenting fish and vegetables, the condiment curled the hairs in your nose when you first smelled it.

Between love bouts in the bedroom or shower, we went all over the island, enjoying the sights and each other's company. Hawaii went out of its way to welcome the GIs on R & R. Every evening, we ate at some beautiful restaurant, and at every establishment we were introduced, along with all the other Vietnam soldiers there with their spouses, to the rest of the guests. That sure made me feel proud. I will always feel a special place in my heart for the warm islands and their warmhearted people. They certainly made me feel welcome and appreciated, and that was at a time when many people in America were spitting at men in uniforms. Of course, we repaid the favor by pouring tons of money on their economy. Hopefully, everyone came out ahead.

Early one morning, we went to the USS *Arizona* Memorial in the waters of Pearl Harbor, and then to the Punchbowl National Cemetery. The quiet peacefulness of the places infused me with a sort of inner strength to continue. I knew if I fell to the enemy, I'd share the ground with brave soldiers and know everlasting peace. It was comforting in a morbid sort of way.

Too soon, it was over and I said good-bye to a teary wife as I fought to stay strong so she wouldn't know how badly it hurt to leave her again. I headed back to CCN, hopeful my last half would go by as fast and as safely as my first. I didn't stay awake long after the plane got off the ground. Love is a many-splendor'd thing, but it is tiring as can be, especially when you go all out trying to set the modern-day record in a week without a few time-outs. After hearing the boasts of fellow returnees to the combat zone, I didn't bother to try and outbrag them; I still have trouble believing it can be done so often, so many different ways, in so short a time. But then, you know how soldiers like to stretch the truth when telling a story.

I would gladly have suffered through the rest of the war the way I had that month, if I'd only been asked; sadly, but not surprisingly, no one did.

9

Swizzle Dick Swanson
or
Fifteen Minutes of Fame

Every man hopes he will be a party to some great event in his lifetime. I was no exception. Fortunately, it happened to me. I was there when Dick Swanson got his immortal nickname. I had the good luck, or maybe misfortune, to know a happy-go-lucky mountain boy from Tennessee named Dick Swanson. Rather, SFC Richard Swanson, soon to be famous throughout I Corps as Swizzle Dick Swanson. His exploits will stand the test of time as one of the best of those whose name is etched on the Wall of Fame in the Kooks' Hall of Heroes.

It all started on a quiet afternoon while I was conducting some business in the headquarters building. Colonel Isler had been promoted to full-bull, and moved on down to Saigon, as head of ground ops. A new lieutenant colonel named Donahue had replaced him. We wondered what idiots were running SF down in Nha Trang, since the new boss wasn't SF qualified. Still, our job remained the same, so we pressed on. The bosses came and went, and the grunts did the dirty work. That was the army way.

"Hey, Nick," the new CCN executive officer, Major Orentes, called to me from his office as I went past. "Step in here a second." The Hispanic officer sat at his desk, doing the unending paperwork that XOs are cursed with as part of their job description. Dark, husky, and every inch a professional soldier, he was a welcome addition to CCN.

"Yes, sir. What's up?"

B Company headquarters. (Author's collection)

A visit to Bon Hai. Pham (right) and his father.
(Author's collection)

The author with Montagnard strikers.
(Author's collection)

A river crossing in the bush. (Author's collection)

The author with the skin of the leopard he KIA'd.
(Author's collection)

On the way to the French fort. (Author's collection)

Getting ready to cook a cow. (Author's collection)

The author, "lookin' studly." (Author's collection)

The CH-34 that crashed, killing the XO.
(Author's collection)

"We're being assigned an SFC from Nha Trang who tore up some bar in a drunken brawl. Apparently, he's a first-class troublemaker, but you're short a recon team sergeant since Holland rotated, so I'm assigning him to you. Try and keep him out of trouble, if that's possible. Name's Swanson, Richard Swanson. He'll arrive tomorrow on the morning shuttle. Get him picked up and processed. Lay down the law, too. No horseshit screwing around, or he'll end up guarding the garbage dump for the rest of his tour, and as a PFC."

"Yes, sir," I answered. "Hey, I wonder if this is the same Dick Swanson I knew back at Fort Bragg? Hell, he's about the best rifle shot in the army. Set the record at the sniper school a few years ago. I hope so. I could use a good sniper-team leader."

"I don't know," the XO replied. "All I have on the man is that he's gotten in more trouble than any three sailors on shore leave. You keep your eyes on him."

Sure enough, the next morning who comes dragging off the plane but the very same Dick Swanson I remembered. He was red-eyed and obviously needing a strong dose of the hair of the dog, but he was indeed Sergeant First Class Swanson, sniper extraordinaire. He casually slid his lanky frame on the passenger seat of my jeep, and forlornly looked at the world around him.

I greeted him, told him who I was, and that he would be serving in my company. "Oh, yeah," he finally nodded. "I remember you, Captain. Glad to be serving with ya agin."

From my first impression, I had my doubts he remembered me or wanted to serve under me, but nodded and kept quiet during the drive back to CCN. Swanson sat slouched in his seat, barely able to stay awake, he was so hungover. Back at CCN, I gave him my standard speech on what I expected from my soldiers, plus a little bit more to satisfy the XO, and dismissed him with instructions to get some rest and show up ready for work the next day. As he left the little office my company used as headquarters, I called for Lieutenant McMurray.

My young XO showed up promptly and had a seat. "You wanted to see me, *Dai Uy*?"

I explained Swanson's skills with the rifle and what I had in mind. "I'd like to give Sergeant Swanson command of Recon Team Asp," I told Mac. "I thought we'd put the best shots from the company in it, and use them as the sniper team. They can support the rest of the company as long-range sniper support on the big operations."

"Good idea, *Dai Uy*. More than once since I've been here, we could have used sniper support. I like it. I'll get with the platoon leaders and draw up a team roster. The radio operator on Team Cobra has been to the 9th Division sniper school down in IV Corps, so I'll transfer him over to Asp as the One-one." (The team leader was called One-zero, and the American radio operator, who was the second in command, was called the One-one. Thus, when we talked on the radio to them, it would be: "Asp One-zero, this is Sneaky Six. Over.")

To my delight, Swanson jumped in with both feet and became a damn good team leader. He worked hard training his men in the techniques of sniper support. I looked forward to the time when we could use Asp in a real mission. In the meantime, Swanson stayed out of trouble, and everything remained calm. I should have known a storm was coming. He was being too good, for Dick Swanson.

As I have previously mentioned, CCN's location was on Da Nang Bay, right at the water's edge. The ocean was a pleasant diversion on a hot afternoon, and just about everyone used it whenever possible. Most of the time, we would just go out the back gate, drop our drawers, and swim in the nude. Rarely was there any reason to wear a swimsuit, at least in our opinion.

In retrospect, I'm a little ashamed at our cavalier attitude toward the Vietnamese women who worked in the camp as hootch girls. I don't think we ever thought of them as much more than pieces of furniture. More than once, I went swimming naked with some of my comrades, paying no attention to the women working just on the other side of the razor wire, washing clothes or polishing boots, and maybe, if they cared to look, watching us.

Down the beach, less than half a mile away, was the 3d Medevac Hospital, with a full complement of female nurses. The highlight of the evening bull sessions at the club would be after one of our soldiers wrangled a date with one of the desirable "round-eyes." The nurses were usually much too experienced as women in a combat zone to ever take a chance on dating a horny-toad Special Forces soldier, especially one from CCN. Our bad reputation had been established long before I ever arrived in country. Our unofficial motto was, "Tomorrow we die, so let's get it on tonight."

Besides, those nurses who did date seemed to prefer the doctors from their own unit. The nurses at least knew what they were getting for their favors. A doctor's future was much brighter than any long-range reconnaissance trooper's could ever hope to be. Not that we gave a damn, but any self-respecting female ought to.

However, the nurses weren't above sitting on their quarters' patio with binoculars and scoping out the scene as we romped buck naked in the foamy surf. We saw them, and heard from our sources that it was a common practice for them when a bunch of us were at the beach. Most of us didn't mind, and some were rather proud to flaunt what we hoped to be an impressive display of masculine hardware.

One sunny afternoon, I was at the beach with a couple of my officers, soaking up some rays, and running into the surf for a cooling dip every so often when Sergeant Swanson and a sergeant named Brian Krause showed up. Brian owned the only surfboard in Da Nang, and he and Dick used it on the puny waves of the bay now and then. They stripped off and splashed around a while, and then came up above the surf line to warm up.

While we were sitting there, the conversation got around to the fact that some nurses were watching us from their patio. Swanson shaded his eyes and looked in the direction we pointed. Then he got up and strolled down to the water, stood there looking at the waves, and then came back.

"Damn right," he whispered conspiratorialy. "One of them gals is a-watching me right now. I can feel her eyes followin' every move I make. By God, I'm gonna go down there and get me a date. I haven't had any round-eye pussy since I left the States."

"Come on, Dick," I scoffed. "Those nurses won't date any slobs like us, and besides, they're all officers. They wouldn't go out with a sergeant, not with all the brass around here who'd give their eyeteeth to get into their panties. It'd just be a waste of energy, walking all the way down there." I rolled over to roast my back a while.

Everyone grunted agreement, and hooted ridicule at poor old Swanson's audacity. Suddenly, I heard someone say, "Damn, he's gonna do it." I looked up in amazement.

Sure enough, Dick had pulled on his shorts and was jogging down the beach, headed right toward those poor nurses, bold as brass.

In about an hour, just as we were ready to go back inside the wire, certain that he was locked up in the Da Nang guardhouse, here he came, jogging up the beach, a satisfied smile on his lean kisser. He wasn't a bad-looking fellow, lean as a mountain lion, black hair, and deep blue eyes. He was as tough as a Tennessee mule, which is where he grew up, and hung just about as good. He'd carried a first-class reputation as a swordsman back at Fort Bragg. A girl could have done worse.

"How'd it go, Casanova?" I asked, certain he'd been shot down in flames.

"Not too bad, *Dai Uy*," he replied. "Got me a date Saturday night with a sweet little nurse. We're eatin' at the Stone Elephant, and then headin' to downtown Da Nang for some serious partying." The Stone Elephant was the navy officers' club in Da Nang city and had the best food in I Corps, bar none.

"Well I'll be a cross-eyed SOB," I muttered. "I never thought you could do it. Congratulations!"

We crowded round, asking questions of the hero of the day. Old Swanson made numerous boasts as to what was in store for the unfortunate gal of his current desires, and we all awaited Saturday with eager anticipation. Dick might just open the doors a little for us with the hard-to-get-at nurses.

By Saturday evening, the whole camp was in a dither, anxious to hear the conclusion to the saga of the nurse and Sergeant Swanson.

I was talking with my XO, Lieutenant McMurray, and he mentioned that some of the TOC officers were going to eat at the Stone Elephant and were hoping to get a glimpse of Swanson's date.

"Good idea," I chortled. "Let's go ourselves. I'd like to see who's crazy enough to date that wild man anyway. I'll take all the company officers with us."

As soon as we were ready, we piled into a couple of jeeps and headed for the Stone Elephant, jittery as the parents of a teenager on his or her first date.

The bar was filled just the way it was most every night, largely with navy officers, a sprinkle of air force and army types adding color. The stools at the bar were filled with mostly younger customers, all drinking hard and shouting to be heard over the general noise level.

We grabbed a table and sat down. Mac nudged me in the ribs. "There he is," he said, pointing with his thumb at the end of the long bar.

"There he is," was an understatement: Swanson was resplendent in a wild, flowered luau shirt and tan slacks, freshly shaven, his unruly black hair plastered down with Brylcreem.

Next to him sat a pleasant-looking nurse, reasonably attractive. Even though her butt was already overflowing the bar stool, that night, in that place, she looked pretty damned good. Swanson was busy trying to sweet-talk her, but she didn't seem to be paying much attention to him. In fact, she really seemed much more interested in the man to her right, an older man, dressed in civvies, by his age probably a major or better. From the way he was monopolizing the conversation, it seemed certain he was shooting poor old Swanson out of the saddle before Dick even got on.

We watched the little drama unfold, Swanson trying hard to be cool and carry on a conversation, and the chunky nurse turning more and more of her attention toward the other guy. After a while, Swanson quit trying, and just sat there nursing his drink. By then, the other two were deep into conversation, faces to each other, oblivious to the world around them. Poor old Swanson was shut out and shot down, and he didn't like it. I could read that on his face, which grew grimmer with each drink that he chugged down—and he was draining them as fast as the Vietnamese bartender could deliver them.

While we watched, awaiting the outcome of the sideshow, the bartender brought another round of drinks to the trio, courtesy of Swanson's date's new friend, and sat them in front of the threesome. Swanson looked at his date. She had eyes only for the guy on her right. Without her noticing, Swanson carefully took his date's drink and turned to face the floor, his back to her. Swiftly, he unzipped his pants, took out his monster weenie, and dropping it in the cold drink, stirred the fluid for an instant. Then, he calmly tucked his whizzer back into his pants, zipped up, and replaced the drink on the bar.

The room became almost deathly silent. Those who saw what had happened quickly told those who didn't. Everyone waited to see the next scene in the little drama unfold. Swanson just sat quietly, nursing his drink, paying no attention to the pair beside him. The whole bar just waited in breathless anticipation. The silence grew deafening.

The talking twosome suddenly realized the bar was quiet, and looked around to see what was going on. The nurse didn't like it. Somehow, she seemed to sense her involvement in a drama, even though she didn't know how.

An annoyed frown on her face, she nervously reached for her drink. We watched and waited, the room absolutely quiet. She lifted the glass to her lips. She took a big gulp . . . The place exploded in pent-up hysteria.

I'm not sure that I have ever laughed so hard in my life. I was guffawing and coughing and pounding Mac on the arm. Everyone was carrying on hysterically except the three main actors. Swanson just sat, stoically sipping his drink and looking straight ahead. The nurse and her friend glared around the room, knowing something had occurred at their expense, but not sure what.

The uproar went on and on, and just when it seemed to be drying up, someone would laugh and start it again. People were streaming in from the outside to see what had happened. When told, their laughter added fresh fuel to keep the fire going.

Wiping tears from my eyes, I went up and grabbed Swanson's arm. "Come on, partner, it's time to get back to camp." Leaning over to the fellow who had won Swanson's date away, I asked, "You'll get the lady home for him, won't you?" I felt like adding, "Be sure not to kiss her good-night." But, I didn't, and I always wondered if he did. If so, and he reads this . . . *surprise!*

I knew the bartender would have the shore patrol there shortly so we piled into the jeep and roared away. All the way to camp, we laughed and hooted at the hilarious conclusion to the evening's little drama. "What the hell were you thinking of?" I asked the more than a little drunk Swanson after we caught our breath.

"Hell," he answered. "I just felt like my dingus was hot and tired and decided to give it a bath. I knew it would have to be a cold one, since I wasn't gonna get no lovin' from that bitch.

'Sides, her drink needed stirrin' and there weren't no swizzle sticks available."

Laughing harder still, I shouted, "Swizzle Dick Swanson, you slay me. You're the craziest SOB I ever met."

Thus, Swizzle Dick Swanson got his name, and his fame endures today, at least in the memory of those who saw it or heard the story. Those who knew Dick never doubted the veracity of the tale, either.

It didn't take long for the story to spread, and Swizzle Dick was the toast of the camp. I don't think a nurse ever went out with a CCN soldier from then on, but so what? We had a man of fame with us, good for free drinks at most any bar in South Vietnam. It was better than any date would have turned out. Swanson became a hero to every grunt who watched the few available women in the godforsaken country date the big brass and ignore him.

Like all famous incidents, Dick's time in the limelight faded fast, and we got back to the business of the war.

Not long thereafter, we received intelligence—see, there I go using that word again—that some VC commanders would be gathering in a small village a few miles west of the VN-Laos border, just far enough inside Laos to feel safe from American warplanes. My company was tasked to raid the village and get them, if possible, and kill them otherwise.

After looking at the map, I noticed that the village was next to a river, with a high bluff on one side. I decided to use Swanson and his sniper team as support from the high ground while we went in from the jungle side.

At sunset on the night picked for the raid, we loaded into choppers about dusk and flew to an LZ about five miles from the village. As we scrambled out of the black choppers, I motioned for Swanson to join me at the edge of the LZ. He was in his tiger suit, his face blackened. A scope-mounted .30-06 was cradled in his arms.

"Dick, you take your team and run point for us. I want to be there by midnight, savvy?" I pointed to the high ground across from the village on my field map.

Swanson took a quick look at the map and nodded. "Gotcha." He motioned to his recon team, and they moved out, the rest of my unit bringing up the rear.

We were there in about four hours, just as expected. Away from civilization, Sergeant Swanson was one fine soldier. He was definitely a field soldier.

I crept to the edge of the bluff and strained to see across the stream to the village just beyond. An American can't imagine just how dark a country is where there is no electricity for lights and little money for gas lanterns. It was one of the hardest things for me to accept. A country so damned dark, once the sun set. A couple of low fires were all that was visible across the black water, but not three hundred yards from where we were lying was a village of huts and people and livestock.

I got sentries out and told everyone else to grab a couple hours of sleep. At four A.M., we were on the march, headed for the rear of the village, while Dick and his team of three Bru Yards and his American One-one watched for problems from the hilltop, across the narrow stream. I wanted Dick to shoot anyone who tried to get away from us by crossing the water and to take out any resistance that he could target when the raid started. I glanced back as I left the RON, but didn't see anything. Swanson and his men had already crawled into the brush next to the bluff's edge, watching the village. From where he was, the village was an easy shot for a sniper with Swanson's talents. I didn't have any worries on that score.

It took us a couple of hours of hard work to get in position around and behind the village. Then we settled into the brush, waiting for enough light to make our assault.

The quiet time before a fight is difficult to describe. There's a lot of pent-up tension, and fear keeps trying to work its insidious way into the brain. It's also a time to remember things because the images seem so fresh and bright. Perhaps because it may be for the last time. Perhaps it's the adrenaline. That time I found myself spending the final few minutes remembering the wading pool I got for my little boys and the fun we'd had "swimming" in it the previous summer. The reverie helped me through the last minutes of darkness.

I could see the foliage around me, so it was time to start the show. Standing up, I motioned my men forward, and soon we were closing in on the unsuspecting village, still asleep, I hoped. As we moved forward, we formed a huge C around the village. The stream would be the back door of the trap.

Just as we reached the edge of the village, a voice penetrated the dimness of the early morning. A sentry had been right in the path of one of my soldiers. My soldier plunged a knife into the shouting man, but the damage had been done.

Shouting at the top of my lungs, I led my sweating soldiers into the village, moving from hut to hut, and sending in a Yard to herd any occupants outside for interrogation. At the far end, down by the river, AK-47 shots rang out, and then the muffled *pow!* of Swanson's sniper rifle. A ragged volley of M-16 shots fired by my troops overwhelmed the enemy fire, and then two M-26 grenades *krump*ed in the din.

I moved toward the shooting, darting past the dark doorways of several huts. Each time, I held my breath, afraid that someone inside would open up on me with an AK-47. By the time I reached the hut where all the firing had occurred, all was quiet. I could see my line of troops reaching the river's edge. The raid was over. I glanced at my watch. It had taken three minutes.

Near a boat drawn up by one of the huts, a man lay dead, his head blown open by Swanson's bullet. A still-smoking AK-47 was lying beside him. I waved toward the bluff, but didn't see any response from the sniper team.

I turned back and entered the hut. It was a mess, with the damage caused by two hand grenades clearly evident.

Strewn about were the bodies of three men and two women, all quite dead.

"Drag 'em outside where we can look them over," I instructed Lieutenant Lawrence. "Check the house for documents and guns. I'm gonna see how the rest of the unit did."

I watched while the two South Vietnamese officers accompanying my unit quickly interrogated the occupants of the unfortunate village. It seemed that all the bad guys were in the one hut, except for guards. We'd killed one guard, and any others had beat feet away from the area.

The four men we killed, along with their two female traveling companions, were indeed VC big shots. We got a regional VC commander, a tax collector, and a political officer, as well as one of their special bodyguards. And of course, the two women, both with pistols strapped to their dead bodies.

"Bring me the radio," I shouted at Pham. I decided to call in Swanson and his team, and extract from the edge of the stream. The choppers could easily land along its flat bank.

Just as I pushed the "talk" button, a burst of gunfire broke out on the bluff above us. We all dove for cover, but the shots weren't directed at us. "Viper One-zero, this is Bravo Six. Come in, over." The noise of the fighting up above us grew even louder and then, just as suddenly, died out. Again and again, I called, but received no answer.

"Saddle up," I instructed my troops, who were all peering up at the high bluffs across the rippling water. I led the way back into the jungle and downriver to the spot we'd crossed just a couple of hours earlier. Moving fast, but cautiously, we returned to the spot where we'd left the five men in the sniper team.

The signs were everywhere. A vicious firefight had occurred here, blood and spent cartridges everywhere. Strangely, there was no sign of Swanson or any of his recon team. I called for my platoon leaders.

"Lawrence, you go east on a five-hundred-meter counterclockwise swing, and Will, you go north on a clockwise loop.

Keep a sharp eye, and watch out for the recon team and each other. I don't want you two bumping into each other and shooting the hell out of yourselves. McMurray and I will stay here, and come a-runnin' if you find anything. Clear? Then get going. I wanta get outa here quick as we can."

The two search units were back in a couple of hours. Neither had seen a thing. I had the troops staying with me look for sign, but the dense jungle had swallowed both Swanson and his men. We never saw them again.

Finally, I gave up and called in the evacuation helicopters. There was too much danger in staying on the ground any longer. For the next few days, whenever the Covey plane flew the area, the Covey rider called on the radio, and monitored for the emergency beacon, to no avail.

Swizzle Dick Swanson dissolved into the dim dusty memories of yesterday, his fame to live on after him, a treasured war story for those of us who knew him and remembered his special time in the limelight.

10

Wallaby's Coming
or
Put the Steaks on the Barbie, Mate

"Captain Nicholson, I want you to take B Company up to FOB (Forward Operating Base) 1 at Vandegrift and stand by to launch operations into Base Area 901 by ground insertion on my command."

Major Skelton, CCN's S-3, tapped the map with his new toy, a collapsible pointer that he carried in his pocket like a pencil and could pull open to about three feet in length like an automobile radio antenna. He liked to slap it against the map, just to hear it pop, I guess. He paused to let me find the designated spot on the map. "We'll send out recon teams to infiltrate across the border, and your reaction company will be ready to reinforce against any major contacts. This will allow us to keep the pressure on Charlie even though this damned rain is grounding chopper inserts."

I was rapidly scribbling down his instructions as he talked. "Yes, sir. You want me to take the entire company? Won't that fill up the FOB to overflowing?"

"You'll make out," the S-3 replied. "There's not much likelihood that this bad weather will last beyond a week or so. You can suffer a little crowding that long, can't you?"

"Roger, sir, if you say so. I'll get the company alerted. I'll have my XO bring by a list of the equipment I'll want to take along. We'll be ready to go by 1600."

FOB 1 was located just outside the big Marine outpost at Camp Vandegrift, only a few klicks east of the Laotian border. A small detachment of CCN people there monitored radio-relay traffic from our teams across the border, and liaised with the Marines if we needed their artillery or air support.

A late-season typhoon had brought in several days of bad flying weather, and more was forecast. Using the FOB as a start point and walking across the border was a good idea. I just hated the thought of two hundred people cooped up in a compound built for twenty. I hoped everyone brought their toothbrushes.

We choppered into the FOB just ahead of another roaring thunderstorm and still managed to get just about everything soaked despite our best efforts. I never saw it rain as hard as it had those few days. It didn't just come down in buckets; it rained solid sheets of water. I pitied the poor grunts out in the bush, who were trying to survive the enemy and not drown at the same time.

We settled in and dispatched the unfortunate recon teams to make their wet, miserable hike into Laos. Those of us left made the best of a crowded situation. The FOB had a big enough bunker/TOC to house the Americans, but the Yards were crammed into pretty close quarters, sleeping in tents around the perimeter of our little camp.

In spite of the wet conditions, a routine was established, and we practiced for combat operation across the line. We didn't stray far from the main wire, since the VC were never far from it themselves. The teams weren't having much success finding any targets of opportunity, so it appeared the trip would be a quiet one. Then, Lieutenant Mac reported that we were running out of rice and foodstuff for the Yard soldiers.

Just about the worst thing you could do to create unrest in the ranks of our mercenary troops was mess up their rice allowance. They were adamant about keeping their bellies full, to the extent that other camps had suffered mass rebellion and desertions when the food ran out. It could be embarrassing and worse if it happened here, so close to Bon Hai, where most of my strikers lived. If they got hungry, they might just cut out for home and some of Momma's cooking.

I called down to CCN on the secure radio and ordered a re-supply run. "Don't know, Nick," the S-4 supply officer replied. "We have no way to get it there right now. The air force is just about standing down while this rain persists, unless there's an all-weather strip to land on."

"Hell's fire," I snarled in frustration. "You know all we've got here at the FOB is a dirt strip, or rather, a mud strip. Still, I gotta have some resupply."

"All right, I'll try the Australian unit at Nha Trang. They sometimes fly when no one else will."

"Whatever it takes, just get some grub up here pronto, or I'll be in charge of a ghost company."

The Aussie fliers, who used the call sign Wallaby, were famous throughout South Vietnam as crazy fliers. They'd fly when the ducks were walking. More than once I had heard how the bravery of the Wallaby crews paid off in big dividends to some hungry or supply-short SF camp. When it came to aerial resupply, they were certainly the favorites of the American Special Forces.

The Aussies flew the de Havilland CV-7 STOL (short takeoff and landing) cargo plane. The twin-engine cargo carrier was ideal for the rough, unimproved landing strips carved out of the jungle beside the isolated camps scattered around the Vietnamese countryside. The U.S. Army had used the plane as its cargo carrier until the air force, fearful that it would lose control of some of the air operations in South Vietnam, insisted the planes be turned over to them. The boys in blue then quickly declared the sturdy but unglamorous puddle-jumpers obsolete and got rid of them.

For the type of work we did, and the primitive airstrips we normally had, the Aussies were the best resupply unit in South Vietnam. If anybody could get through, the Wallabys could, and regularly did.

When I passed the word that Wallabys were bringing in the supplies, a satisfied murmur went around the room. We all looked forward to meeting the nifty chaps of the Royal Australian Air Force.

The next morning was unchanged from any that week, drizzly and gray. Low clouds came to within a few meters of the ground. I could have thrown a baseball into the air and seen it swallowed in the swirling mist. It was a miserable day for flying, at least anywhere around the FOB. Because we were in the mountains on a plateau surrounded by other mountaintops, no pilot in his right mind would try and get low enough to find us. The chances of being splattered on the slope of a surrounding hill were just too great.

About noon, the radio blasted the eagerly awaited message. "Hello, Yanks! Wallaby's coming. Are you there?"

"Roger, Wallaby, we read you. Be advised that the ceiling is less than two hundred feet, and the runway is extremely muddy." The FOB radio operator was all business; he wanted the plane to make it down safely.

"Not a care, Yank," was the cheery reply. "We're starting through the overcast now. Let us know when you think we're right over the camp."

We all hurried outside to listen, fearful of the sound of the Aussie plane slamming into the side of a mountain.

"You're right overhead," the RTO shouted into the mike as the roar of the engines reached a crescendo. The crazy Aussie flyboys were easing down in a tight circle directly over the camp, hoping to break out of the overcast before they ran out of airspace. Lower and lower the circling plane descended, while we willed it to break free of the enveloping mist. Then suddenly, there it was, the red kangaroo painted on the tail, like a travel poster, breaking free of the mist with less than two hundred feet to spare before they plowed into the ground.

With a roar of reversed engines, the gangly old airplane slipped to a halt in front of us, its wheels buried well past the axles in red clay mud. Cheering in admiration for the flying skill of the Aussie pilots, we slipped through the muck to the door of the craft, anxious to be the first to welcome the Aussie pilots to the FOB.

"Cheerio, laddies," a red-haired Aussie with a ferocious handlebar mustache shouted from the door of the aircraft. He dropped to the mud, followed in turn by his companion, a sandy-haired younger man, or really, youth was a fitting description for the copilot. I don't think he could have been out of his teens. Two grizzled RAAF flight NCOs dropped out after the two pilots, and everyone sort of gathered around our new arrivals, anxious to greet them.

Shaking hands all around, the pilot introduced himself and the rest of his crew. "Barney Clybourne and Peter Knolls, Royal Australian Air Force. These are my crewmen, Flying Sergeants Bobby Rader and Reggie McQuade." All the Aussies greeted us like long-lost cousins, and we them. After meeting each other, we all headed for the team house as the Aussies wanted some beer to wash down the collective dryness in their throats. I'm certain the landing hadn't been the piece of cake they pretended it was.

First Sergeant Fischer got the strikers to quickly unload enough rice and dried meat to last the company for a month, if necessary. Barney and his flight sergeants walked back to the airplane after a couple of beers to inspect its wheels, which were buried in the red-orange clay of the airstrip.

"We're stuck here, laddies," Barney announced at supper that evening. "The boys and I will have to wait until the ground dries a bit before we can taxi. Hope that'll not slip a cropper into your operation here."

"Hell, no," I answered, and was promptly chorused by the others. "Glad to have the company. Anything you want, just ask."

"You know, Captain, there is one thing I'd rather like to do, if you could work it out." Flight Lieutenant Clybourne grinned at me conspiratorially. "Neither I or any of my crew has ever flown about in one of your Huey helicopters. I'd give a bloody hoot for the opportunity. Can it be arranged?" He brushed his rather long brown hair off his forehead, and winked confidently at me. Apparently, the Aussies didn't make their soldiers cut their hair as close as we Americans did.

The other Aussies nodded enthusiastically. "Right on, Barney. That's a capital suggestion," Sergeant Rader chimed in. "Maybe even out there where the bloody dinks are messing about. I'd like to take a shot at just one of the muggers before I go back to Queensland. That'd be a fair dinkum way to spend a day." The slightly built Rader would have lasted about a day in the bush against the NVA. He appeared to be about as vicious as a little puppy dog.

I shook my head. "I'll have to see. The only way we can get a chopper is to borrow one from the Marines. It might take some doing, but, what the hell, I'll give it a try tomorrow."

"Bloody marvelous," Barney pumped my hand. "Now, come on, we've got beer to drink and lies to tell. Let's get to it."

My head protested when it came time to get up the next morning, but a cold spray at the rudimentary shower stall washed the misery away. Even a few beers brought back memories of the party at the village. My head would never be the same. The rain had stopped, and there appeared to be a good chance that the sun would come out. I borrowed the FOB jeep and drove over to the Marine S-3 (Air) office with the NCOIC of the FOB, Harvey Saal, a legend among SF troopers. He had been in South Vietnam about as long as any man in country. In fact, we did not know it, but he was at that moment AWOL from a field hospital that intended to ship him Stateside to recover from a previous wound.

We crowded into the little cubicle that the harried Marine officer who served as S-3 (Air) used and made our pitch for a helicopter. He peered at me over his glasses, skepticism on his face. "We really would only need it for a couple of hours, Captain Bassett." I pointed to the map pinned on the wall behind his desk. "I thought I'd take them out to Antelope Valley and look for some deer. If we get any, I planned on having a barbecue, and you'd be very welcome to attend."

The aptly named Antelope Valley was home to several herds of deer, and a hunting trip from the chopper would be a great way to entertain our guests. We could flush the deer from cover with the noisy helicopters, then blast them from above without hardly getting our feet dirty.

Bassett thought for a minute. "No way I can give you choppers for an unauthorized deer hunt, but if you were to ask for a couple to practice combat assault landings, I suppose I could send you some." He pulled out the required forms. "Now, just what type of assault training did you have in mind . . . ?"

The sun finally peeked out of the clouds around noon, and shortly thereafter, the familiar *whomp! whomp!* of Huey blades slapping the air announced the arrival of our assault training choppers.

I briefed the Marine aviators on the true intention of the flights and offered to provide troops for assault insertion if either chopper crew wanted to really fly a training mission instead of screwing around hunting deer. I'll bet you can guess the answer to that question.

We put a pair of excited Aussies in each chopper plus a couple of my SF officers, and off we roared, mighty hunters of the sky. I flew with Barney and McQuade in my chopper. The Marines did a great job of flying low, showing the Aussies their skill in nap-of-the-earth flying. Before long we popped over the last hill and the wide expanse of Antelope Valley lay below us.

The natural amphitheater was ten miles wide and maybe five long, with much of the area covered in waist-high grass rather than trees. From our vantage point in the helicopters, we would have little trouble flushing out deer to shoot. It didn't take long. A few swoops over the scattered copses of trees, and a small herd of Vietnamese deer broke cover and darted across the grassy slopes.

The smallish deer were about the size of the American white-tailed deer, although with much smaller horns. I pointed out the running herd to the pilot, and he banked the chopper hard, those of us in the back whooping with excitement, with the other chopper close behind. We closed in behind the running animals, and I nodded at the two Aussies and shouted above the roar of the chopper, "Let 'em have it. Don't forget to lead, or you'll hit behind them."

Both Aussies leaned out of the open door of the helicopter, tightly gripping borrowed M-16 rifles. As we swooped over the terrified deer, both opened up with a full load of twenty rounds, kicking up dirt and grass, but all missed the deer, which darted to one side and scampered into another grove of trees.

Shouting and laughing, we cruised on down the valley, shooting at anything that moved. The aerial hunters got better with every try, and within an hour there were six dead animals slung under the chopper. "Time to head for the barn," the pilot announced as we tied the last animal to the skid of the aircraft. "We've just about burned up a full tank of jet fuel." His face was hidden behind the silvered sunscreen of his flight helmet, but you could hear the excitement in his voice. The pilots had enjoyed the chase as much as we had.

We dropped the load of meat at the edge of the FOB airstrip and invited the flight crews to that evening's cookout. In return, we got their promise to return the next day, to "continue the training," if the weather cooperated and more important missions didn't get their choppers.

We had a grand barbeque with lots of venison and beer, and more laughing than I'd had in a long time. The Aussies were in rare form, telling outrageous tales, and every one of them crocked to the gills. It was a great party.

I saved one of the racks from a little buck. It now hangs in my office. The chase was hardly sporting, and today when I think about it, I feel a little ashamed at the cavalier way we killed the little animals so cold-bloodedly. Perhaps we were so hardened by the killing of humans that the slaughter of defenseless deer seemed unimportant. At the time, it was just a big lark. Later, I paid a more haunting price for the memory.

Low clouds and gusty winds kept us and our Aussie friends grounded the next day. We had satisfied our hunting lust, and each Aussie owned a souvenir rack of antlers. I suggested that we fly over toward the Laotian border, and "sightsee/recon" the place where Charlie lived.

"Bloody marvelous," Sergeant Rader crowed. "Maybe I'll get me that shot at a dink after all." He proceeded to check his borrowed M-16. The Aussie NCO was positively bloodthirsty.

The next morning as we climbed on the waiting choppers, I quickly briefed the pilots where to fly, then we lifted off, the wind knocking the straining chopper about, and finally headed due west toward the dark mountains of Laos, visible through the wispy cloud cover. Everyone clutched his weapon a little tighter as we swooped over the tree-covered landscape not far from the border. The Aussies were all hanging out of the doors, scanning furiously for any sign of the bad guys, while I was talking with the pilot and watching him fly the aircraft. Like the previous day, I flew with Barney, and with Flight Sergeant Rader, who was the biggest cutup of the crew, even more so than McQuade. Sergeant Saal also came along, hoping to add some spice to what was mostly a staff job, although awfully close to where Charlie owned the territory.

We made a couple of passes along the border area and turned back into Vietnam, meandering toward the FOB, when I saw the copilot's head snap up, and he poked the pilot's arm. They both talked on the radio for a couple of seconds and then banked the chopper hard toward the north. A quick turn in a helicopter is enough to bring your breakfast up fast and leave you quite breathless.

"What is it?" I asked over the intercom as we headed toward a line of dark green mountains to our front.

"A Marine recon team has run into some trouble, and we're the closest aircraft to the scene. They need an extraction ASAP."

He turned back to his flying and talking on the radio, while

I sat back, fastened my seat belt, and starting checking my weapon.

"What's up, mate?" Barney asked, seeing the seriousness of the expression on my face. He and Rader looked around, their faces suddenly reflecting extreme discomfort.

"Trouble ahead." I quickly briefed them as to what I knew. "Fun and games are over, Barney. You two do exactly as you're told, and nothing else, got it? If we get shot down, stay close to me." You should have seen the look on their faces at that statement: they were green, fast turning white.

We waited as the chopper roared on, the tension so thick you could cut it with a knife. Suddenly, the chopper swerved in a steep bank and dropped, leaving me looking straight down at the ground several hundred feet below. I looked out the door. Off to the left, yellow smoke was swirling away as the downdraft from the chopper blades hit it. A couple of dirty Marine grunts, carrying a body between them, ran toward our settling chopper. Our skids had not touched the ground before the men were pushing the limp form on board and jumping in themselves.

With a roar of full power, the pilot forced the Huey back into the air, and as he did, I saw the other three Marine recon troopers clamoring onto our companion helicopter. As we banked hard, clawing our way into the air, the door gunner opened up with his machine gun at numerous dark shapes bursting out of the tree line and converging on our landing site. Where the bullets hit, they kicked high splashes of water and mud into the air, just like on television.

I saw the orange and gold twinkle of rifle muzzles as the NVA shot at us. "Open fire," I screamed at the two Aussies, and I did the same. The noise of our firing precluded any talking. We all shot as fast as we could load and squeeze the triggers. Of course, we didn't have a snowball's chance in hell of hitting anything, but maybe it kept the enemy from aiming as carefully at us.

A crack whistled past my ear, and helicopter insulation

fluttered down. One of the VC bullets had hit the side of the chopper. I glanced at Barney and Rader. They were wide-eyed and pale. The levity of earlier that morning was dying as fast as the Marine lying at their feet.

We pulled higher into the cloudy sky, and the door gunner ceased his continuous firing. The two dirty, sweat-streaked recon grunts lay aside their rifles and turned to their injured companion. He'd been shot in the chest, and foamy red blood was everywhere, from his mouth to his waist. His face was white in fear or shock, and it was pinched tight with pain. With practiced haste the one Marine tore open a field bandage and pressed it over the bubbling hole in the wounded Marine's chest. The man's labored breathing slowed, and I think he passed out. Luckily for him, he might live, since we had gotten there so quickly. If his friends had had to drag him around longer, he would have bled to death.

"Hold this," the Marine commanded of Rader, who was the closest man to him. He pushed the terrified Australian's hand down against the bloody field dressing. The Marine put another bandage on the hole in the wounded man's back, and settled down to ride out the trip home. It was old stuff to the Marine, who might have been twenty, going on fifty. I smiled at him and lit a cigarette, which I put in his mouth. He nodded his thanks and relaxed a little. He was safe, comparatively speaking.

Rader's face got paler as he did what he'd been commanded to do. Blood had oozed over his fingers, and I could see he desperately wanted to wipe them clean. The bloody froth finally slowed, and the wounded man lay still, held securely in his buddy's arms. Barney's countenance had a decidedly green cast as we hurried through the warm air toward the LZ at Vandegrift.

We unloaded the wounded man at the waiting ambulance. Then we bid our brave chopper crews farewell and trudged over to the truck sent for us by the FOB crew. It was a subdued bunch of Aussies who rode back up the hill with me to the FOB.

The next morning, it had dried enough that we were able to dig their wheels from the sticky mud and ready their plane for departure.

A quieter Australian clumped over to me, shaking drying mud off his combat boots. "Cheerio, mate." Barney shook my hand. "I think we're bloody content to just hop in the old crate here and scoot on back to Da Nang. We'll leave the ground work to you chaps."

Suddenly flashing his patented cheery smile, he climbed into the waiting plane, and they gunned the engines into the takeoff fury required to break free of the muddy earth. As they gained altitude, they turned and roared overhead, the wings of their plane wigwagging a last good-bye.

The radio crackled. "FOB, this is Wallaby. Airborne and homeward bound. Cheerio and good luck. Wallaby out."

We watched the Aussie plane fade into the distance. Our feelings of comradeship and affection had increased with the time we had spent together. It's a shame all people couldn't share the same sort of feelings we did just then. If they could, we'd have been home instead of where we were. "Roger, Wallaby. Have a safe flight. FOB One, out." I walked out of the commo bunker and glanced up at the heavens. I could still faintly hear the roar of the Aussie plane as it climbed toward the blue sky, somewhere above the cloud cover. It looked like rain.

11

Angel Flight
or
The Meaning of Sacrifice

Every four weeks, on a rotating basis, one of the two combat companies in CCN was the alert company for two weeks. The alert company had to be ready to launch within fifteen minutes to provide support for any ongoing operation. The one we most wanted to support was what we sometimes called an Angel Flight, the search and rescue of a pilot downed behind enemy lines. I think Bright Light was the official name for an SAR operation.

The chance to go in on an Angel Flight didn't occur very often. The entire time I had the raider company, we went only once, but it was one wild afternoon.

It was sunny for a change, and since the rainy weather had grounded the air force a lot over the previous several weeks, the boys in blue had put just about everything that could fly into the air.

It was midafternoon when the alert came in. An F-4 fighter with two men on board had crashed just over the border in Laos, about sixty miles southwest of Da Nang.

The S-3 sent for me. "Nick, I want you to take a reinforced platoon out to cover an Angel Flight extraction. The choppers are on the way. You've got ten minutes to get ready for liftoff." Major Skelton pointed to the spot on the map where we were headed. "You're gonna be close to the entrance to Base Area 910, so there's a good chance Charlie has a lot of triple-A (antiaircraft artillery) in the vicinity. There may or may not be ground troops to bother you, but be on your toes. A rescue beacon has been activated, so somebody must be alive. There's a Covey headed to the spot, so you'll have air support if you need it."

I hustled off to get my reaction force armed and ready for the pickup. "Hell," I eagerly announced to Lt. Ray Lawrence, my gangly, redheaded platoon leader, "I'm coming with you. Who knows if we'll ever get another one of these?" Judging from his less-than-enthusiastic reply, I don't think he was thrilled with the idea. But, I loaded my pack with ammo and rations and hustled out to the helipad just as the five green Huey choppers from the 101st were making a landing approach.

Pham and a couple of other Yards were with me as bodyguards, and Sergeant White, the supply sergeant, came along as a supernumerary. He'd been begging me for a long time for a chance to go into the bush; now he would get his wish. He was as excited as I was.

Huffing and puffing, the NCO was wearing even more gear than I was. Between the two of us, we could have fought off a VC battalion. He grinned as I waited for him to get loaded up. "Thanks for rememberin' me, *Dai Uy*. This is gonna be fun."

We scrambled on the first helicopter and lifted, and once again I had that sickening feeling that the shuddering contraption was never meant to fly. To this day, I tip my green beret in amazement at the bravery of pilots who fly helicopters; nobody in his right mind would want to fly such an ungainly beast for a living. Our pilots were aviators from the 101st, the best in the business, so I was in good hands.

We *whopp*ed across the green and brown Vietnamese landscape and entered the high mountains of the border region. The pilot informed me that we would fly clear around the crash site and come in from the west: "Less ack-ack on that side."

"The CAP (combat air patrol) drawing ground fire?" I asked. I instinctively squeezed my buttocks a little tighter together as I awaited the answer.

"Bad, man," the busy pilot replied. He had his silvered faceplate down, which was how I remember all the aviators I saw in country. There must have been some regulation about their always looking cool and collected. Maybe to give us terrified passengers confidence.

"The CAP says there's fire from all over the valley." The CAP were the cover planes assigned by the air controllers that I had flown with when I went to Thailand. Their job was to suppress the ground fire enough so that we could land and effect the rescue. It was a tough assignment, since they had to stay close to us and low to the ground. Every NVA in the area would be shooting at them.

"What size?" I asked, praying that he'd say BB guns and slingshots.

"Everything, right up to 40mm and even more," was the less than heartening reply. I was squeezed so tightly by then that the others in the chopper with me, who couldn't hear what had been said, could see my tension. Theirs reflected mine, without a word being passed between us. With a tension that squeezed the breath out of our lungs, we waited in silence for the end of the ride.

The young warrant officer pilot in command swung his ship in a tight spiral, and the ground rushed up to meet us. He'd spotted a small clearing and was putting us in it. He spoke to me over the headphones. "The crash site is about half a klick due north of the LZ, Captain. I'll get into orbit and hold until my fuel starts to go. When I call, you've gotta come, no matter what, 'cause I can't wait."

"Roger, I understand. We'll cut an LZ at the crash site if we can."

As the skids of the shuddering Huey touched the ground, I jumped off the chopper and waddled over to the edge of the trees. Already, I was sorry that I'd brought so much stuff. I assumed that we would land right on top of the site, not half a klick away through heavy jungle.

I watched while the rest of my troops unloaded and the

noisy helicopter lifted off. It would find some safe spot and circle while we raced to get to the crash site before the chopper had to come back and pick us up again.

I whispered to Lieutenant Lawrence, even though any VC within miles knew where we were, "Ray, head due north about five hundred meters."

We could hear the sound of planes zipping overhead, AAA fire off in the distance, and the mighty *ka-boom!* of five-hundred-pound bombs impacting. The blasts were shaking the ground we walked on.

"Move out," I gave the command, and the troops pushed into the dank underbrush. It was a tight-assed time, and right behind me I could hear Sergeant White cursing with every step. "Goddamn, oh, God and sweet Jesus. What am I doing here?" The gravity of our situation had finally sunk into his hard head.

"Quiet," I snarled softly. "There's NVA all over the area. You want them to hear you?"

The mumbling quieted, but I still could hear a soft muttering of *hells*, *damns*, *shits*, and *fuck mes*. Sergeant White was quickly getting his fill of ground combat.

The point squad moved as fast as was humanly possible given the treacherous conditions. They knew we had to get to the crash site, find the pilots, and be ready to extract when the choppers ran low on fuel or we'd get left; nobody wanted that.

The jungle was interrupted by a smoking circle about forty meters in diameter, blasted out of the heavy brush. The F-4 had come in hard and exploded upon impact. There was no sign of anyone around the crash scene.

"Ray," I said, "Put a three-sixty defensive perimeter around this spot." He moved his troops out, and soon all I could see were my personal Yards and Sergeant White.

"Come on," I instructed White. "Let's check the wreckage." We carefully pushed our way through the smoldering debris. "There's one," I said, pointing to a blackened lump of what looked like a red and black pile of burned trash. The limbs were gone, either in the crash, or from the heat of the fire. As we got closer, the stench of burned flesh overwhelmed the smell of jet fuel and burned plastic. It was what was left of a man's body, all right.

White was retching into the pile of shredded metal as we scooped what we could of the remains into a body bag. I blew a breath of relief as we zipped it shut. That cloying smell, like burned bacon, is forever imbedded in my memory. Unfortunately, once smelled, it's never forgotten.

"Covey Two-two," I whispered into the radio. "Recovered one KIA at the crash site. No sign of the other."

Covey replied, "Roger, Bravo Six. Move at a heading of nine-zero degrees from your location for about three hundred meters. A parachute is hanging from a tree."

"Roger, on our way. Keep an eye peeled for hostiles. I'm surprised they're not all over us."

"The CAP has engaged a group about two klicks east of you. (That was the aircraft firing I was hearing). "They're staying low, but the triple-A is starting to increase, so move it."

"Roger, Covey. On my way." I got the platoon moving in the desired direction. I assigned Sergeant White and my two Yard bodyguards responsibility for the body bag. We'd want to take it with us when we extracted. I could hear White's wheezing as he struggled to stay up while carrying the awkward load. His cussing never ceased except when he drew another breath of air into his lungs.

Overhead, I counted half a dozen aircraft zooming in and out of the valley, dropping bombs, shooting their cannons and rockets at troops or AAA targets.

As we reached the general location of the pilot's parachute, mortar rounds started to impact ahead. Somebody had spotted us, and was laying a barrage in our direction.

I called the spotter aircraft high above: "Mortar rounds headed our way. Get somebody on 'em ASAP. We're gonna be in deep shit in just a few minutes."

"Roger, Bravo Six," came the reassuring reply. "They're on the way. Pop your smoke, now."

"Negative, Covey. That'll just give the VC a clear idea of where we are. Just tell the planes to stay away from the parachute. We're close to it."

"Roger, Bravo Six."

The jets roared over, and the leaves sifted down on us from the impact of bombs not far in front of us. The mortars shut up, and we moved forward, until one of my Yards pointed at the orange and white parachute dangling from a high tree to my front.

"Damn it," came the anguished voice of the Covey pilot. "One of the fast-movers just went in." As he spoke, we heard the distant *boom!* of the jet slamming into the ground.

I looked around the area where the chute was hanging. There was no sign of anyone, not even footprints. I don't know if the mortars and bombs had dropped enough leaves and foliage to cover them, or if the pilot had covered his tracks as he moved away from the spot where he landed.

"Covey, there's no sign of anyone here. We'll fan out and look, unless you want us to proceed to the crash site of the second plane."

"Don't bother, Bravo Six. There were no chutes, and the plane went in nose first. They're dead. See if you can find the first pilot." The Covey pilot's voice was matter-of-fact, as if he were ordering pizza.

"Roger. Are you still receiving his rescue beeper?"

"Negative, Bravo Six. It's been quiet for the last one-five."

"Roger, Covey. Any signal from the plane that just went in?"

"Negative."

I sent two squads on a circular search around the tree where the parachute was hanging. In a very few minutes, they called in with a negative result.

"Okay," I decided. "Fall back to the crash site. We'll call for extraction."

I could see the relief on the faces of the troops as we pulled back. We were too damn close to way too many bad guys to be comfortable. We reached the crash site, and I put the three squads in a 360-degree defensive perimeter. Just as I started to call for the choppers, the first bullet snapped by my ear.

"Second Squad, we're taking fire," I shouted at the men to my front. "Do you see them?"

I moved to where the American platoon sergeant, named Crowley, had his little hole scooped out behind a splintered tree stump. He was as quiet and unassuming a man as I would ever want to meet back in camp at CCN. Here, under heavy fire from the hidden enemy, he was cool as a cucumber. As I flopped down beside him, an automatic weapon sprayed the ground beside me with a dozen bullets. They screamed away, whining just like the ricochets you heard in the movies.

"A bunch of gooks moving over there, Captain. On that little hill there." He pointed at a small bump in the landscape about three hundred meters away. His face was calm, his voice sounding as if he were telling me the time of day. But I noticed his dark brown eyes never left the spot from where the enemy fire was coming.

"They moving in on us?" I gasped as I caught my breath. I eased up just enough to look at the offending spot of real estate. What I really wanted to do was bury my head in the dirt and hope the NVA would go away.

"Nope, looks like they're diggin' in."

"Goddamn the bastards. They know they don't have to rush us. All they got to do is keep the choppers away until dark, and they'll have us by the short hairs." Another bullet whizzed by my head, warning me it was time to duck down again.

I gulped down the fear that was trying to boil out of my throat and forced myself to scoot around the defensive circle to where Lieutenant Lawrence was located. I found him, well hidden in a fold of earth, trying to call me on the platoon radio.

"Ray, we're in the deep shit. The NVA have set up on that

hill there, and we're under sniper fire. Keep your men alert in all directions. They may try and rush us from somewhere else while they distract us from the hill."

"Roger, *Dai Uy*. Want me to take some men and flank the bastards?"

"Jesus, no. That's just what the little cruds want. Get us divided up and then wipe our asses out. Just stay down and watch your front. I'll sic the air force on them. Maybe they can blast them out, at least long enough for the choppers to get in and pick us up."

I left the fire-eating lieutenant and moved across the burned area in a jerky, scuttling run. A couple of quick shots drove me behind a large rock where Sergeant White was frantically digging a fighting hole. With every breath, he cursed his decision to come along.

It was a good place to hide while I was on the radio to the air force, so I motioned Pham over with my radio.

"Christ, Captain Nick," White complained. "That radio antenna will draw the fire of every gook within five miles. Why don't you go find your own rock?"

"Sorry, Sergeant. Haven't got the time. Besides, if they get you I'll put you in for a medal, posthumously."

"Not funny, goddammit. Them little mutherfuckers mean to kill me."

"That they do, Sergeant. Don't sweat it. You're doing just fine. I'll bring you with me the next time we come."

"The hell you will. Don't even think about it. I got more sense than to put this black ass on the choppin' block more than once. I'm a-stayin' behind my desk in supply from now on."

I was grinning as I explained the situation to the Covey pilot, still circling high overhead. I glanced at my watch. The choppers would be coming soon. We had to get something done, and quick. I called the air force for a bomb drop on the hillside.

"Okay, Bravo Six. I'll run a bomb drop on the hill at your

one-three-five, distance three hundred. See what it does to the locals camped there."

"Just what we need," I muttered. "A comedian running our air support."

Two fast-movers swooped down over the hill, and I watched four dark shapes detach themselves from the underside of the wings and arc toward the earth. They hit with a mighty *kaboom!* in four-four time, and four fountains of dirt, smoke, and greenery rose up as if in slow motion. As the shock wave passed, I got up and ran to the spot where Sergeant Crowley was lying.

"Keep your eyes peeled. I'm gonna call in the evac choppers now. If the NVA get dug in over there, they can keep our ride home from landing."

"Gotcha, *Dai Uy*. Send over all the M-79 gunners, and we'll pop a few rounds to keep their minds occupied." The calm demeanor of the man was steadying even to my frazzled state of mind.

The single-shot, 40mm grenade launcher would be straining to reach the little hill with any accuracy, but the nasty warhead did a good job of discouraging troops from getting too visible.

"Good idea. I'll get 'em over ASAP." Shortly thereafter, the three strikers who had M-79s as their main armament were crouched behind the broken trees, thumping their snub-nosed grenades in the general direction of the knob of ground. I could see the dirty gray puffs of explosion every time one hit the ground.

The air-ground battle at the far end of the valley was dying down as the planes expended their ordnance against the few targets located by the airborne controllers.

I called for the evacuation choppers just about the same time they decided to alert me their fuel was running low.

"We're inbound, Bravo Six. Be at your location in five. What's the situation at your LZ?"

I hesitated, afraid the chopper pilots would chicken out if I told them just how bad it might be when they showed up, but decided they deserved the truth. These were 101st Airborne helicopter crews, and there were none better.

"It's liable to be hotter than hell, Eagle Three-six. We've seen several NVA moving our way. We're trying to pin them down, but be on your toes. They're on a little knob about three hundred meters to my one-three-five direction."

"Roger," was the laconic reply. "I'll have the door gunners alerted. You have any casualties?"

"Negative, just one AF KIA that we recovered from the crash scene. Couldn't find the other pilot."

"Damn, too bad. Well, here we come. Be ready to enplane as soon as we touch down."

"Roger. You don't have to worry about that," I answered. That was no exaggeration. You couldn't believe how fast scared men could scramble onto a waiting chopper when it was their only way home.

Just as I spotted the first chopper darting over the hills behind us, a sniper round pinged off the ground at my feet.

"Covey," I screamed into the radio, "those bastards are at it again. You've got to put their heads down for couple of minutes so we can get out of here."

"Roger, Bravo Six. I've got a couple of slow-movers with me carrying fire. I'll lay 'em on a north-south pass, and the flames and smoke should cover you."

"Roger, Covey. Sounds good." Slow-movers were propeller-driven airplanes, as opposed to jets, or fast-movers. Carrying fire meant they had napalm to drop on the target. The jellied gasoline was a fearsome weapon, burning everything it touched. The NVA hated it; I loved it.

The two A-1Es came lumbering in, low and slow, dropping four silver tanks that blossomed into a massive fireball of black and orange, swirling around the rising, expanding demon of fire in the center of the maelstrom. There would not be a peep from anybody on the hill the rest of the time we were on the ground.

"Way to go, Covey," I said into the mike. "You creamed 'em good. Give a well done to the Spad drivers (A-1E pilots)."

I was watching the two airplanes turn to the right, in perfect tandem, as I talked to the overhead controller.

Suddenly, the trailing A-1E spouted a long streamer of black smoke and nosed upside down, straight for the ground.

My heart lodged itself in my throat. I couldn't speak or move. All my focus was on the diving plane. It looked like a toy, falling back after being thrown in the air by a child. Tragically, it was real. The terrified crew was riding it down to a shattering, fiery death.

I tried to reach out with my mind and hold it up. I really tried, but to no avail. The plane smashed into the ground and exploded much like the bombs it had just dropped.

With heavy heart, I reported to the spotter. "Covey, one of the A-1s just bought the farm. About three klicks north of the drop zone."

"Roger, Bravo Six. Any sign of a parachute?" The voice was as calm as if he were directing Sunday traffic at church.

"Negative, Covey. He rode it in. The plane exploded in a million pieces."

"Roger. I'll make a pass and check it out. Call as soon as you're all picked up or if you get any more ground fire."

"Roger, Covey. And thanks."

"No sweat, Bravo Six. All in a day's work."

We scrambled on the hovering choppers and pulled away from the crash site. In the distance, two slender spirals of smoke marked where two brave men had died that afternoon while trying to save a man they didn't know, had never met, or even seen.

I thought of the Biblical saying: "Greater love hath no man than this, that a man lay down his life for his friends."

I should have been filled with bitterness at the deaths of fine men, highly skilled, superbly trained warriors, loved and missed by their families at home, families that would never see them again, except in photographs. Thankfully, all I felt was admiration and pride at their unselfish bravery, their dedication to saving others regardless of the risk to themselves. What magnificent beings American soldiers can be when the chips are down.

I honor their memory still today.

12

Bomb Damage Assessments
or
Run for Your Life, Charlie Brown

"Nick, I'm sending you back up to FOB One." Major Skelton held up his hand to stop my protest. "I know, I know, you just got back. Sorry, but something else has come up." He flashed his most easygoing grin at me. "I hear you had a pretty easy time of it last trip, anyway."

I grinned back. "Guilty as charged, I guess. Still, it's just tough to live up there in such close quarters. Life here has softened me. What's up?"

The major tapped his fancy pointer at an area of the map showing northern Laos. We had already nicknamed the region "the Bottleneck." It was one of the exit points of the Ho Chi Minh trail from Laos into the northern section of South Vietnam. What the newspapers called the Ho Chi Minh trail was in reality a spiderweb of trails and rough-cut roads leading down from the western side of North Vietnam through eastern Laos and Cambodia. There the trails branched out into western South Vietnam, from the border between North and South clear to the South China Sea. Dealing with NVA infiltration would have been much easier if there had been just a single trail to plug.

"Air force HQ has informed us that they have programmed a series of B-52 Arc Light (the code name for B-52 bombing missions) strikes on suspected supply caches and truck parks in this area, and they want us to run some BDAs on the results." BDA is the abbreviation for bomb-damage assessment. For reasons I'll soon explain, nobody liked doing them.

"Oh shit," I groused. "Major, you sure know how to make my day, don't you?" I gave him my most appealing grin, but it did not work. He had made his mind up and, once the major had done that, no baby-faced captain was going to whine his way out of the job.

The mighty bombers, usually flying all the way from Guam, or perhaps Udorn, in the southern tip of Thailand, could drop fifty thousand pounds of bombs per plane. The impact zone would be several hundred yards wide and two to three miles long. The damage done was incredible, and causing it was quite an expensive undertaking.

Since the bombing campaign started, the army had been tasked with providing teams of men to run BDAs through the impact zone, evaluating the effects of the bombing strike.

In theory, it should have been an easy and relatively safe operation. A team of men would be waiting in helicopters, orbiting a few klicks away from the bomb run. They would swoop down on the target right after the bombers made their strike and offload at one end of the impact zone. The helicopters would then fly to the far end of the drop site and orbit, awaiting the BDA team's arrival.

The men on the BDA would run a zigzag course through the bombed area, looking at the damage and attempting to get an idea of the effects of the bombing mission. The idea was to get in and get out before whatever dazed enemy was left alive nearby had time to react.

A five-hundred- to thousand-pound bomb going off in your face or right over your head was enough to leave a person groggy, if not very dead. Factor in the effect of a hundred and fifty or more striking all around, and you see that Arc Light strikes were a first-class example of high-tech carnage—which is what the big shots somewhere way to the rear were thinking when they pronounced the Arc Light BDA mission a safe one. But all things dreamed up by thinkers instead of doers usually have a slight flaw in the "best laid plans," and the BDA operation had a beauty: Although it was true that anyone caught in the blast zone was too busy counting his fingers and toes to be much of a problem, anyone just far enough away not to be affected yet close enough to get there in a reasonable amount of time came a-running to see if there was anything he could do to help those caught in the blast zone.

As people who were on the same side of the SOBs who had just dumped the deadly explosives on their heads, the assessment team was not going to be received in a friendly manner by the NVA. Thus, the BDA missions became a dash to get in and get out before the NVA rescuers arrived in numbers far greater than the four men involved by our side.

For some reason, that never occurred to the bright boys who dreamed up the BDA assignment originally. Nobody really wanted to do the damned job, and nearly everyone who did complained about the dash to the far end of the drop zone. The unofficial name for a BDA job became "Run for your life, Charlie Brown."

Therefore, the call sign was changed to Charlie Brown One-zero," for all radio communication with the assessment team members on the ground. The Charlie Brown One-zero would be talking and running, as the four team members made a dash for their lives through the debris of an Arc Light strike. The speaker would be panting and puffing so hard he was difficult to understand over the radio.

It wasn't unknown for a team to vanish before it reached the far end of the run, gobbled up by those left alive after the B-52s' visit.

"Take two recon teams and a reaction platoon with you," Major Skelton finished his instructions to me. "I'll have the choppers here at 0700 tomorrow morning."

I thought about complaining that two recon teams were insufficient for a BDA assignment; if the big bombers were in any way active, there might be two or three BDAs a day to complete.

Nobody wanted to run the damned things more than once a day; that was a given. Then I reconsidered. More than likely, the reaction platoon wouldn't have much to do. Rarely did the BDA teams uncover anything after a B-52 strike that required a platoon insertion into the area. I could make additional teams from the soldiers of the platoon, and give a couple of my lieutenants something to write home about. I decided to take two extra lieutenants as supernumeraries. That way I could field five BDA teams, with myself and First Sergeant Fischer as the fifth and last to go out, if needed. Our call sign would be Charlie Brown Five.

I made the assignments that night, and received a positive re-action to my plan. One nice thing about young lieutenants, they were so gung ho dumb, they'd go anywhere. A person grew to love them, just like little puppies, not quite paper-trained.

We lifted off the helipad the next morning, loaded down with the tools of our trade and anything else that we thought would make our stay at the FOB comfortable. As the strug-gling chopper dipped its nose and gathered forward speed, I realized I was anticipating the coming mission. Damned if I wasn't as eager as the ell-tees riding with me. I leaned over to Fischer, who was stoically puffing on a smelly cigar and watching the ground below. He was probably daydreaming of better times.

"By God, Top. I sorta hope we get a chance to make a run, don't you?"

The wise old NCO just looked at me as if wondering, "Is this guy a candidate for the psycho ward or what?" He just grunted, probably hoping I would outgrow whatever was temporarily affecting my reasoning.

We arrived at the FOB, still tucked alongside the Marine position at Vandegrift. We were met by Sergeant Saal. He re-ported that the NVA had recently started to shell the base with long-range 122mm rockets.

"We've got a bomb shelter dug," he told me. "Usually, it's not needed. The NVA can't get the right trajectory on their launchers to hit us." FOB 1 was located on a slope at the top of the basin above the main compound, which was in the valley below. The Marines down there weren't quite so lucky.

Saal continued, "It means if they pop off a few rounds, especially if it's after dark, we can sit outside the shelter and watch the rockets go over and slam into the Marines below. When they hit something, it's quite a show."

"Better them than us, I reckon," I replied. "Anything to make the time go by, right?"

Saal just laughed. "You'll see. The Marine artillery that fires counterbattery is over there." He pointed directly east of us. "When they shoot back, the shells go right overhead. It's a blast."

We settled in and put away a few cool ones while the trusty barbecue was heating up. After a delicious repast of barbecued Spam, beans, potato chips, and beer, we relaxed and watched the Marines, busy below us in the main camp. From our position, they looked like tiny ants hurrying about on ants' business.

Before long, the sound of men at ease ripped through the darkness. The beans were doing the job Mother Nature intended. All a person could do was ignore the lack of etiquette, suck on the cold beer, and dream of home. Mixed with the sounds of evening—bugs, noise from below, and jets high overhead flying off for the night interdiction raids on the supply lines of the enemy—it wasn't all that unpleasant. I was just about ready to call it a day, when a siren cut through the din.

"Incoming, Captain," Saal shouted. "Get to the bomb shelter."

"I thought you said they couldn't hit us?"

"Haven't yet. You want to sit out here and see if they have figured it out?"

"Point well taken," I agreed as we dashed to the heavily sandbagged dugout.

We hadn't even made it inside when the first rocket arced overhead, several hundred feet above us, and dropped toward the massed humanity below. It hit with a loud *boom!* next to the piled supplies behind the main complex of buildings far below.

From where we were, the rocket looked like a giant roman candle, spewing red sparks as it rode through the sky. It was easy to follow its path toward the Marines huddled below. They must have felt like fish in a barrel, waiting for the impact.

The big rocket sounded like a runaway train rumbling through the dark sky. All in all, it was a spectacular way to end the evening. The Marine artillery promptly responded, shooting the big 155mm shells right over us toward the unseen enemy in Laos. The shells headed out and the rockets coming in passed overhead. The roar was like standing in a tunnel hearing semis whiz by at ninety miles an hour.

Several more rockets streaked over us, one impacting right on top of a crowded bunker, sending sandbags and timbers flying and causing two ambulances to race from the hospital area to the aid of the unlucky Marines inside. Their lights and sirens added to the carnival atmosphere. After the all-clear sounded, I made my good-nights and went to sleep, satisfied that I'd seen a real rocket attack, up close. Just like front row seats at the Fourth of July fireworks show back home when I was a boy. I didn't spend a lot of time thinking of the cost to the unlucky Marines below. It would only have interfered with my sleep. I suppose my callousness would have been less pronounced if they were army troops; it would have turned to pure outrage had it been Special Forces soldiers taking the pasting.

I woke up the next morning in a good mood, and we proceeded to get on with the business of BDA runs. For the next two days, things went smoothly. We only had two or three runs a day to make, and the enemy wasn't a bit active in the area after the bomb runs. Most of the Arc Light strikes did more damage to the jungle vegetation than to the bad guys. Every now and then, one would catch the NVA, and I guess the carnage was horrendous. Most of the time, at least as I saw it, we were a day late and a dollar short with our intended targets. Like everything else wrong with the damned war, the bomb strikes had to be approved at both Washington and Saigon political levels. By the time the poor air force got approval for the strike, the enemy had moved on or died of old age. The men who risked their lives flying the overladen bombers off the ground and to the target in twenty-year-old planes to attack empty jungle didn't get a say, unfortunately. Welcome to the war, air force.

You could say it's similar to today, trying to build a dam or highway someplace. The paperwork takes longer than the project itself. I often wondered later if environmental impact studies were filed before we bombed the enemy jungle. I would not have put it past the bureaucrats running the war.

The first two days were easy, with very little to report from the bomb strikes. The third day was something else. Charlie Brown Two didn't show up at the end of the bomb area. The chopper pilots had radio contact with him until about halfway through the run, and then silence. Repeated calls were not answered, and finally the choppers returned empty.

I met the first chopper back and talked to the pilot. He was a grizzled warrant officer (WO), the predominant rank of army aviators. Judging by the master aviator wings sewed over his left pocket, he'd been driving choppers a long time. He looked older than his years, the fatigue of a long flight on his face. His eyes squinted at me in the sunlight, showing the sun wrinkles around the sockets. He wiped a sheen of sweat off his upper lip with the sleeve of his green flight suit, the heavy kind, made of Nomex material, which was supposed to retard the flames of a crash. It was required wearing for the flyers, but it must have been like wearing long johns in the desert.

"I swear, Captain. We stayed right up till we were short of fuel. The team just never showed up. I flew down the entire length of the DZ callin' on the radio. Not a peep. There was ground fire, though. Charlie was back in business, quicker than usual."

"Well, shit fire," I groused. "What the hell happened to them? You didn't see any bodies?" The weary pilot shook his head. I looked at the rapidly setting sun. "It's too late to make another run today, but you be here at first light tomorrow. I want to be over the last place you heard from them as soon as we can see. Okay?"

"Wilco, Captain." Slowly, he climbed back inside the Plexiglas cockpit of his Huey and started the whining, turbojet engine. The choppers lifted off, heading for their pad, where the maintenance crews would spend the night working on them. Like most of the soldiers in Vietnam, the hard-working men who kept the "iron birds" flying didn't get anywhere near the recognition and praise they deserved.

The old WO was as good as his word, and the next morning, we had twenty men in four choppers racing the rising sun to the spot where the BDA team had disappeared.

While I got on the radio, calling for the missing team, the choppers swooped down into the chewed-up jungle. Every man strained to catch some sign of the missing men. The pilot motioned me to put on the headphones hanging by my seat. Coming over the air was the welcome sound of the team leader's voice. "This is Charlie Brown Two. Come in, Eagle flight."

I grabbed the microphone. "Charlie Brown Two, this is Sneaky Six. Are you okay?"

"Roger, Six. We're poppin' yellow smoke. Do you identify?" I saw the bright yellow cloud of smoke rising into the sunshine about three hundred meters in front of us.

"Roger, Charlie Brown Two. You're at our two o'clock. We're on our way. What the hell happened to you anyway?"

"This is Charlie Brown Two. It's a long story. I'll tell you when we're outta here. Now hurry up. Charlie has been all over this area all night."

"Heads up," I warned the pilot. "Could be a hot LZ."

He nodded and spoke into the mike clipped to his flight

helmet. The four choppers fanned out, and two went into an orbit over the other two, which spiraled down to an area where a bomb blast had knocked over all the vegetation.

As soon as we touched dirt, two men darted toward us, each carrying another man, fireman-style, across his back. They threw the wounded men into the doorway of the chopper and scrambled in the door. The pilots were watching the men run toward the waiting chopper, and as soon as their butts touched the floor, we were airborne. Not a shot was fired at us, and we were well on the way back to the FOB and safety.

I grabbed the team leader, Will Turin, and shook his hand. "Good job, Will. What the hell happened to you all?"

Lieutenant Turin wearily shook his dark-haired head. He was covered with dirt, dried sweat streaks down his cheeks. The dark circles under his eyes and the exhausted expression on his face revealed a long night, spent very much awake and plenty uptight.

"They hit us just about halfway down the lane. We had just started a new leg and got split up. The two Yards went one way, and my One-one and I went the other." He paused and took a swig of water from the canteen I gave him. "All night, we laid low in a pile of knocked-down debris while the VC crawled all over the area looking for us. Then, this morning, they moved out and we found the two Yards, both wounded, hiding out and waiting to see if we showed up."

I nodded. "Of course, one of the Montagnards was carrying the radio, wasn't he?" I'd seen the One-one climb into the chopper. He didn't have the all-important radio on his back.

My crestfallen ell-tee nodded, a little sheepishly. "Sorry, *Dai Uy*. We'd just switched off, taking turns. It's damned hard to run the whole way with that heavy SOB of a radio on your back."

I nodded. He was right, the damned thing was heavy. And carrying it while running was like having twenty-five pounds of sharp-angled steel strapped to your back, digging in painfully at every step.

"You were lucky, Lieutenant. That's why we tell you to always have an American toting the radio. Live and learn, right?"

I smiled at the worn-out young officer. I doubt he ever let his Yards carry a radio again. At the same time, word would get out to the other Americans in my command, reinforcing my standing orders that only the Americans on the recon teams carry the radio on operations. I didn't carry mine, of course, but then when I was out, there was always more than just one radio along.

We shipped the wounded men off to CCN and our hospital for indigenous personnel. I sent the rest of the Charlie Brown Two back as well. The team would not be fit for combat work for the rest of that mission anyway.

I still had four teams available, and the BDA mission was winding down. In fact, I started plotting how I could make a run, just to see what it was like. On the last day of the bombing raids against the area, I got my chance.

I'd sent out teams 1 and 3 the day before, and decided to schedule teams 4 and 5 for the final two runs, the last day. I could tell Sergeant Fischer wasn't any too thrilled with my announcement of the schedule, but he was the consummate professional soldier and swallowed his resentment. He briefed the rest of us on what we would be doing. Since I was taking Pham and another of my bodyguards, Fischer was the only one who'd ever run a BDA before, and that had been during an earlier tour.

The key to the run is to make a zigzag sweep from side to side of the bomb zone, always moving toward the waiting helicopters at the far end of the run. You could never forget that the helicopter could only stay so long, and then it was gone, with you on board or not.

At two P.M. we were in the choppers, lazily circling about ten klicks south of the intended bomb drop zone.

"Here they come," the air-control relay warned us. We couldn't see or hear the high-flying bombers but I watched out the door of the chopper, eagerly awaiting the impact of the bombs.

Suddenly, the entire world turned to hell along the long axis of the bomb run. Explosion after explosion chased one another down the line. The three bombers were laying a carpet of 150 or more five-hundred-pound bombs into the drop zone. White shock waves rippled away from the blast, and trees and dirt rocketed into the sky as our choppers shuddered and rocked in the concussion of the bombs. The noise permeated our senses, overwhelming the racket of the helicopters.

It seemed to go on and on, yet in less than a minute, it was over, and a pall of dirty gray smoke and dust obscured the area of the bomb drop. Our choppers turned toward the melee, and the pucker factor kicked in. Hurriedly we checked our weapons and gear. In another moment, we would be on the ground.

Too soon, we hammered in, *whap, whap, whap,* jumped out, and received the thumbs-up salute from the pilot, who was watching to insure we got away from his whirling blades, and then *whop, whop, whop,* our ride was gone. We were alone, on the ground, with who knows how many nasty VC anxious for our heads. Suddenly, for whatever foolish reason imaginable, I thought of how different the sounds are that a helicopter makes when it's coming for you as opposed to when it's leaving you behind in harm's way again.

I immediately felt very lonely and very vulnerable. Fischer pulled out his compass and took a quick look at the azimuth he wanted to take for the first leg of our zigzag.

"Come on, Captain," he growled, letting me know just how much he appreciated me cutting him in on my little party. "Let's get the fuck outta here before we get our asses shot off. Head for that big tree blown down over there." He pointed at a

150-foot tree that had been blasted off at ground level and was sticking upside down at the edge of a big bomb crater.

The area was stirred, as if a giant tornado had swooped across the land. Trees and brush were piled up in giant clumps, like the aftermath of a careless job of raking by some monstrous gardener. Holes were blasted out of the ground about every hundred feet or so, the dirt piled around the edge like a humongous mole's hole. And the area was quiet, too quiet. I didn't hear a sound except for the rasping of my breath.

We started the first leg, skirting downed trees, shattered limbs and trunks that had been tossed about like used matchsticks. At the end of the first leg, I was gasping for breath. The going was anything but easy, and we had a long, long way to go. The four of us spread out a bit, and we pushed off on the second leg.

For the next half hour, it was a marathon of fighting our way through the debris of the bombing, trying to stay on line, and worrying with every step that the next thing we saw would be a thousand nasty-tempered NVA soldiers.

Our survey legs were nice, crisp forty-five-degree offsets at the start. By halfway through, they were widening out, and by three-quarters of the way down, we were hi-diddle-diddle, straight down the middle. Even so, I was sweating out the concern that we might not reach the end of the run before the choppers had to leave.

When we finally reached the waiting choppers, I was so tired I could barely drag myself on board. I was afraid I'd need to have someone get out and push on my butt as I crawled on for the ride home.

I was soaked in sweat, emotionally drained, and dirty as a pig. And I hadn't seem a damn thing except dirt, brush, and splintered wood. One of the Yards said he spotted some damaged supplies from a destroyed bunker so that's what we turned in. "Numerous bunkers destroyed, with associated supplies." A million-dollar bomb run was in the books. Only ten thousand more to go.

Everyone was happy, and I had my fling at being a BDA hero. I had my only "Run for your life, Charlie Brown," experience of the war. That was fine with me.

13

Pie (Plate) in the Sky
or
Where Do You Pee, up in a Tree?

"New toy's a-comin'."

"How's that?" I asked the operations officer, or S-3, Major Skelton, who stopped by my chair on his way out of the mess hall. I was just finishing up my breakfast, canned tomato juice heavily laced with Tabasco and Worcestershire sauce, which disguised the tinny aftertaste of the tomato juice to the point that it was almost bearable. Normally, I love tomato juice, but in Vietnam it took half a bottle of hot stuff to make it palatable.

All the canned beverages we got in Vietnam tasted, well, metallic. Perhaps it was the long ride on rolling ships, or the fierce Vietnamese sun that beat down on the pallets of soda, beer, and juice back at the distribution centers while they awaited transport to the numerous camps. Whatever the reason, what we finally drank was a disgrace to the manufacturer's efforts.

I finished my glass with a shudder and looked up at the bemused face of our S-3, who had the unenviable responsibility of telling those of us who *did*, what it was that those who *didn't*, wanted us to do next.

"I just got a message from MAC-SOG in Saigon." Major Skelton watched as I gulped down the last of the fiery red breakfast drink. "They've come up with a new gadget, and they want us to try it out in the field. You're elected. Put a couple of recon teams on alert, and a security detail."

"How big a security?" I hoped he would say the whole

company. I needed to get everyone in the bush for a spell. The soldiers had had it too soft for the previous few weeks.

The seasoned S-3 hemmed and hawed for a second. "I don't suppose you'll need more than a squad. This thing won't last more than four or five days, and I'm gonna put you in Area 92. It's been quiet there for the last month, so you'll most likely not have any problems with the pie plate."

"What the hell is a pie plate?" I supposed it was some new type of land mine or movement sensor.

"Nick, you'll never believe it. Be at the heliport at 1600, and you'll see. Come by the TOC at 1300, and I'll give you your AO briefing. Your people better plan on insertion around the day after tomorrow."

Major Skelton turned to leave and then turned back. "Oh, yeah. You'd better go in with them. We'll want a senior field commander's evaluation of the gizmo to send back to Saigon."

"Christ fire, Major. I just got back in camp. 'Sides, I sure get nervous with less than a company of soldiers around me in Injun country."

"TS, soldier. What do you think the taxpayer's spending all that money on you for? He wants full value for his buck. That takes some sacrifice by us poor mud-eaters."

Major Skelton moved away, pleased with his attempt at humor at my expense. As a rule, majors are notoriously grim. They're too busy scheming to become lieutenant colonels to enjoy the nuances of a good joke. Major Skelton didn't hear my acerbic reply, which was intentionally very quiet: "What's this 'us' crap? You got a bird in your pocket?" We captains have a talent for the witty repartée. Comes with our natural good looks and superior brainpower.

I really liked Major Skelton and didn't want to put him down, so I grabbed a foil pack of dried prunes and headed back to the company orderly room to put the necessary people on mission alert. I would take my two newest recon teams, and ten men from the platoon who had been in camp the longest. It wasn't long before they were scattered to the four winds assembling the myriad of items needed before they could go into the badlands.

If the previous month was any indication, the AO was a relatively safe place to go. The periodic recon patrols in the area found very little sign of enemy activity, and contacts were few and far between. Since I had been struggling with a touch of upset stomach, I really wasn't too anxious to charge all over hell's half-acre fighting bad guys.

One part of the briefing had stressed that we were to take a five-gallon can of water for every two men. That meant we weren't going to be moving around much and that we were going to be someplace without water close by. I was a bit uneasy about that, but when I started to question the reasoning, Major Skelton just said to wait until 1600 hours at the heliport and all would be clear. By then, my curiosity was piqued, so I was on time for the surprise that was coming by helicopter.

Sure enough, at 1600 hours, the faint *fump, fump, fump* indicated the approach of an incoming helicopter, and shortly, I saw a big chopper headed our way. As it got nearer, I could make out that it was a CH-47, the army's big transport helicopter. The twin rotors were carving great chunks of air as the olive-drab aircraft worked its way toward the tarmac where I waited with Major Skelton and several interested onlookers.

Slung underneath the chopper, spinning like a bicycle wheel laid on its side, was a weird object. Even from a distance it looked big. The nearer the chopper got, the bigger it became.

"She-it fire, Major S," I exclaimed. "What on God's green earth is that?" By now, everybody in camp who didn't have anything to do was headed to the chopper pad to take a look at the thing coming our way.

"The folks down in Saigon have given it the code name Pie Plate," Major Skelton replied. "They want us to give it a field test. That's where you come in."

Suddenly, I got a sinking feeling in my gut. "I have a suspicion I'm not gonna like what you say next, Major. So go ahead, what am I supposed to do with that thing?"

The big chopper flared in to deposit the object at the far end of the tarmac. I almost didn't hear Skelton's reply over the noise of the rotors. He had to shout it in my ear: "We're gonna drop that thing in a treetop somewhere, and you'll use it for a portable patrol base."

"Jesus Christ," I screamed. "You gotta be shittin' me!" My world had just gotten a whole lot more complicated.

Major Skelton watched as the gauntlet of emotions flamed across my face while the chopper hovered, disconnected the sling holding the device, and thundered again into the humid air, leaving an explosion of dust in its wake that settled on the object and the onlookers alike.

Finally, he spoke again. "Not in the least, *Dai Uy*. We're gonna drop that thing in a tree somewhere, and you're gonna run operations off it. Then we'll pick it up, bring it back, and write the report some desk puke in Saigon wants, and hope we never see it again."

The thing was appropriately named pie plate. It was made of PSP, or perforated steel planking, which looked exactly like its name: a twenty-four-inch-wide plank of steel, about a quarter-inch thick and ten feet long. The steel is waffled for strength, and two-inch-diameter holes are punched throughout to reduce its weight. The engineers use the stuff to lay down as hard cover over dirt runways.

Some bright boy must have come up with the idea of welding the stuff together to form a circle, about twenty-four feet in diameter, and setting it on eight steel pipes that radiated from the center and reached about ten feet past the edge of the steel plate.

The legs were slightly bent, so the whole thing looked like an inverted pie plate on ten-foot-long spider legs. Strung between the legs just like a spider's web were five lengths of thin steel cable, starting about two feet from the outer edge of the plate and circling it. Every two feet another cable was welded to the legs.

I walked around the thing, looking as dumbfounded as a hillbilly in Las Vegas, trying to visualize it in a tree. Major Skelton tried to make it easy for me.

"The theory is simple. We drop it in the top of a tree. The steel and cables rest on the branches. The tree limbs support the weight of the thing. You drop off the insertion chopper onto the pie plate, and then you simply rappel down ropes to the ground. Run your patrols and come back, where you then climb up the ropes, pull them up after you, and there you are. Safe and snug as a squirrel in his nest. High off the ground, away from Charlie, hidden, yet easy to find from the air."

He smiled at me as if I were a half-wit cousin. "Now what could be easier than that?"

"Pardon me, Major," I snarled with barely an attempt to maintain military courtesy, "but I've hunted squirrels in Arkansas all my growing-up life. Nothing I loved better than for them to run into their nest. Then all I had to do was plink away until I shot 'em all out. Hell of a lot easier than trying to hit them on the run."

I waited for his reply, but he just shrugged his shoulders and walked over for a closer look at the pie plate. Then he strolled away, with me right behind him.

Anxious to convince him of the folly he was proposing, I headed back to the TOC. "We'll be sitting ducks up there for Charlie. He figures out where we are, and a ton of lead is gonna be headed up my ass. Not some headquarters quack's down in Saigon, but my ass, mine. And that's a painful way to get a Purple Heart."

"Well, you'll just have to make sure Mr. Charles doesn't see where you're headed when you start for home."

It was all I could do to keep from screaming. "Of course, we'll just ask him to shut his eyes and count to a hundred while we hide each night. There's no such thing as making sure when Mr. Charlie's involved."

"Sorry, Nick. Them's the orders." Skelton was decent enough to sound contrite. "I'll pick a spot where the jungle is triple-thick canopy, and where activity has been light. Then it's up to you, and good luck."

"All right," I groused unhappily. "I just wish the asshole who thought this one up was gonna be there with me when Charlie goes squirrel huntin' with me as the squirrel."

True to his word, Major Skelton found a perfect place to put the thing. I watched from my transport chopper as the CH-47 dropped the plate over a big tree on top of a hill right in the middle of heavy jungle somewhere close to the Laos border. We were higher than any other hills nearby, so nobody could get above us.

The plate appeared to be nice and steady as my chopper hovered over its middle. The men in the chopper with me followed as I dropped off. Quickly, I directed them to move to the edge of the metal disk so the cargo chopper could leave and the one carrying the recon teams could land. As they jumped on the plate, with the water, rations, and ammo for twenty men adding to the total weight, the platform settled deeper into the top of the tree. I began to wonder if it would ever stop going down, but, after settling five feet or so into the foliage, it did.

Once my heart slowed down to a calm five hundred beats a minute or so, I had to admit that if we were as invisible from the ground as we were from anyone who climbed up another tree to look for us, then we were well hidden.

The choppers faded into the dusk and silence returned to the area. We liked to insert just as the sun was setting. It made Charlie's job, finding us, just that much harder. The usual drill was to move a few hundred yards away from the LZ, set up an ambush, and hunker down until morning. Then, we would be off and running the operation.

The night was quiet and uneventful. I stayed awake a long time, listening to the night noises to find out if bad guys were camped under us, just waiting for daylight and target practice.

Eventually, I drifted into a troubled and dream-filled sleep, which seemed to consist of me hobbling through life without an ass to sit on. Seen from the top of a hundred-foot tree, the sunrise was pretty spectacular.

As soon as it was light enough to see, I decided to rappel down a ways and check out the ground. I took the two recon team leaders with me. Quietly, we dropped the rappelling ropes over the side and stepped off the edge of the plate. The first ten feet were tough going; the jumble of compressed branches took some effort, a lot of sweat, numerous curse words, and way too much noise to get through.

After what seemed an eternity, we dropped through the first tree canopy and into the second. Our main tree was over a hundred feet high, with most of its branches in the top thirty feet of the trunk. At about sixty feet up, we hit the second layer of tree canopy and descended through it with much less difficulty. We hit the bottom layer of the triple-canopy jungle about thirty feet up, and stopped for a look around.

By that time, I could see the ground, and it appeared no unwanted visitors were camped around the base of our tree. I looked up and the forest seemed undisturbed. Not a sign of the huge steel platform resting in the topmost branches was visible. Maybe the thing was going to work out all right.

"Look over to the north," I whispered to the two recon leaders. "That gully yonder is rocky and steep. Use it as the route away from and back to the tree. That way you won't be leaving footprints all over the area as you come and go."

They both nodded that they understood. "I'm going back up," I whispered after a last look around. "I'll send the teams down, one at a time, starting with Sidewinder, and then Python." The two recon leaders settled into the branches to await their teams' arrival before going the final distance to the ground.

The night before, I'd reviewed the recon plan with the two teams. Each would leave in its own direction, loop out for one day, then come in the next. At the end of four days, we'd have a 360-degree recon coverage of the area and could be picked up at daylight on the morning of the fifth day. If the recon teams found anything of interest that required additional firepower, I'd insert the remaining ten men I had with me. Otherwise, I planned to keep them up in the tree, away from the ground, and out of trouble.

The climb back up made the trip down seem like a walk in the park. I was sweating like a hog in a heat wave by the time I reached the Eagle's Nest, as we had covernamed the pie plate. I sent over the five men from Sidewinder, and then those from Python. As the teams reached the ground, each leader called me on the PRC-25 radios they carried. "Eagle Six, this is Sidewinder One-zero. Departing azimuth nine-zero. Over." As commander of the nest my call sign was Eagle Six.

"Eagle Six, Roger. Hourly check-in until RON (remain overnight) location. Then radio silence until 0500. Eagle Six out."

"Python One-zero, Wilco. Out."

A few minutes later, Team Python took off at a 270 azimuth, and we who were left behind settled in for a two-day wait. That is, unless a team's luck was bad and they ran into VC or NVA. Then it would be run, shoot, pray, and shag ass back to the tree. I had warned the team leaders that I wouldn't let them up the ropes, which I'd pulled about thirty feet off the ground so they couldn't be seen by passersby, until I was sure no bad guys could see the team members disappear into the trees.

I went over to my squad NCO, a bright young kid we called Sergeant Wojo, as his name had about thirty letters in it. "I want you to make damn sure none of your squad has a loaded weapon. You check every damned rifle personally. Spot check all day long. Then again, every rifle at dark. I don't want some jerkoff firing a round by accident and telling everyone within two miles we're here." Wojo was a chunky Polish kid from New Jersey, and a rock-solid soldier. His head looked like it had been shaved, his hair was cut so short. He was young for an NCO, but he was a good kid, and tried hard. "Roger, *Dai Uy,* I gotcha."

By the end of the first day, the novelty of our new home had worn off, and several real problems were developing. I was surprised nobody thought of them, including me.

One, where do ten men relieve themselves a hundred feet up in a tree?

Two, how about the trash generated by ten men eating packaged foodstuff?

Three, where do ten men go to stretch their legs? Talk? Sleep?

The answer to question three was easy: I let two men at a time walk back and forth while whispering to each other; I had the others lie on their bedrolls, clustered around the edge, with their heads all pointing out from the center.

Question two wasn't all that hard. I couldn't let any trash accumulate and fall on the ground, where it might be found by the bad guys, so everyone had to eat in the center of the platform and then put the trash into an empty rations box. By the end of the mission, I had three boxes full of trash.

Question one was the tough one. I didn't want the men taking a wizz off the edge of the platform, although by the time it had passed through the many layers of leaves, it would have probably been reduced to a fine mist. It was the smell I worried about. The urine from a dozen men would stink like blazes by the end of the mission. Anyone within a hundred yards of the tree would know something was going on. So, I had them fill the water cans as we emptied them of water. By the end of the mission, I had better than twenty gallons of urine to take out.

The really difficult one was the other waste product we humans produce. In desperation, I had the men erect a little cubicle at one edge, using branches and a poncho. Then we started filling the rest of the empty food boxes with solid waste. By the time we were ready to leave, we ended up with five boxes of putrid, smelly crap.

The rest of the time, we monitored the radio, stayed in touch with the recon teams, checked in and out at the assigned times with Prairie Fire control, and waited for the time to pass. Every four hours or so, I sent a couple of men down to the thirty-foot level to look around, as well as to burn off energy. We didn't see or hear anything, but I still felt awfully vulnerable in our perch in the trees. My nights were neither restful nor short.

The second night, both recon teams climbed up from below, tired and dirty from sneaking through the bush. We fed and rested the men who were doing all the work, then sent them out the third morning to cover the other two legs of the search pattern.

It rained for a while that afternoon, giving those of us on the platform a chance to grab a hasty shower, and we certainly needed it. Then, the wind picked up a bit, which caused the Eagle's Nest to settle another foot into the treetop. It was in so deep by then that we couldn't see above the top leaves. It made for a claustrophobic last day.

However, that's not what made the last day memorable.

The day prior to our departure started off quietly enough, although by that time, the stench from the waste boxes was searing the membranes in our noses. Any NVA downwind must have scratched their heads in wonder. Were the trees farting? The cloudy sky meant a cooler day. Even so, the platform got plenty hot in the bright afternoon sun. At the noon check-in, I made arrangements for an early morning pickup the next day. As the afternoon wore on, I started looking ahead to a hot shower and meals. The LRRP (long-range recon patrol) rations we were eating, although filling, left much to be desired in terms of gastronomic satisfaction.

Around three P.M., Team Python showed up. It was a little early, but not worth making a scene over, so we dropped the ropes and the five hot, sweating, dirty soldiers scrambled up like monkeys and were soon asleep or quietly eating and chugging water. It had been a hard but uneventful recon mission. They saw nothing, heard nothing, found nothing. I assumed Team Sidewinder was in the same boat.

Trusty Pham, who was with me as my radio operator, suddenly moved to the south edge of the platform. He stood quietly, as if listening for something.

"What's wrong, Pham?"

"*Dai Uy,* someone is shooting that way." He pointed south.

I strained to hear, but wasn't successful. I whispered loudly to the others. "Everybody quiet. Listen. Does anyone hear shooting?"

The whole platform tipped as everyone moved to the south edge. "Go back, get away from the edge," I ordered, fearful the thing would tip on us. "Just listen."

Several of the Montagnard soldiers agreed with Pham. Somebody was shooting far out to the south. I wondered if Sidewinder was in trouble. Not one of the Americans with me could hear a thing. Too much rock and roll music in our decadent youth, I suppose.

It wasn't long before I got confirmation. The radio buzzed, and Pham handed me the headset.

"Eagle Six, this is Sidewinder One-zero. Over."

"This is Eagle Six. Go ahead, Sidewinder."

Over the static of the radio, I could hear the panting wheeze of the speaker. "We just ran into a mess of NVA. We've broken contact, but they're right on my ass. We're headed back. Get them ropes down, ASAP."

I grabbed the hand mike. "Negative, Sidewinder. You've gotta be sure they're not right behind you before we pull you up. This thing's a sitting duck if they see you headin' up."

My team sergeant gave it right back to me. "Goddammit, you're not down here with half the fuckin' NVA army on your ass. We gotta get up there."

I forgave the indiscretion of the scared team leader. It was only his second recon insertion, and he'd not had a contact on his first operation. "Understand, One-zero. Now listen up. Are you ahead of them now? Can they see you?"

"Roger, we're ahead of 'em. We dropped everything we had on them when we ran into 'em. I think we're a couple of hundred meters in front. Over."

"Cool, Sidewinder. Go hard for twenty minutes in your current direction. Then do a ninety-degree loop for ten minutes." I paused to allow him to digest the orders. "Now listen, One-zero. As soon as you've looped for ten minutes, shoot a round like someone accidentally fired his weapon. Then loop back on the original heading for the Nest. Call as soon as you're close, and if you're not in eyeball contact, I'll send down the ropes. If they're too close, you'll have to keep on going, and hole up somewhere until dark. Understand?"

"Roger, Eagle. Wilco."

The NVA had learned the hard way not to bust through the brush chasing a recon team. We had the nasty habit of looping back and setting up an ambush or putting booby traps in on the trail. What they liked to do was keep pushing the team, like hunters push deer, toward some spot where the terrain or manpower favored them. I figured if Sidewinder could divert their pursuers away from the hill where the Nest was, they'd have a good chance of getting up without being seen.

Suddenly, I heard a burst of firing off to the south.

"Sidewinder, you all right?"

"Roger," a satisfied voice answered. "We saw some dinks crossing an open area about two hundred meters behind us. I hosed 'em down good. We're moving again. Just about ready to loop. Over."

Roger, Sidewinder. Be sure you draw 'em that way before you loop back toward us. Over."

"Roger, Eagle. Sidewinder clear."

The time dragged on, every second punctuated by a drop of nervous sweat falling from my nose. I was in a quandary. Should I take everybody down, where they had a chance if the NVA found us, or stay up here and hope we were not discovered?

The radio broke my deliberations. "Eagle Six, we're firing the single decoy shot now. Over."

"This is Eagle Six. Roger."

We all heard the solitary rifle shot. I hoped it would pull the NVA hunters away from our hilltop and set them off in a different direction.

"Eagle Six, this is Sidewinder One-zero. We're starting the loop. Over."

"This is Eagle Six. Roger. Make it wide, and be sure you clear Charlie before you turn back here. Call as soon as you're within five minutes of home, and we'll start down. Over."

About an hour later, Sidewinder called in. "Eagle Six, we're at the bottom of the hill. No sign of Charlie for the past hour. Send down the elevator. Over."

The patrol leader may not have seen Charlie, but he was out, and in force. We could hear the positioning shots from their AK-47s every so often as they tried to encircle the elusive quarry, namely us.

I took a radio and rappelled down to the top of the lowest tree level. This put me about forty feet above the ground. I settled into a fork of two sturdy branches, and called up to Sergeant Wojo to lower the five other rappelling ropes on down to the ground. They had barely arrived when team Sidewinder came puffing up the hill. Even in their haste to get away, they moved by bounds, one or two men always covering the movements of his comrades.

The team leader, a young sergeant, started to call on his radio, when I whispered down to him. The sound caused him to jump like a startled rabbit.

"I see you, Sarge. Get on up here. Keep it quiet."

The five men started up the ropes, climbing and using the branches as steps. It was the fastest ascent I saw in my time on the platform. The team leader stopped by me for a second.

"Thanks, *Dai Uy*. I was feeling awfully lonely out there for a while."

"I know the feeling," I answered. "How many do you think are coming?"

"I'm not sure. A whole bunch. More than a platoon, but not a company. Say fifty or sixty."

"Okay." I looked one last time at the ground. "Get on up, but for God's sake, be quiet."

The shaken young sergeant didn't need a second invitation. He scooted up that rope. I wasn't too far behind him. At the middle level of trees, I stopped for a few minutes. I was well covered from anyone below, but I could hear much better than higher up. I waited and watched the ropes jiggling and bouncing as the men squirmed their way to the top. Suddenly, the ropes disappeared into the foliage, and I knew they were at the platform.

I waited a few more minutes. It was dusk by then, and the breeze was rustling through the forest. Abruptly, I heard a voice. The enemy. He was close by, looking for the trail. Someone called softly. The sounds below me moved toward the gully. The searchers had seen the signs of traffic in the gully and were following them. They moved away from me, and it grew quiet. I stayed where I was for a little longer, but heard nothing more. Finally, I carefully moved on up the trees to our little home at the top.

I crawled over the edge and pulled up the rope. I gave Sergeant Wojo his orders. "They're down there. Some went past our tree about ten minutes ago. I don't want any noise tonight, so be quiet. Have two men awake at all times. They're to wake anyone who snores or coughs, you got it?"

I'm telling you, it was a tense night. Several times, we saw what had to be flashlights shining up in the treetops. Whether the bad guys were looking up for us, or it was just carelessness, who knows. I can tell you we held our breath more than once. Nobody slept, and not a peep was heard the entire night.

At dawn, I sent Sergeant Wojo and one of the recon team leaders down to the lowest treetop. All was quiet. I called the extraction choppers in. "This is Eagle's Nest. Ready to go home."

"Roger, Eagle Nest. This is Covey. Your big bird is ten minutes out. Slicks (troop-carrying helicopters) are with him. Be prepared for extraction. Is your LZ hot?"

"This is Eagle Six. Negative, Covey. LZ is cool as ice. Come on down."

The sound of the approaching helicopters was a welcome one. As we waited, I thought about the last five days. I hadn't touched the ground once. I hadn't seen a single NVA, although I did hear them. All in all, it was a strange way to spend time in Indian country.

The choppers arrived, and we scrambled onto the slicks. A single crewman jumped off the CH-47 and hooked the sling cable from the pie plate to the big hook beneath the cargo chopper then jumped back inside.

I watched as the big machine pulled the platform free from its leafy home and chugged into the blue morning sky. I'd piled the filled cans and twenty boxes of the men's daily deposit in the center of the platform. As the big circular platform started to spin, the boxes and cans went sailing off to land in the jungle below.

I could just see the face of some unlucky VC, thinking he's found a box of Yankee field rations to eat, he opens it up and finds a big box of human shit! The joke would be on Charlie.

It was a good feeling to see the miles slip past. We had gone into enemy country, put our ass on the line, and come back whole. I hadn't lost anybody, and no one had been hurt. We were safe and soon to be clean and full of hot chow. I wish I could have experienced that feeling of contentment more often in the years since; I'd be a happier man. I may never have hit a homer for the Yankees or walked the halls of Congress, but I took men down into harm's way and brought them back alive. It was a special feeling, and I savored the moment.

We arrived at CCN safely and got our hot shower and hot chow. I spent a good deal of time writing a report on the tactical advantages and disadvantages of the tree platform. I closed by pointing out the need for a portable toilet to be included in its equipment list, explaining along the way how we had solved the waste disposal problem.

The Eagle's Nest sat on the tarmac for a couple of days and then was picked up by a big chopper and taken away. I watched as the monstrosity, spinning in its harness like a top on a string, faded in the distance. I never saw it again.

14

POW Snatch
or
Going for the Gold

In a unit like CCN, every week seemed to bring some new objective, or command emphasis mandated by the powers that be in Saigon at MAC-SOG HQ. This week, the fifty-dollar hot button was "Prisoner of War."

Of course, POWs were always important, and we continually hoped we could bring in some poor VC slob to tell us all he knew about his unit: its mission, strength, location, and weaknesses. Believe me, very few of the enemy had the capability to withstand the American methods of interrogation: we didn't even have to torture them; we just promised them that they could stay out of the South Vietnamese prison system, go to work for us at a hundred times the money they'd ever hope to make in their lives, and hold out the promise of eventual emigration to the U.S. with a green card. As I say, very few could resist the offer, and most spilled their guts at the first opportunity.

Those few who resisted our inducements were passed on to the South Vietnamese Army, and even they talked eventually. Of course, many of those spent the rest of their lives without sex organs, teeth, fingernails, and so forth. Thanks to the reputation of the SVN prisons and the ARVN's vicious interrogation methods, most NVA soldiers talked to us sooner, not later.

Anyway, the word came down that Saigon wanted prisoners, and to sweeten the offer headquarters was throwing in some special incentives: any POW delivered by CCN soldiers would be worth five hundred bucks of fun money and a week in Taiwan, courtesy of the MAC-SOG Special Ops Fund. Special Forces had a safe house in Taipei, Taiwan. The stories brought back from those lucky enough to use it made the offer mighty tempting.

Every night at the club, we listened to one another brag how we soldiers of CCN were going to capture all these high-value POWs. I had high hopes that B Company would get a chance to get in on the gold rush. I was anxious to get a taste of the high life in Taipei. I'd had my R & R with my wife, tasted again the joys of the flesh, and convinced myself that a little fling on the wild side wouldn't hurt me and would certainly help when it came time to sit around the campfire and boast to my drinking buddies of sexual triumphs past. Things I certainly couldn't talk about doing with my wife. Our Hawaii reunion had to be off-limits for bragging to my way of thinking. Thailand had faded in memory, and I needed new ground upon which to build my campfire reputation. Therefore, it seemed clear to me that I needed a little foray to the fleshpots of Taiwan to round out my tour of duty away from the land of the free, home of the brave.

Major Skelton developed a convoluted plan that put recon teams out looking for good ambush spots to grab enemy soldiers. Places like rest areas or heavily traveled roads were the kind of prime locations the recon teams were looking for. Once they'd been located, a heavily armed reaction force would insert and make a sweep, policing up any unfortunates who stumbled into its path.

The thorn in the rosebush, at least for my company, was that Dick Meadows's company would be first to go. Dick was the finest soldier I ever knew, a born warrior, the first man on the ground on the Son Tay raid later in the war, and brave beyond belief. Having been commissioned out of the NCO ranks while in his thirties, he was very old for a captain. Tall, calm, confident, he was my idol, and what I wanted to be like when I grew up.

As luck would have it, he got a good potential snatch situation right off and took in a reaction platoon on a suspected hospital area. They shot up a bunch of NVAs and brought back one alive, as per instructions. With barely concealed envy, I watched as Dick left for Taiwan amid wild speculation as to his nights of glory.

All he said when he returned was that there were great restaurants in Taiwan. Then he smiled benignly. It made me all the more determined to bag a POW and make the trip myself. I spent several fretful days awaiting the call I hoped would come. "POWs ready for pickup, just like cash in the bank." I don't know where I got such a silly notion. Nothing in Vietnam worth a cup of bat shit ever came easy. No way was I gonna scoop up five hundred bucks just lying around waiting for me to come get it.

I had about given up hope, when the magic call came through. One of the recon teams was shadowing a major route of travel. Several large formations of Charlie had passed by their hiding place in the last day.

The plans were made. I'd take in a platoon of forty men and lie beside the trail. If a small group went by, we'd jump them and take one or more alive. Two POWs meant two trips to Taipei. Hell, we might get a dozen. The whole company could go on the trip. I'd be the most popular commander in the SVN theater of war.

I checked out from the arms room a couple of .22-caliber Huntsman automatic target pistols with silencers. The deadly little handguns would be ideal if we got close to some bad guys and wanted to snuff them without alerting any others close by. Besides, I wanted to try the silenced weapons on the enemy. The sound they made when fired was hardly louder than a skeeter's cough. Of course, when the silenced pistol was added to all my "normal" gear, I could barely hoist my ass onto the helicopter for the ride out to Charlie country.

Lieutenant McMurray was with me as the assigned platoon officer. Lieutenant Cable was off on R & R for a week, and I didn't want to command the unit myself, just go along as the "superboss." Little Pete was always ready for a romp in the brush, so I wasn't losing anything by having him in the backup role. I liked Mac better than any other American soldier in my command, although I considered myself blessed because I liked all my men. Command of B Company had been a wonderful experience to that point.

"Ready to go?" I queried my friend and XO as we climbed onto a black-painted whirlybird that was trembling as if the iron monster was impatient to get back into the air.

"You betcha, *Dai Uy*," McMurray answered. "I got a good feeling on this one. We're gonna strike gold."

"Sounds good to me." I waved at the inquisitive face of the pilot, and he turned back to his controls and got us airborne.

Once again, we banked hard over the rice paddies that surrounded Da Nang, then headed west toward the blue-green haze of Laos. The recon team that had spotted the troop movements was waiting at the selected LZ, so we had the luxury of going into a landing area we knew was probably clear of waiting NVA soldiers.

The chopper flared into the waist-high grass, and we piled off, heading for the edge of the tiny clearing in the middle of the Laotian jungle. The other three birds dropped their loads and roared away, leaving the usual ominous silence in their wake. As we moved away from the LZ, my tension level soared skyward. We were in Indian country again, and over there, on that side of the border, the game was for real.

The slight nausea of vulnerability I always felt right after the choppers left us was gnawing at my gut. I never did get used to that "abandoned" feeling, not once in two years of combat. I was always ready to go out, but watching those choppers headed away, without me, did bad things to my nervous system.

We moved a couple of hundred meters away from the LZ and went into a defensive perimeter while Mac and I discussed the situation with the recon team leader, Sergeant

First Class Boker. He was so well camouflaged in stripes, war paint, and brush that even out in the open he was hard to see.

"What's the drill?" I asked the grimy, sweat-streaked NCO, who was unfolding the map he carried and smoothing it out on the ground at my feet.

"We ran into a series of heavily traveled trails right here." He pointed to the 1:50,000 map, carefully tracing his grimy finger along a ridgeline. "That's over to the west about five klicks. We can ease down there tomorrow and set up ambush sites for the next morning. The way foot traffic has been going on 'em lately, we should have contact before the day's done."

I marked the spot on my map. "Looks good. What numbers have they been traveling in?"

Boker scratched his black-and-green-painted cheek. "So far, pretty big. We've not seen anything less than a company-size unit. A hundred-plus in each party. That's why we didn't take a chance on going after one ourselves."

"Shit, man. We're not big enough to take on a company. I only brought thirty-six men."

"I know, *Dai Uy*, but sooner or later there's gotta be some stragglers or somethin' headin' south. We'll just have to find a place where we can see the road without them seeing us. Then, it's just a matter of gettin' lucky."

I nodded. "I guess so. Okay, lead us to a good spot for an RON. I wanna be on the trail at daybreak tomorrow. The quicker we get to the road, the quicker we can get an ambush set up."

For that mission, we had to bring several boxes of Italian Green along. The heavy boxes of booby-trapped mortar ammunition were supposed to be left near ammo dumps or troop bivouac spots. As soon as Mac and I were satisfied we had all the poop we were gonna get from Sergeant Boker, I signaled for the men to gather their gear and get ready to move.

"The first trail we come to," I whispered to Mac, "we're dropping this crap. We'll make our own ammo dump." It wasn't too long before we crossed a tiny little path, and we quickly put a pile of mortar rounds out in the middle of it. If I had to guess, I'd say the stuff is still there, molding away in the jungle. The idea might have sounded good at head-quarters, but the pukes who thought it up never had to hump eighty-pound boxes of booby-trapped 82mm mortar rounds through steaming hot jungle. As I mentioned earlier, I had a real heartburn with the concept.

We went into our RON perimeter a few hours later, along-side a footpath that appeared to be heavily used. I set up the classic L-shaped ambush, and we settled in for the night. Like all trips into the bush, we had to suffer through the unceasing assaults of bloodthirsty mosquitoes and no-see-ums. The first night was always the hardest. Bugs and nerves made sure no-body slept, and the dawn always seemed a long time coming. In my case, the bugs' absolute rapture over the taste of my blood made worrying about the enemy a distant problem. We didn't take insect repellant on operations because of its dis-tinct odor, one that Charlie would recognize. All I could do was roll down my sleeves, pull a mosquito net over my face, and suffer.

Like every morning before or since, dawn finally came, and we moved out toward the waiting rendezvous with the enemy. He was close; everyone could sense it, so we moved slow and careful.

We headed for a spot I had picked on the map that seemed ideal for an ambush site. It was about six klicks according to the map, maybe eight klicks' actual travel distance from where we were. But, it took us all day. That's how thick the jungle was. We came to a particularly tangled section of jungle and slowly penetrated into its dank interior. Suddenly, the column came to a halt. "What the hell's the matter?" I hissed up the line toward the front. "Get moving, the day's almost over."

"The point's stuck," came back down in reply. "We're gonna have to back out."

"Hold it right there," I commanded. "I'm coming up to the

point. Pete, you take charge of the main body. I'll kick some ass and get us started again."

I moved up, fighting my way around the file of immobile soldiers jammed up like commuters in a freeway pileup. I finally inched my way to the front of the column. We were completely surrounded by a gigantic growth of wait-a-minute vines. These were famous throughout Vietnam as the toughest, thorniest, nastiest bushes ever grown by the devil. The thorns were sharp and long and resisted any movement once some poor soldier got caught in one, hence the name.

I'd never seen such an abundance of wait-a-minutes in one spot before. The area to the front and side was one impenetrable barrier of pain-giving thorn branches, some several inches thick, twisted and tangled together. "Goddamn," I exclaimed to the point squad leader, Sergeant Garrett. "How did you get in this mess?"

"Fuck me like a virgin if I know, *Dai Uy*," he answered, gasping for breath from the exertion necessary to cut a path through the thorny impasse. "We just sort of got in and couldn't get out. Now it's so thick all around us that we can't go any way but back the way we came from."

He was right. There just wasn't any way to go ahead, or even sideways. I carefully worked my way back to the rear of the column, and we backtracked until we could see a way to circumvent the hazard. We had to circle several hundred meters to clear the worst of the stuff. By the time we made it to a spot I liked on the map, it was well after sundown. I pulled everyone back into a good location to RON, and we spent another night slaking the thirst of the insects.

Just before we turned in, I gathered all the Americans around me, and we went over the next day's plans.

"We'll use the bramble bush as our rally point if we get hit and have to bug out," I told them. "Get back in there and hole up. We'll not have to worry about any VC coming up on us without our knowing it."

"Damn right about that," Sergeant Garrett, the first squad

leader, mumbled. "Pull a couple of branches over our trail, and Charlie will never know we was there."

"Sergeant Boker, how far to our objective?" I looked at the recon team leader.

" 'Bout three hundred meters ahead. Just on the other side of this hill. I scouted it just before you got here. It's perfect for an ambush. There's a walkin' trail built along the far side of this big hill, with a steep drop-off to a creek at the bottom. We can get in position above the trail, in good cover, and still be close to it."

I nodded. "Okay, first thing tomorrow, we'll sneak in slow and easy, set up the ambush, and see who comes along. I don't want any firing, and for sure don't let your men move around once we get in position. I'll start the shindig with my trusty little ol' silenced pistol, and we'll see how it goes from there. Now, get some sleep, if you can."

I spent another night fighting a war against the bloodsuckers, losing it badly. The morning sun was a welcome visitor. "I'm gonna be bled dry before we even get a chance at a snatch, the way these bugs are after me," I grumbled to McMurray.

The recon team took off, and we settled in to await their signal to move up. In about an hour we got the call. "I've found a great spot," Sergeant Boker called back. "Head out at a direct 180 from the RON, and we'll pick you up just before you reach the trail."

"Roger," I whispered back. "Any activity on the road?"

"Negative. All quiet."

I got the platoon going and stayed up front with Lieutenant McMurray. "We'll run into the recon team just ahead. Don't get trigger-happy," I cautioned.

"Gotcha, *Dai Uy*," was all he said. Mac knew his business, but it made me feel better to remind him.

Sergeant Boker suddenly stepped out of the bushes with one of his Yards. His unexpected appearance almost made me forget my own advice. The brush was as thick around there as anyplace I ever saw in South Vietnam; fighting would have to be at extremely close range. That meant it would be easy to lose anybody after us, as well.

"We found a great spot, *Dai Uy*," he reported. "Follow me." He headed off to the right, down the steep hill.

Sure enough, it was a great spot for an ambush. The trail followed the side of the huge hill, and the far side was a steep drop-off, covered in heavy brush. Two small ridges came down almost to the edge of the trail, giving a perfect spot for the snatch team—McMurray, Pham, and three Montagnard soldiers. Sergeant Garrett had the rest of the platoon on the second ridge, where he could cover the snatch and our retreat up the hillside. To watch our backs, I put Sergeant Boker and his recon team on top of the hill above me. It was tactically sound, and it got him away from the trail. I certainly didn't want him or his men, instead of my platoon, grabbing a POW. Once everyone was situated, we settled down to wait for some poor schmuck to come diddy-bopping down the trail. My plan was that I'd shoot him in the leg with the silenced pistol, grab his ass, and beat feet to the pickup point. Then, fame, fortune, and a fabulous time would all be mine. I silently hummed a tune as I waited for my gold mine to arrive.

By the end of the day, I was all out of tunes, and we hadn't seen a soul, except for high-flying fighter-bombers headed somewhere along the myriad of trails that comprised the Ho Chi Minh trail complex.

At dusk, I pulled the men back to the place where we'd spent the previous night. The men had laid at the ambush site all day, and biological functions had to be attended to. Besides, we couldn't do any good after dark since the enemy would probably lay up until morning. We really needed daylight to snatch and run.

"So, we were unlucky," I said to McMurray after we settled in for another night. "Maybe tomorrow. The only thing is, I may be dead from loss of blood. What is it about me that these damn mosquitoes love so?"

"Shit, *Dai Uy*," Sergeant Garrett laughed as he listened to me complain. "These Vietnam bugs are smart. They know better than to get after us dust-grubbin' foot soldiers when there's blue-blooded officers around to gnaw on."

He chuckled smugly, and settled in the little spot he'd made for the night, his head and rifle pointed away from the center of the camp, the way we always slept, ready to take on any unexpected enemy assault.

"If I thought these bloodthirsty bastards had that much savvy, I'd field promote you to general, my good Sergeant," I grumbled as I tried to make myself as inconspicuous and comfortable as possible.

The next day was as unproductive as the one before. We spent it lying quietly, suffering the sun and bugs, without any sign of foot traffic. "I wonder if the NVA has quit sending troops south?" I complained that night. "Maybe the war is over, and they forgot to tell us?"

I scratched in the dirt while describing my next bright move. "Let's split up tomorrow. I'll stay here with ten men, Pete, you and Sergeant Boker each take ten and cover the next two trails to the west. If anybody snatches or gets hit, we all pull back to the extraction LZ together. We'll put up a stand there if there's a bunch of 'em. Sound all right to you?"

They all agreed it was as good as any other plan they could think up, so we settled in for another night battling the bugs.

The next morning, we split up, and I took my bunch back to the same place we had spent the last two days. By midmorning, the other two teams were in place along smaller trails to the west, and we sweated out the hours.

About two, I thought I heard the faint popping of gunfire. My men did as well, and their eyes turned to Pham, who was waiting by the radio. "Snatch Six, this is Five. Over." It was Pete McMurray.

I grabbed the radiophone and whispered a reply, "This is Six. Go ahead. Over."

Pete's voice came back, excitement in his every word. "This is Five. We have a score. Headed back to the LZ. Over."

The lucky little bastard, I thought to myself, Why wasn't it me? I answered softly, "Roger, Five. Any pursuit?"

"Negative, Six. There was just four of the little mothers. We popped three and grabbed one. We're headed out now for the Lima Zulu."

I acknowledged and put in a call for Sergeant Boker's team to pull back to the LZ as well. He rogered, and I turned to signal for my team to wrap it up, when Pham grabbed my shoulder.

"Dai Uy," he whispered and pointed with his head. "VC come."

Sure enough, two dudes came waltzing around the corner, rifles casually slung on their shoulders, jabbering it up like Mutt and Jeff on a Sunday walk in the park. I had to make a quick decision. Did we take them, or lie low and scoot as soon as they disappeared down the road? I knew we didn't have much time, but I wanted my own POW badly, so I gave the signal we were going to make a snatch and waited in the bushes by the edge of the road.

As the two soldiers got close, I took a quick look around. Not another soul in sight. It was going to be a perfect snatch, better than John Wayne did in the movies. The two unsuspecting targets walked closer and seemed oblivious to us.

Grinning in anticipation, I eased the bulbous nose of the silenced pistol free of the bush I was hidden behind, aimed and fired. *Sfitt!* The sound was hardly loud enough to bother a skittish cat. My .22 hollow-point round took the first guy right above the ear. He started folding like a limp dishrag, just barely alerting his companion that anything was amiss. The second fellow was just starting to turn when I popped him in his right knee. He fell with a shallow squeal, more like a startled baby than a wounded man. Pham and I were all over him before he even reached the ground. I grabbed his rifle, and Pham smacked him on the head two or three times with the leather sap he was carrying. The wounded man was out like a light.

I threw his rifle to Pham and gathered up the limp body, throwing it over my shoulder like a sack of flour. The skinny NVA didn't weigh a hundred twenty pounds; I would have no trouble carrying him to the pickup point. I was so excited I was almost whistling in glee. I had my POW! I suppressed an urge to shout out Tarzanlike in victory.

Just as I reached my hand up to the others for help back up the steep bank, I saw Pham's eyes widen. I glanced in the direction he was looking. Coming around the bend was the whole fuckin' NVA Army, or so it seemed. They saw what I was up to and, touchy bastards that they were, they reacted badly to the little drama unfolding before them. Their rifles were quickly being swung onto shoulders, and their scowling faces showed no appreciation for the humor of the situation.

"Jesus Christ!" I screamed. "Give me a hand. We gotta get outta here."

The ten men in my covering squad opened fire, and the NVA did the same. The bullets of both were passing about a foot over my head. It was as close as I ever was to fainting from fear, but it gave wings to my feet. I charged up the steep slope, still carrying my precious cargo, the rest of my men shooting and retreating right behind me.

There was a *lot* of shooting going on, but I don't think either side hit anyone from the other. My guys were fast catching up with me, burdened as I was, but I was not about to drop my golden prize, no matter how much he impeded my progress up the hill. We passed the only semiclear spot on the hill just before we went over the top, and some joker on their side took a shot at us with his RPG (rocket-propelled grenade), a bazooka-like antitank weapon the NVA liked to use as much as we used the M-79 grenade launcher. It played hell with troops in the open, and that's what I was at the moment.

The RPG hit behind me about twenty yards. The noise temporarily deafened me, and I felt a stinging in my back, and wetness on the backs of my legs. I must have taken some shrapnel from the blast, but everything still worked, so I kept running. Even with my load, I was pulling away from the angry NVA soldiers, who didn't like chasing us around in the bush. It probably meant they would be late to their next stop-off station and a chance to rest their weary feet; those dudes had probably been on the trail for three hundred miles or more, headed on foot to the war.

"Head for the wait-a-minutes," I gasped to Garrett, who was in the lead. "Then, cut left and circle the worst of it. If we're lucky, Charlie will rush in and get stuck, just like we did." I was whistling for breath.

Garrett nodded and kept on humping, not bothering to waste his breath answering me. He led us right to the center of the stuff and peeled off, leading us around the thorny hazard. As the last man made the turn away from the sticker bushes, Garrett threw some branches on the path we left. It might fool the NVA long enough for them to get caught in the wait-a-minutes.

Sure enough, we came out the far side well in front, with the curses and shouts of the entangled enemy sounding ever fainter as we headed for the rendezvous with our comrades and the soon-to-arrive helicopters. "Pham," I gasped, "call ell-tee Mac. Tell him to get the extraction choppers on the way. We're being chased and will arrive in two-five minutes."

After an exhausting run through the dense jungle, we reached the desired spot and joined the rest of my soldiers anxiously waiting for us. Did they look lovely, watching our rear from hasty fighting positions as we ran up the hill toward them.

I leaped over a fallen tree and dropped my prize next to the tied-up soldier who was McMurray's POW. He didn't look any too happy at his predicament, but he was money on the hoof, so what did I care.

"How long we got?" Mac asked, looking at the bush behind me.

"I think we got way ahead of them," I answered, looking back nervously at the way we had just come. "We led them into the wait-a-minutes."

"Good," McMurray replied. "The extraction choppers are inbound. We'll be history in twenty minutes."

I twisted to look at the back of my legs. "Oh, God," I moaned. "Lookie at all this blood. I must be hit bad. Check me out." I pulled up my shirt, a sudden chill of fear shaking me right down to my deepest core. I just hoped I'd survive until I could get back to Da Nang and the Medevac hospital.

"You ain't hit bad, *Dai Uy*. Just a little nick on your back. It's hardly bleeding."

"Well what the hell? How'd I get all this blood on the back of my legs?"

Pham was rolling over my POW. "It belong to VC. He dead, *Dai Uy*."

"Fuck me to death! He *can't* be," I cried as I hurried to my prize. Pham was right, my golden POW was deader than a mackerel. A piece of shrapnel had damn near taken off the top of his head, and it was his blood that was all over me. I'd carried the dead man all that way, while he dripped all over me. I was devastated; my prize was gone, NVA were looking for us, and choppers were on the way. My live POW had become dead meat.

The choppers came, and we scrambled on, flying away from the bad guys, who were still probably hung up in the thorns. My glum face was quite a contrast to the happy countenance of McMurray's. He was already talking about *his* trip to Taipei.

"You know," he gushed, "I missed my regularly scheduled R & R because of my bout with dysentery. This'll make up for it."

Hell, what could I say? I'd already had two trips out of the combat zone. I couldn't pull rank on him and take this chance away from him.

Making the best of a bad situation, I smiled and replied, "You got it, Ell-tee. Do a couple for me."

"Can do, *Dai Uy*, can do."

Lieutenant McMurray went off on his little reward trip, and I started a new training cycle in the company. He returned in a week, bubbling over with war stories about the booze ingested, steaks digested, and whores invested.

But I was involved with a training program for the company, and time was at a premium, so I never heard all the delightful details.

15

Operation Dipstick
or
The Raid on the Pipeline

Combat is just a matter of luck. Luck, fate, roll of the dice, karma, call it what you will. If you hang around fighting long enough, you're gonna get your ass kicked and handed to you on a tarnished platter. My time to roll craps came up. The ones who had to suffer for my bad luck were the men with me.

Pete hadn't been back long from his R & R when we got alerted. One of our recon teams ran across an honest-to-goodness pipeline, constructed through the jungle way up by the Muy Ghia Pass, where the Ho Chi Minh trail enters Laos from North Vietnam. Of course, its discovery created a sensation. The team had seen it only from a distance as they were running from contact with the local NVA units that were guarding the pass area from people just like us. It was six to eight inches in diameter and well camouflaged from observation aircraft.

Two more teams were promptly dispatched to see if they could verify the discovery. My company was put on insertion alert, and everyone waited to see what the teams would discover. We were all excited at the prospect of inserting against a target of such importance. If it was a pipeline and its purpose was to carry fuel, then its destruction would be a big coup for CCN.

In preparation for the launch, I took the company up to Camp Eagle, where we would wait out the decision to go or not. Camp Eagle was farther up country than Da Nang and meant a quicker trip to the target area. Even so, the target was well over a hundred miles away, which meant a long flight in the choppers before we unloaded. It also meant not much chance of quick extraction or resupply. We'd have to take all we needed with us, and be prepared to stay against opposition.

The news was good. A second team had spotted the pipeline, farther west of the original discovery. That is to say, they saw it. The rugged country and lots of bad guys let them no nearer the pipeline than binocular vision. They reported it ran straight west as far as they could follow it, up and down the rugged terrain. That part of Northern Laos was truly rugged, much like the hills outside of Honolulu, but covered with triple-layer jungle as an added impediment.

The brass eagerly received the latest report, and ordered us to insert. They decided to send in two platoons of troops. Since I'd been counting on taking the entire company rather than just half, I put in a call to Major Skelton. He was already over at the radio relay site in Thailand, where he could monitor the ground operation and still have commo back to CCN.

"What gives, sir? I've got two hundred men up here ready to launch and you tell me to only take half?"

"That's a big rog, ol' son," he replied. "It's just too damn far away. It would take twenty choppers to get all your guys delivered. As it is, it'll take ten slicks (unarmed troop carriers) and four guns (armed gunships) to get your people there. We'll hold the rest of your soldiers in reserve. If you find something really good, like a refueling depot or something, we'll bring the rest in ASAP."

"Damned if I like it, sir. The NVA will be all over me like stink on shit if I get close to anything that good. I sure don't like going in half strength."

"Don't worry so," was his airy reply. "You'll be in and out so fast, Charlie won't know you're there until his oil supply suddenly goes up in smoke."

I surrendered. "Roger." I wasn't going to get any satisfaction arguing with the major. He probably was right. If we were lucky, we'd be gone before any of the bad guys knew we were even in the area. Soon, ten slicks full of troops with four Cobra gunships for company beat their way north toward Laos.

I took my two best platoons, even though one of the platoon leaders, Lieutenant Lawrence, had a severe eye infection and was in the evac hospital in Da Nang. Lieutenant McMurray was temporarily in command, and I took Pham and two husky Yard soldiers for my personal bodyguards. I would run the operation and leave Lieutenant Cable in charge of the stay-behinds. He would bring them in as rapid reinforcements if I called for them.

As we beat through the humid air above the jungle, I looked around at the ten men in the chopper with me. Everyone had green and black camo paint on his face and hands or, like me, was wearing black gloves. I had a nice pair of driving-type gloves made to my hand measurements by a leather tailor in Da Nang. We all wore tiger suits of irregular green and black stripes. Every man was loaded to his personal load-bearing capacity with ammo, grenades, explosives, knives, garrotes, pistols, and, for all I knew, rocks to chuck at the bad guys. We also had three days' worth of water and chow, stuffed in wherever. Add to that maps, radios, batteries, claymore mines for the RON defense, first-aid kits and blood expander, compass, clean socks, poncho, and a hammock for resting. Add to that signal flares, flashlights, strobe lights for night signaling, smoke grenades for day signaling, and cameras to record the damage. It's a wonder any of us could walk.

The chopper pilot signaled back to me, and I put on the offered headset. He had bad news.

"One of the choppers has a warning light from his engine. He's turning back."

I leaned out the open door and looked behind us. A trailing chopper was already returning to the launch site. I had just lost ten men. It wasn't a very good way to start the operation.

I couldn't tell who was on it, but silently prayed it wasn't the one with Lieutenant McMurray. I relied on his unceasing bravery and common sense in tight situations. I wanted him with me on that mission.

We flared over a tiny clearing, where we jumped out and rushed into the heavy brush so another chopper could come in. It took a good while to get everybody off the choppers. In the meantime, the Cobras were flying orbits around the circling slicks, and anybody alive within ten miles knew that the Yanks were coming.

Twice as many ships would have been a mess, doubling the unloading time, so Major S had been right about that. The big, noisy, ungainly Hueys certainly proclaimed our presence to any watchful NVA scout.

And there was one watching.

Looking back, it seemed easy to understand. Suddenly, there were American scout teams snooping around where we'd never been before, close to a certain pipeline built through the jungle. It didn't take a genius to figure out where nine chopperloads of the NVA's most hated enemy troops were probably headed.

After the last chopper had lumbered away from the LZ, I gathered my leaders around me. Another sign of the bad luck I was suffering: The chopper that had turned back earlier carried Lieutenant Turin and his radio operator. The 1st Platoon was leaderless.

"Mac, I'll take the 1st Platoon. Move off four or five hundred meters to the west and then turn due north. I'll parallel you from right here."

We knew we had landed south of the pipeline. I hoped that by splitting up, we would have a better chance of finding it in the heavy brush. Separated by only five hundred meters, we could still support each other.

"Roger, *Dai Uy*," he grinned. "We'll race you to the damned thing. First platoon there gets free drinks from the loser when we get back."

"Okay, Pete. Be careful. Move out and call me as soon as you make the turn north." I watched as Pete and his men eased off through the heavy underbrush. I motioned to the American platoon sergeant assigned to the 1st Platoon, Sergeant Crowley.

"I'll take the point squad with Pham. You bring up the rear. Keep your eyes open for trackers. Sergeant Margier, you stay in the middle with the second squad."

Margier was the company medic, who didn't have any assignment but to care for the wounded. He could run a platoon in an emergency, as could any SF soldier in CCN, but I didn't want him worrying about it as long as Crowley was available. He was a medium-built kid, with medium brown hair, medium height, medium looks, medium . . . , you get the picture. He even wore medium-size glasses. I didn't think of him as a fighting soldier, but he was as courageous as any soldier I had.

The NVA always operated the same when they didn't have a good fix on our units. They'd put out trackers until they crossed our trail, and then they would follow along behind, firing a single shot every fifteen minutes or so. The other NVA units would listen, get an idea of our location and direction, and try to get in front of us. Then they would set up the inevitable ambush and wait for us to walk into it. It was obvious why we hated the trackers; cats hate dogs.

I got Pete's call in about thirty minutes. He had made his turn north, so I immediately got everyone under way. We headed due north, right against the lay of the terrain, which favored east-west movement. It was tough going and slow. We were constantly climbing up or down sharp ridges, forcing our way across country covered with almost impenetrable undergrowth.

The plan had been for us to reach the area of the pipeline around dusk. That way, we could follow or blow it, whichever seemed the best idea, then disappear into the darkness.

Dark came way too fast. I hadn't seen hide or hair of any man-made object, and neither had Pete.

"Hole up for the night," I ordered him. "We'll stop right here, and start off at first light. Stay in deep cover. You know Charlie's bound to be out lookin' for us."

"Roger, Six. This is Five saying nighty-night."

The night slowly passed, and we were ready to go just as soon as it was light enough to see. We thrashed on, fighting our way across endless ridges, through brush-choked gullies. Sweat and energy were expended in copious quantities, and still no pipeline.

Suddenly, a shot sounded somewhere to our rear. "Oh, shit," I groaned. "Somebody just got lucky, and it wasn't us." I got on the horn to McMurray. "Pete, you hear that?"

"Roger, Six. It was from your direction, I think."

"Sounded like it to me, too. Pick up the pace before they get us triangulated. I'm gonna turn on 'em and see if they fall for it."

"Roger, Six. We'll keep on going straight. Maybe we'll get lucky and find the damn thing soon."

I took my platoon in a right-angle turn and headed east. Why I didn't go west, toward McMurray, I'll never know. I just didn't think. The going was easier, and when we heard the next shot from our diligent tracker, he was quite a bit farther behind us. Still, I had to go north to find the target, so I eventually turned again and headed in the original direction.

We put out a dozen M-14 toe-poppers, hoping the tracker would step on one and blow his damn foot off. No luck, because it wasn't long before we heard his next shot. He was still with us. He would have died from embarrassment had he heard all the nasty things I called his sorry ass in the next two minutes. The next time we turned, I stopped the men and set up an ambush, hoping to draw him into killing range. No luck there, either. He just stayed out there, about half a mile, watching and waiting.

"Sneaky Six, this is Five, over." Mac wanted me on the radio.

"This is Six, over."

"We found it, *Dai Uy*. We found the damn thing." His voice was fairly shaking with excitement.

"Good job, Pete. Where are you?"

Pete read his coordinates to me over the radio. He was about a kilometer to the west and two to the north of me. In this jungle, I'd be two hours getting to him. I had to let him make the decision: blow it, or follow it. "Pete, it's your call. I'm too far away. I'll start in your direction now, but you decide. Blow it away or follow it. Over."

"Six, this is Five. I'm worried about that dink following you. I say I'm gonna blow the SOB and hightail it to LZ Blue. The damn thing's built right along a mountainside. We'd have hell following it. I can't even get there from here without using ropes. I'll blow it and scoot. You start now for the LZ and get a defensive position built. I have a feeling we'll need it before we get picked up. Over."

I agreed. "Roger, Five. Blast it to smithereens. We're boogying outta here right now for LZ Blue. See you there."

"Roger, Six. Look for the fire. Charlie's gas line is going up in smoke in one-five. This is Sneaky Five, out."

LZ Blue was a high, flattopped hill three klicks behind us. We'd picked it out the day before as one of several possible LZs to return to when it was time to go home.

Disappointed that I'd come all this way and not even seen the famous pipeline, I turned my platoon back to the south. But I wasn't about to keep going ahead. We now had three trackers shadowing us, and I knew it wouldn't be long before we would be boxed in good. I was plenty nervous and well on my way to being damned scared.

We slowly worked our way toward the rendezvous, accompanied by tracking shots every quarter-hour. The single *crack!* in the humid afternoon air bode ill for us, but I didn't know what else I could do. We had tried everything I could think of to discourage our pursuers and still hadn't shaken them off our trail. These boys were damned good.

Unexpectedly, we came to a large clearing in the jungle. A

fire had burned there some time ago, and the trees hadn't recovered yet. I made a hasty decision.

"We go straight across," I told the point squad. "Pham, you and the bodyguards stay with me. We'll set some more toe-poppers just beyond the tree line. Maybe we can get the trackers as they come out of the forest."

Pham gathered up a dozen of the small antipersonnel mines from the strikers who were carrying them, and we planted them across our trail, which was obvious in the six-foot-high saw grass. Carefully, we camouflaged them and crossed our fingers the enemy trackers would step on one, or more.

Then, we hotfooted it after the rest of the platoon. As we reached the far side, we got behind cover, just at the edge of the heavy growth of jungle. The trail was slightly uphill, so we had a clear view of the far side.

We waited, silent and sweaty, while the sounds of the rest of my men faded into the distance. I could see how a skilled tracker could avoid our turnaround ambushes. He would just have to stay far enough behind to barely hear us, and when we stopped and things grew silent, simply stop where he was until we gave up and started out again. He had the advantage on us. We had to get somewhere; he didn't.

The time dragged on, and I made a fatal mistake. Growing impatient, and afraid to let the main body get too far ahead of me, I gave up waiting and stood up. "Let's go, dammit. The sumbitches either are too far back, or we've finally lost them."

Just the opposite was true. The little slimeballs were across the clearing, watching, waiting.

Pham stood beside me, worried at my carelessness in exposing myself. "*Dai Uy* . . ."

I turned my head at his address, and the bullet cracked past my cheek, so close I could feel the displaced air from its passing. It hit Pham right in the mouth, puffing out his cheeks and snapping back his head. Blood sprayed in tiny red droplets like fine mist, splashing against the brush behind him.

My brave radio operator and friend dropped hard, wheezing like an old man with emphysema.

"Pham, Jesus, Pham. Over there! Open fire, Godammit! Fire! You son of a bitches. I'll kill you all, God damn you."

The other Yards fired their weapons at the place I was pointing, while I scrambled to Pham's side. He was hit bad, the bullet having gone out the back of his neck, just below the hairline. My friend had been shot with a bullet meant for me. I prayed we could save him from dying.

I wiped at the hot tears flooding my eyes. My hand came away red. I was bleeding around my mouth. I poked at the spot with my finger, and felt a prick of pain. It was a piece of one of Pham's teeth, sharp as a razor. It had stuck in my upper lip.

"Pham, hang on, buddy. You'll be okay. Just hang on." I grabbed the radio and called for Sergeant Margier, the medic. "Get back here with everyone, ASAP. Pham's been hit."

"Roger, Six. We're on our way. Be there in five. Out."

I put Pham's knapsack under his head and stripped the radio from him. Looking up, I asked the other two soldiers if they'd seen or hit anything. They both shook their heads, and looked morbidly at my wounded comrade.

"Hang on, Pham; *bac si*'s (Vietnamese for medic) on the way." The young soldier just looked at me, trying to say something with his shattered jaw. I was busy trying to put a compress bandage on the gaping exit wound. Pham tried again to say something to me, but it came out as a frothy red gurgle. He held onto my arm with his hand, his eyes questioning. Then a vague sort of surprise filled his face, and he fell slack, the heavy, last breath spraying my hands and arm with red mist. Pham, son of the chief of Bon Hai, died in my arms. He wasn't yet eighteen.

The others burst out of the underbrush, and Margier rushed to my fallen friend. "He's dead, *Dai Uy*," he uselessly informed me. I knew it. I was there when it happened.

Sergeant Crowley came up to me. "What do you wanna do, Captain?"

I glared across the opening at the place where the shot had come from. "Get over there and see if we got the mutherfuckin' SOBs," I snarled.

"Captain, we need to get going. The day's going fast, and we're a long way from the LZ yet."

"Do what I said, goddammit. I'm not going until I see if we got the sumbitches who shot Pham. The sooner you go, the sooner you get back. We put toe-poppers on the trail, so circle around."

Reluctantly, Crowley moved the men across the clearing and disappeared into the woods on the far side. I knelt down by my faithful Pham. He'd been at my side since I took over the company, never flinching, and cheerfully carrying the heavy PRC-25 radio, no matter how rugged and impassable the terrain. I couldn't think. All I could do was grieve for him and curse the ones who killed him.

Crowley showed up. "No luck, Captain. They got clean away. Now they're probably trying to get around our flanks. We gotta get goin'. You hear me, sir?"

I dumped a lungful of pent-up air. "Okay, I hear you. You're right. Saddle up. Let's get outta here."

"What about his body? You wanna try and take it with us?" The tone of his voice told me what he thought.

"No, we can't do that." I looked down, grief-stricken, at my friend. "Sorry, Pham, old buddy. We've gotta leave you, dammit to hell." I pointed off to the side at a big tree surrounded by thick brush. "Drag him over there in that thicket. Maybe the gooks will miss him in the chase." We were on the run, so Pham's body would hold us up too much. As much as I hated to, I had to leave him behind.

We headed on toward the hill where Pete and the others were going to meet us. I looked back, just once. The place where we left Pham would haunt my memory forever. Dark, green, dank, foreboding, alone. I gave the radio to one of the other men and pushed on through the brush. My loyal young friend, Pham, stayed behind. He rested in the place he now owned forever.

Suddenly, the solitary *crack!* of a tracker's rifle shot shattered the jungle stillness. They were still back there, God-damn their eyes.

16

Hell on a Hilltop
or
Fire from the Sky

"What's wrong, *Dai Uy*?" Sergeant Crowley panted as he struggled to talk and walk at the same time. In the tangled brush we were forcing our way through, that was some accomplishment. My face must have reflected my profound grief and guilt.

"I should have brought out Pham's body," I mumbled in both sorrow and self-pity. "I wish I'd never left him behind. He deserved better. I should have brought him out."

"It's too late now, sir," the square-jawed NCO beside me panted. "We can't go back. I'm not even sure we could find it if we wanted to. Besides, the damned trackers are right on our ass as it is. We got to get to the LZ before dark. A stiff would only slow us down. You know that."

"I know, I know." I wasn't about to debate my feelings with him. "I just know we shouldn't have left him back there. We would never have done it if it had been an American."

The sweating NCO remained silent. He knew that was true. We busted chops to bring the American bodies in. What right did we have to abandon the Yard bodies like so much roadside trash?

I was hurting inside. It burned in my gut that leaving Pham was a bad decision, and I felt a lot of guilt. It was standard policy to bring out the American dead, no matter the risk. Yet, we regularly left the Montagnard bodies behind if it was inconvenient or risky to the Americans. Looking back, I'm surprised that they put up with our infidelity. And even more bewildering, they also risked their lives with us when we went after American bodies. Their trust and devotion to us were a wonder to behold. Simple and loyal, the Yards were a lot like a beloved old dog from my childhood. He never gave up on me. No matter how badly I mistreated him or took him for granted, his devotion remained unwavering.

Somehow or another, the Montagnards forgave us our fallibility and fought their hearts out for us, even though we didn't deserve their sacrifice. It sickens me to think that we abandoned them to face the victorious NVA's reprisals when we cut and ran from Vietnam in 1972. I suppose the vast majority of them were slaughtered shortly thereafter.

The trail the point squad was hacking through the heavy growth was mostly southwest, at least when the terrain allowed it. This forced us to go up and down the sharp ridges as well as through the brush. At least we were moving away from the pipeline, toward our LZ and extraction out of this green hell. On the map, the spot was a good choice, high and apparently flat on top. That meant easy access for the choppers to land in and pick us up for the ride home.

I kept humping through the brush, scarcely noticing the passage of time. Suddenly, I realized that the day was almost over, and we weren't anywhere near where we were supposed to rendezvous with Pete and his platoon. I cursed myself for deciding to separate my command. I had meant for the two halves to stay close together, but the terrain and circumstances had forced them much too far apart. We were not going to make the LZ location in time for pickup tonight. That meant that we'd have to sit it out until tomorrow. If the NVA were close, we were in for a long night.

As if to punctuate my dilemma, the solitary shot of an AK-47 proclaimed to the world that our unshakable trackers were still behind us. I motioned for the radiophone from my new operator, a tall Yard a few years older than Pham.

"Sneaky Five, this is Six, over." I talked quietly, hoping only Pete could hear me.

"This is Five, over." Lieutenant Mac was right there on the phone. "You getting close to the LZ?"

"Negative, Five. We're a long way yet. How 'bout you?"

"This is Five. We're almost there. Charlie still on your tail?"

"Roger, Five. He's right behind me, like a shadow. He's shooting his rifle about every ten minutes now."

"Okay, Six. You want me to call in the extraction choppers?"

"This is Six. You'd better not. We're gonna be late. If I'm gonna spend the night there with bad guys all around me, I want you right there at my side. You get to the LZ first, you start setting up fighting positions. We'll hustle along and be there as soon as possible."

"Six, this is Sneaky Five. We're almost there. I'll be waiting. Get your ass here, pronto. All of a sudden, I've got a funny feeling about this place."

"I know exactly what you mean," I muttered to myself. The day was flying past. I do believe it was one of the shortest days in recorded history. We were in a race against the sun, and it won. It was just at the far horizon when Sergeant Crowley came back to me from the front of the column.

"We're close, *Dai Uy*. I can hear someone choppin' trees ahead. It has to be the 3d Platoon."

I nodded in agreement. "Hustle it up. I'll call Ell-tee Mac and tell him we're on our way in." Now that I had stopped walking, I could hear the sound as well. McMurray had his men cutting trees down to clear a landing zone and to open fields of fire. "I got a feeling we're gonna need defensive positions before this day's done," I remarked to Sergeant Crowley.

I grabbed the radiophone again. "Sneaky Five, this is Six. We're coming up the hill now. Hold your fire. Warn your people not to hose us down."

"Roger, Six. Tell me, where did I go on R & R last month?" Pete was no dummy. He was making sure I was who I said I was, and not some English-speaking NVA trying to sneak in close.

"Taipei, you little fucker. And on my ticket."

"In a million years, your ticket! Come on in. Even Charlie couldn't guess the answer to that one."

We headed for the top of the hill. We had made a lucky choice. The hilltop was nice and flat and shaped like an oval. The sharp ridge leading up to the flattop made it impossible for more than a few soldiers to come at us from the side, and the back of the hill was so steep that nobody could approach from our rear undetected. That meant if the enemy came at us, it would have to be up the steep slope to the front.

Pete had cleared away almost all the trees, and we had a flat surface 150 feet by 30 feet, at its widest, to defend.

"Hi, *Dai Uy*." He watched me clamber over the brush and debris at the front edge of the hilltop. "Not a bad spot to defend, is it?"

I walked around the top with him. He was right. The sun was going down fast, so I gathered all the Americans together. "We'll sit it out here tonight. Lieutenant McMurray will take the right, and I'll take the left. Each platoon will send out a three-man listening post. If they get pushed in, they'll become the platoon reserve and will dig in behind the front of their platoon's perimeter. Pete, you keep a sharp eye on the ridge approach on your right. Not many could come that way, but a few might get real close before you see 'em. I'll set up there, by that big tree stump behind the 1st Platoon. You NCOs put two men to a hole, all along the front rim of the hilltop."

By the time we had everyone spotted, it was almost completely dark. I felt good about our position on the flattopped hill. We had cover from the enemy's direct fire and were on the high ground. Best of all, we wouldn't have to fight any direction except to our front. Unless, and the thought kept nagging at me, the enemy sneaked up along the ridge to the far right. I crossed my fingers that Pete would keep a sharp eye on that avenue of approach and went back to the hole my bodyguards had dug for me beside a dead tree stump. I jumped in with my radio operator, the other two men of my personal entourage on the other side of the stump in their own hole. We would be the reaction reserve if any enemy assault broke through the outer line of defense to the front.

It was going to be a dark night, hardly any moon showing in the clouded sky. I had just wiggled into a comfortable position and called for a first-light extraction the next morning, when it dawned on me that I hadn't even asked about the damned pipeline, the reason for this whole operation.

I clicked the squelch button on the radiophone, causing a soft static burst in Pete's phone. He was about twenty-five meters to my right, in his hole.

"You call, *Dai Uy*?" he answered.

"Yeah," I whispered back. "I forgot to ask. What happened when you blew the pipeline?" From where we were, I hadn't seen a thing when Pete's men blasted the line.

"Shit, Captain. The son of a bitch was dry as a bone. All we got was some dust. I don't think the damned thing was ever even used."

"Well, I'll be double-damned. We came all this way for a dry hole. Wouldn't you know it would be that way? And it cost me Pham."

"I heard. Sorry about that, Captain. I know he was a special friend to you."

"The worst thing was leaving him behind. I wish I'd insisted on bringing him with us. If I'd have known we were gonna be too late getting here to get out tonight, I'd have made the effort."

Suddenly Pete's voice dropped an octave. "*Dai Uy*, my outpost just came in. I'll go see what's up and call you back. Five out."

I gave the phone to my radio carrier and listened hard. Something was up to the front. I could hear a commotion as the outpost soldiers scrambled through the brush we had piled in front of our position. I hurried over to where Sergeant Crowley was sharing a hole with the medic, Sergeant Margier. "What happened, Sarge?"

"The outpost just pulled back. Says there's a lot of activity at the bottom of the hill." He whispered a name, and a Yard scooted over to us.

"What you see?" I questioned him in the pidgin English we used with the Yards even though many could speak and understand the Queen's own.

The man's face reflected the fear I could hear in his voice. "Many VC, *Dai Uy*. All around." He pointed to the front, the only way anyone was going to come up the hill. "I not see, but hear many voices and men moving this way."

"I'll call for some air support right now. Sergeant Crowley, put these men at the far end of the line. Make sure they know to watch the approach up the spine of the ridge. Got it?" I stood to go. I whispered low, "They're coming, fellows. We can't go anywhere, so you gotta stop them. Stay alert."

I headed back to my hole and told Pete what I'd learned. His men had confirmed the report. Many NVA were working their way toward us through the dark jungle. Shit was gonna hit the fan.

I called for Prairie Fire airborne control and requested air cover. I listened to the calm voice of the controller, flying high above me somewhere in the endless circle of their patrol route. It brought back the memory of the days I'd spent doing the same thing a couple of months earlier. The stress levels from where I was then to where I was now couldn't have been any farther apart.

"Roger, Sneaky Six. I've got a Spooky on patrol about three-zero minutes from you. I'll send him over. His call sign is Lima Two-six. You got a strobe for him to access on?"

"That's a big roger, Prairie Fire Control. I'll have a strobe out at the center of my position. Tell Spooky that the bad guys are in a 180 around me from nine o'clock to three o'clock, with twelve at due north. You copy?"

"Roger, Sneaky Six. I'll pass it on. Stay on this frequency. Good luck. Prairie Fire Control, out."

I hurried to put my little strobe light out in the center of the hill. It had a long sleeve that allowed it to be seen only from above and not from the side. Spooky would see its blinking white flash in the dark jungle like a beacon in the desert. I began to feel a whole lot better.

A Spooky was a converted World War II–era C-47 cargo carrier which had been converted to a deadly, flying gun platform. It had a pair of six-thousand-rounds-per-minute 20mm Gatling guns sticking out the side. The pilot could fly over and deliver a bullet every square foot in a zone one hundred feet wide by as long as he held down the trigger. The old carriers were death-dealing SOBs, and those of us who received fire support from them loved them.

I called Pete and passed on the news and sent one of my bodyguards to tell Sergeant Crowley. I signed off the radio by quipping, "All we have to do is be lucky for thirty minutes, and Charlie's ass is grass." I surely should have kept my mouth shut. The gods of war overheard me.

Only minutes after I spoke, the NVA started firing RPGs (rocket-propelled grenades) at us from below. Most went over our heads without exploding and then tore up the woods well to our rear. Some did hit the ground below the edge of the hilltop, showering the men in the front holes with dirt and some with hot shrapnel.

Then, the probing NVA soldiers opened up with everything they had. Bullets were cracking overhead or thumping into the tree trunks and dirt. I saw the green tracer bullets from East Germany mixed with the orange ones from Czechoslovakia zipping past, and heard the *krump!* of the Chinese grenades. Even as I cowered in my hole, I thought to myself, "I wish those bleeding hearts back home could see the help the North Vietnamese are getting from their Commie friends. They wouldn't be so quick to claim the NVA is fighting us alone. I wish they were with me right now."

Most of the stuff they shot at us was going too high, and my troops were firing back down the hill. It sounded like there was a bunch of them, but we were keeping them back. Then an intense outburst of firing and grenades went off to my far right, where Pete's men were located. I saw movement. Someone was crawling my way. I couldn't tell who it was. The flashes of gunfire and tracers gave a ghastly illumination to the dark shapes.

An RPG round whizzed overhead. From the glow of its exhaust, I saw the distinctive shape of the pith helmet of an NVA soldier.

"NVA," I screamed and opened fire, as did the other three men with me. The running figure turned to fire at my voice, but his head snapped back and he fell in a sliding heap right beside my hole. I could have reached out and touched him if I had wanted to.

Lieutenant McMurray was urgently calling for me on the radio. "Captain, they broke through from the side. Some got past me. They're coming your way. Jesus, here come some more." He stopped talking and started shooting again.

I jumped from my hole. "Come on," I called to my three bodyguards and headed for Pete's location. We saw two more dark shapes running our way and cut them down in a blaze of automatic rifle fire. I could only hope they were NVA instead of my troops.

We reached Pete's hole, and I squatted down beside him, safe from the snapping bullets flying overhead. "What's up?" I gasped, trying to swallow the wad of cotton that had suddenly lodged itself in my throat.

McMurray pointed with his rifle. "They came out from the finger of the ridge, just like you said. My right squad is gone, either run off or dead. Some NVA headed your way."

"I know. We got three. Any more?"

"I'm not sure. I got a couple and some headed toward the front of the hill. I'll go make a check. What do you want me to do?"

I thought for a second. It was hard to decide. When you're in a firefight, the adrenaline seems to take over and you run on pure instinct. Thinking is tough. I pointed toward the center of the hilltop.

"Pull back the rest of your people toward my men. Bend them around so you block more of the right flank. Dig in and hold on. Spooky will be here soon, and we'll be all right then. Try to get me a count of what men you have left. I'm going to Crowley's hole and then back to mine. Meet me there in a few minutes." I sent my two bodyguards back to their hole and headed for Sergeant Crowley's position.

The old NCO (he was nearly forty!) didn't stop firing his weapon as I crawled up beside his hole. He had a good spot, with a large tree limb overhead to protect him from airbursts. He was grimacing, and his face was streaked with sweat and grime. I shouted in his ear. "Everything okay?"

He nodded, his faced highlighted by the muzzle flash from his rifle. "We stopped 'em cold. Musta kilt a dozen or more right out in front. Did some get in behind us?"

"Yeah, a few. I think we took care of them all. You got any casualties?"

"Not sure, I'll go check as soon as I silence the last of these mutherfuckers shooting at me."

I spotted the muzzle blast of an enemy soldier, down about fifty feet below the top from us. A green tracer round snapped up past us into the sky. I grabbed a couple of the little grenades I carried and threw them one after the other at the spot where the gunman was hiding. The double *krump! krump!* of their explosions settled the enemy's wagon. He was either dead or gone from that spot. At least, he quit shooting our way.

The fire from the bad guys was dying down, so I called for everyone to cease fire. We had only so much ammo with us, and it had to last. I went with Crowley, checking out the troops while Margier worked on those wounded men he could find. Crowley had four dead and six hurt, but only one serious enough to consider beyond saving. Lieutenant McMurray was at my hole when I arrived.

"Eight KIA and twelve gone, *Dai Uy*. They must have panicked and run down the back side of the hill in the first attack. I wonder where the hell that Spooky is?"

"He'll be here. Keep alert on your flank. The enemy may try and come that way again. Also look out for those MIAs. They may try and get back up here, now that it's quiet."

"Roger, that. See you later, *Dai Uy*."

Pete took off in a crouching shuffle for his hole. I was down a third of my men, and it still was not ten o'clock. If Spooky didn't hurry up, it was gonna be a bit of hell on earth that night.

The sound of an airplane broke through my fear-numbed brain. A voice came over the radio. "Sneaky Six, this is Lima Two-six. We have your strobe in sight. What'd you boys want?"

"Lima Two-six, this is Sneaky Six. Two hundred plus NVA are to my front, due north, from nine to three on the clock. Hose 'em down at fifty meters out from my light. Can you do that?"

"Can do, Sneaky Six. Stay on the horn and make your corrections. Here comes the devil's piss, fire from the sky. Charlie's in for a big hurt tonight."

The night heaven suddenly turned to orange-red fire, and a long arcing stream of hammering hell descended on the unlucky enemy below the lumbering gunship. It was just like the pilot said. It seemed as if a very big, very bad giant was pissing fire down on the unfortunate men. Sparks, ricochets, and debris flew in every direction. It was like listening to a lead hailstorm. The plane made a pass, turned, and made a second. Another offering of fire and hell from the black sky. The pilot called back, a hint of satisfaction in his voice.

"This is Lima Two-six. That ought to give them something to think about. We'll orbit this area for a couple of hours. If you want another hosing, just say the word."

The jungle to our front was silent, save for a few muffled moans like someone had been kicked real hard in his crown jewels. The surviving NVA were headed for safer ground as fast as they could claw through the thick brush. It grew very quiet around our little hilltop.

Before our airborne saviors left us, they came back for two encores, once when we thought we heard some noise to the front like someone was trying to sneak up on us and once just before the gunship had to return to its home base to refuel and resupply its depleted ammo. It poured the remaining rounds all over the area to our front.

"You fellows ever get to Da Nang," I called on the radio, "the drinks are on me. Thanks a whole bunch, Lima Two-six."

I could hear the pilot chuckle. He'd probably heard that pledge before. "No sweat, Sneaky Six. All in a night's work. Good luck to you guys."

The plane's propellers droned away, and the night grew quieter. I checked everything out then moved back to my little hole. Now we just had to wait out the rest of the night, and the extraction choppers would be on their way at first light. Sergeant Margier reported that the badly wounded soldier had died, so I now was at thirteen KIA and twelve missing. I crossed my fingers that would be all. The night dragged on, making up for the fast day before. That way it came out even after twenty-four hours.

The dawn eventually came, and I got the welcome call that the choppers were fifteen minutes out. I had the dead soldiers wrapped in their ponchos and placed at the edge of the LZ. I went to the edge of the hilltop and peered over the side. The ground to the front looked like a scene from the moon. Trees were blown away or completely denuded of branches and leaves. The tremendous amount of fire from Spooky had stripped the area bare for a good three hundred feet in all directions.

I could see several bodies lying crumpled and silent out there. I sent a couple of men to go through their pockets to see if they were carrying anything our military intelligence types could use.

Then I remembered the dead man who had laid so quietly beside me all night. I decided to check him out as well. He was still there, the top of his head blown away, with brains and blood all over his back. I grabbed his arm and rolled him over.

"Good morning," he spoke quite clearly to me.

"Jesus Christ! This sumbitch is still alive," I cried as I opened fire at him with my rifle.

Lieutenant McMurray came running over and grabbed my arm. I guess I was as white as a ghost. "The damned gook was still alive," I stammered out, as I gained control of my senses.

Pete smiled and shook his head. "Naw, *Dai Uy*. He just belched when you moved him. Musta had a gas buildup in his gut during the night." Pete poked at the dead soldier, who looked like he was about Pham's age. "You sure got him now, though. You musta shot him twenty or more times."

I was still shaking as the first chopper flared over the little LZ we had cleared on top of the hill. We pushed in the dead bodies and loaded the living, ten to a bird, until only me, Pete, my radio operator, and a badly wounded Yard, whom Pete had thought was dead until he made one last check, were left on the ground.

The last of the big, black H-34 Choctaw choppers made its approach. The two little Vietnamese pilots seemed tiny in the cockpit of the helicopter, but they maneuvered it right over the clearing and settled down, the huge tires just touching the ground. I jumped on board and pulled the wounded man inside. Pete sat in the door, his feet dangling outside, watching for signs of enemy fire. I moved to find a support for the wounded man as the chopper rose, dipped its nose, and flew forward to pick up air speed.

The hidden NVA machine gunner had waited patiently for a helicopter to get close to his position. He was rewarded when the last one, carrying me and the others, flew right at him. He opened up at the twin white flight helmets of the pilots.

Sensing more than hearing the bullets that chewed up the two men in the cockpit, I glanced up to where the two pilots sat in a raised cockpit that was very hard to reach from the passenger compartment. I saw the blood and gore splashing down the front wall. Instinctively, I started to stand as the chopper dipped and plunged to the left, back toward the hill we had just left. I was thrown against the opposite side of the interior with an impact that drove the wind from my lungs.

Fortunately, we weren't very high and we struck the ground tail first before the heavy chopper slammed counterclockwise into the side of the hill. Again I was smashed against the side of the interior and, for an instant, was too stunned to move. The massive motor screamed insanely as it ran wild, and the chopper blades snapped and tore themselves to pieces against the side of the hill.

I spent a horrifying moment waiting for the ship to explode, but it didn't happen and I forced myself to move. The NVA would be coming on the run to get what was left of us. My radio operator was okay, so I pushed him out the twisted door and gave him the Vietnamese crew chief, who had been knocked unconscious in the crash. There was no sign of Lieutenant McMurray.

I jumped out and started up the hill. I found the wounded striker, thrown up against the shattered trunk of a small tree. He was clearly dead. I motioned for the radio operator to drag him to the top of the hill, while I took the crew chief with me. I was supporting the semiawake crew chief as we scrambled around the nose of the chopper. Both pilots had been chewed to pieces and didn't need any help. Helping the crew chief, I headed for the top myself.

Partway there, I found my young lieutenant's body. He'd been thrown out of the spinning chopper and one of the blades had hit him right in the chest. Damn near every bone in his body was broken. My little Pete, the best friend I had left at CCN, was dead. Grasping his pack strap, I dragged him over the top of the hill to the LZ then took the radio handset and called for one of the departing helicopters to come back for us.

To my relief, the last of the string of black choppers circled and returned, picking the five of us up, just ahead of the advancing NVA soldiers. Three alive, by the grace of God, and two dead. We scrambled in, and the heavily loaded chopper thundered into the air. All the way home, I held Pete's head in my lap. I didn't have any tears for my friend, not yet. But it was all I could to just sit there and not scream like a wounded animal, again and again and again . . .

When Pete had returned from Taipei, the pace of the company training cycle made it impossible for me to listen in on all his adventures while there. But I wish I had, and I hope he's reading this somewhere in the next world, where good soldiers do nothing but laze on a warm, sandy beach, with lovely companions lounging nearby.

Pete, little buddy, my friend. I hope you had a dozen beautiful ladies lying before you, and you left them all dazed and breathless with your studliness. You were a good soldier and a good friend. You deserved the best.

An odd sort of postscript to this story: The day was July 22, 1969. That afternoon, after the debriefings and a hot shower, I sat in the O-club and watched TV newscasts of Neil Armstrong taking the first steps on the moon. The feelings I experienced watching the TV were surreal. I had just spent a hellacious night on an insignificant hilltop, killing my fellow human beings, and the following day watching men moonwalk in the heavens. The incongruity of it all continues to perplex me when I allow myself to think about it.

17

Road Kill
or
Starlight Snipers at Work

The days following Pete's and Pham's deaths were long and bitter for me. I had lost friends before, but not two so special, who died so close together. Our mission to destroy the pipeline was recorded as a glorious victory. We destroyed the line and wiped out a whole slew of NVA soldiers, but the scoreboard totals didn't begin to placate my sense of loss. We turned in a total of one hundred of the enemy KIA to our twenty-eight KIA and missing, so we met the guidelines laid down by the big brass, i.e., more of them than of us. That way, some PR puke could release carefully crafted news briefings claiming we were winning the war. Pete was sent home to be laid to rest before his grieving family. Pham was left in the bush to mix with the earth and return to the dust of his creation.

My only salvation from the devastating guilt was ironically found in the Montagnards themselves. Their strong faith that the dead are reborn in another body comforted me. Their calm acceptance of the loss of so many of their friends was an inspiration. I prayed that their belief held true for my friends Pete and Pham, and that they would have a joyful and long life the next time around. That prayer, mixed with my own Judeo-Christian upbringing, sustained me through the worst days.

I made Lieutenant Lawrence, the 3d Platoon leader, the new XO for the company. He had missed the pipeline raid and was eager to make a good impression on me and the unit. He was tall and lanky, redheaded and freckle-faced. He looked about half his age but was a fine young officer. I sensed that he wanted to get closer to me because he had become my XO, but I stayed as aloof and distant as possible. I had learned a bitter lesson. Make friends and suffer the agony of their loss, or maintain your distance and sleep better at night.

Being an officer in wartime was damn tough. Officers care deeply about their men, yet they have to be willing to send them into the fires of hell when necessary. It wasn't an easy thing to do. At least for me, the less personal attachment I had to my men, the easier it was to overcome their loss. I know Lieutenant Lawrence was disappointed in the way I treated him, especially after seeing the way Pete and I had worked together, but I hope he understood before his time in Nam was over.

To this day, I shy away from close friendships, and I know it has hurt me socially and professionally. And, I doubt if anyone who has not "been there" would truly understand.

I tried to stay busy and, except on rare occasions, I quit going to the club after duty hours. I wrote home more often and rebuilt my stock of in-the-field letters, letters home to my wife or my folks that I wrote in advance, saying little, but making it seem as if I were safe in camp rather than out in the bush with Charlie on my tail. A staff officer would mail one every other day while I was gone. I don't think my wife ever knew when I was out, the plan worked so well. But she must have thought I wrote the most boring letters in the world.

Time was passing by, and I knew I didn't have many more trips across the line left in my tour. My nerves were going, and I was having trouble sleeping at night. The slightest sound would wake me up, shaking and sweaty.

I sucked it up and waited for the next mission, determined that I could make it through a few more. In the meantime, I spent a lot of time retraining the 1st Platoon. It had suffered 50 percent casualties on the pipeline raid and was being refilled with new recruits from Bon Hai. I didn't have the nerve to go up and recruit them myself, so I sent Lieutenant Lawrence.

I nominated Lieutenant Cable to go up to FOB 1 as a launch officer. Through bad luck and illness, he had missed the last two operations involving his platoon and I was afraid that his troops might have lost confidence in him. The unit needed new blood anyway, to start off fresh. The new platoon sergeant would be Sergeant First Class Garrett, and a new junior lieutenant from 5th Group headquarters named Jefferson was made platoon leader. He was a slender, black kid from Chicago, and easy to get along with. His warm brown eyes and chocolate coloring were about the same shade as his Bru troops. I hoped they would get along well with him, and as it turned out, they did. With the experienced Garrett as his platoon sergeant, I didn't worry about the platoon's command.

More time passed, the pain diminished a little more every day, and the war went on. I stayed busy, and continued to count down my days left in country.

"Hey Nick! You hear the news?" One of the S-2 officers stopped me coming out of the supply warehouse, where I'd just had another lesson in Scrabble from Supply Sergeant White.

"What news?"

"Big Momma was going over to Tan An to work in the village clinic. His jeep hit a mine on the road about a mile south of here."

"Jesus, Big Momma. He get hurt?" Big Momma Jackson was the best and kindest and most gentle man I knew in Vietnam. He was the head medic at our little camp hospital and was just about the best non–school educated doctor in the business. He was as big as a house and a solid soldier. Everybody was crazy about him. Coming from a poor family of black sharecroppers in South Carolina, he was a confirmed career soldier. His hands had magical healing powers in them. One soft touch from his big fingers, and the pain just seemed to disappear.

He had gotten the nickname Big Momma because of his motherly concern for the health of those under his care. He was warm and friendly and a genuinely beautiful human being. The Yards were as crazy about him as we Americans, and those he treated in the village clinic owed their good health to his dedication and medical skill.

He spent a lot of his off-duty time working at the little clinic he had started in a fishing village near the far end of the bay. I have always wondered if the black medic played by Percy Rodriguez in John Wayne's movie *The Green Berets* was patterned after Big Momma Jackson.

"Yeah, he's got a broken leg and some other stuff. They took him over to 3d Med Hospital by chopper. He'll probably be medevacked back to the States."

"Damn! He's the best medic we'll ever have. That's sure bad news for us." I glared over toward the village across the shining waters of Da Nang Bay. "God damn the mutherfucker who set that mine. That's about the fifth one someone's hit in the last two months. We're gonna have to get serious and kill the sneaky SOB before someone else gets hurt."

Before that day, it had been Marines or army-supply soldiers who had hit the mines so cleverly planted by our unknown VC saboteur. But he had gotten one of ours. It was time to get serious about ending his little reign of terror.

After the word about Big Momma got out, our CO, Lieutenant Colonel Donahue, called a commanders meeting for later that evening. All of the unit officers were there. "I want some suggestions on getting the bastard who's been putting those mines along the MSR (main supply route). Anything you think might work." Colonel Donahue stood waiting, his jungle fatigues bright green and freshly pressed, showing just how new he was in country.

The ideas offered from his officers all revolved around using the night-vision scopes we had recently received for just that sort of thing. Everybody was fishing for some clever way to get the shooters out along the road, where they could watch with the high-tech devices.

I held up my hand. "I think I might have an idea." The CO nodded and I went up to the map of the area hung on the wall. "Here and here," I pointed to two fingers of forest that jutted out toward the road, which ran smack through large fields of flat, open rice paddies. "These two fingers come down to about three hundred meters of the road. What if B Company goes out on a training mission along this area, and then moves on south about to here, near the village of Coi Hung, and RONs. The next morning, you send the camp trucks to pick us up.

"A couple of days later, we do it again, only this time, we leave a stay-behind ambush in each of these spots. The VC sappers may not be able to resist putting out a mine to get the trucks, which they will expect us to send, just like before. One or both of the stay-behind teams may have a good shot at anyone who tries to dig along the road." I swept my hand across an area of the map. "We'll have the road covered from here, just south of Marble Mountain, to here, near the exit to the village of Tan An."

"What if they put out mines before the first truck convoy?" The question from Major Skelton was a good one.

I shrugged my shoulders. "I don't know. It will just be a gamble that we'll have to take. There's always been a time gap between the mines placed on the road. Usually long enough for the patrols to get careless or discontinued. I am hoping the VC will see the trucks come for us the first time and figure that's what we'd do the second time. Maybe he'd get careless and go for a hit earlier than usual."

We knocked around several other ideas, and the boss made his decision. "Okay, we go with Captain Nicholson's plan. Start your first exercise day after tomorrow, and we'll schedule the second for next Tuesday, providing . . ." he grinned wickedly at me, "providing you don't get your ass blown away the first time."

His closing remarks evaporated any satisfaction I might have felt at the acceptance of my plan. But, I got the men started on the plan to run a two-day exercise starting from the camp and moving south along the road until we reached the end of the cultivated area that was about eight miles farther west of CCN.

We practiced assaults into the woods bordering the cultivated area, marched in a column along the rice paddy berms, and showed anybody watching the typical training activities of a unit. The six big trucks that came for us at the end of the exercise must have seemed an awfully tempting target to any VC skulking around as we rode back to camp. Over a hundred men were packed into the vehicles as they lumbered slowly down the narrow dirt road to CCN.

As we reached the gate to CCN, I ordered my driver to pull over to the side of the road. I watched as the bait rolled into camp, breathing a sigh of relief. We'd made it without hitting any mines, and since I'd been in the lead vehicle, every bump had jarred my clenched buttocks like a hammer blow.

I walked over to the old grandma-san who sold cold drinks from her pushcart and bought a Coke for myself, my driver, and Lieutenant Lawrence. We sat there and enjoyed the cool refreshments while we quietly talked about the makeup of the ambush teams. I knew the next trip would make this one seem like a walk in the park.

I sipped the cool soda as I explained my plan. "I think Garrett and Sergeant Crowley will be one team, and you and I the other. We're the best trained of any of the snipers in the company. Let ell-tees Turin, Jefferson, and First Sergeant Fischer take the rest of the company down to the RON. There are so many of them, I doubt the VC will bother them during the night, so it won't matter that we're not along."

I nodded in agreement with my superior logic. "I think that will work." I squinted into the bright sunlight. I could just make out the heavily wooded, green outline of the first finger thrusting down from the steep slopes of the mountains that surrounded Da Nang. "It won't be fun lying quiet all day and then staying alert all night. There's liable to be bad guys out, and there for damn sure will be more bugs than you'll ever want to meet again. It's a long shot at best. We're more likely to spend a long, uncomfortable night and then go home without a hit, run, or error."

"Yeah, but I want to do it anyway. Please, *Dai Uy.*" The plea in Lawrence's voice reminded me of his disappointment and guilt at missing the pipeline raid, even though it wasn't his fault.

"Okay, we'll do it that way. Get Garrett and Crowley over to the firing range tonight at 2200 hours. We may as well get good zeros on the starlight scopes."

Ray grinned like a kid with a new bike for his birthday. "You betcha, *Dai Uy.* I'll have'em there." He flipped his Coke bottle into the ditch, alongside mine and the driver's, and we headed for the gate and a hot shower and some shut-eye. The old grandma-san's young granddaughter scrambled to retrieve the cast-off bottles. They were worth money in return deposits. The old gal looked to be as poor as a church mouse and needed every penny she could get. She was a fixture along the highway, selling her drinks and smiling at all the Yankees hurrying along the road.

The army's newest toy, the starlight scope, magnified whatever ambient light was available. In the darkest night, you could see two or three hundred yards, and even farther if there was any moon at all.

By midnight, we all were satisfied that we had a good zero on the scopes, which were mounted on Winchester hunting rifles that had been converted to army sniper rifle specifications. That meant a heavy barrel and a very sensitive trigger. We were right on target at four hundred yards and felt comfortable that if we could see anyone, we could hit him.

I reported to the CO that we were ready. "Okay," he nodded. "You go day after tomorrow. I'll have the pickup trucks come into camp before dark on Wednesday. If anybody's watching, the word might get back to our little sapper friends (sapper was what we called the VC mine planters, bombers, sabotage engineers, etc.—among other more descriptive and derogatory nouns). If you see the son of a bitch, you pop his ass good, hear?"

"You got it, Colonel." I headed back to my hootch, satisfied that all was in readiness. It was just like fishing. Cast a little bread on the water and see what comes up to get it. Sleep was a long time coming for me that night. I was definitely about to run out my string. Every night I had to fight harder just to keep from coming down with the shakes.

We moved out early the next morning. I took out one hundred twenty men so I felt confident that nobody would spot the six men in the stay-behind teams. Each team had a Yard radio operator along as well as four modified rifles with bulky, blackened starlight scopes in padded bags.

The men were in good spirits. They hadn't a clue as to what the real reason was for the exercise and thought it was just another field exercise, away from the endless details that are the plague of every soldier in garrison.

We marched here and there, and then we lined up and assaulted the first finger about a mile south of camp. We came back out of the woods and continued on toward the second spot I had picked for an ambush site. These two spots were just far enough apart that a person could split the difference and be safe from either of the two teams, but he would have to be awfully lucky in his choice of location.

In about an hour, we were at the second spot and moved into the trees. When the unit came out on the other side and continued on, Lieutenant Lawrence, myself, and our radio operator stayed in the dense brush, about a hundred yards above the location I had in mind.

"Get comfortable," I whispered. "We'll stay here in the deep cover until dark. Then, we'll move down to the very edge of the tree line." Crawling under a thick bush, I hid the entrance hole I had made. The other two wormed in close by, and we settled down to wait out the day. Soon, the forest animals grew accustomed to us and started up their night melodies. I even dozed a little.

Around dusk, First Sergeant Fischer checked in. He had the rest of the company bivouacked on the outskirts of Coi Hung, about a mile south of where my team was hiding, and everything appeared secure for the night. I whispered my final instructions and clicked off. It was almost time. We wanted to be in position after sundown, but before it got so black that we couldn't locate a good spot to watch the road.

I signaled my comrades, and we slipped out of our cover and sneaked toward the edge of the tree line. There was what I wanted: a downed tree, lying so we could use its trunk for a gun rest and its branches for cover. "Over here. Ray, you set up here. I'll be right beside you. No moving once you get settled. None. Piss where you are. Savvy?"

"Gotcha, *Dai Uy.*" The young officer grinned at me, confident excitement all over his face. I nodded my head and moved to the spot I'd chosen, about ten feet to his left. Youth! There I was, an old man of twenty-eight, shaking my head at the antics of a twenty-three-year-old kid. One aged quickly in Vietnam.

The night grew quiet as we watched and waited. "Ray," I whispered. "Look through your scope, straight ahead. Do you see that mound just off the road?"

I sensed him looking where I had directed. "Got it, *Dai Uy,*" he whispered. "Looks like an old honey pot." The farmers used human waste from their toilets to fertilize their fields. They kept the stuff in big earthen jars we called honey pots. The rumor was that on a night attack, an American soldier dashed across a field and fell headfirst into a filled honey pot and drowned. No matter how many times I heard the story, which was probably as much bullshit as most war stories are, I still shuddered at the thought of such a malodorous death.

"You watch to the right of the pot, and I'll watch to the left. No talking unless you see something."

Ray was smart enough not to even answer, but I could make out his movement as he swung the starlight scope up and down his assigned sector of responsibility. I slowly moved my scope from the field back to the left, toward the lights of Da Nang. The magnified intensity of the scope gave me a tremendous view. The objects were cast in a greenish glow but with an incredible sharpness. If the VC sapper came down to plant his mines in our area, we had him.

All night we watched the road, fighting the desire to sleep and the ever-present bugs that thirsted for our blood. But no VC sapper showed up. I was disappointed, but it was a long shot at best.

As dawn turned our world gray, I whispered over to Ray to get back up the hill to where we had hidden the day before. After dividing up the daylight hours into sentry watches, we settled in and tried to sleep through the hot, humid daylight. The coming night would be our last chance. The trucks would arrive the following morning.

After sundown, we again crept down to our tree location. Lieutenant Turin reported that he'd worked the company all day in assault training and patrol techniques and would stay at a crossroads about four miles from where I was. He had seen nothing of the enemy, which was good; I didn't want my company in a fight and me stuck a couple of miles away from it. The other sniper team had also seen nothing the previous night, and would resume its vigil after dark.

We settled in at the downed tree and started the monotonous scanning of the empty road. About midnight, Ray whispered toward me, "*Dai Uy.* Movement on the road to your right. About three hundred meters from the honey pot. See 'em?"

I swung my rifle to the right. Sure enough, two people coming down the dark road, way out at the edge of the seeing distance on the scope. "Got 'em. Watch 'em close. This late, it has to be someone up to no good."

I swung back to my side of the honey pot. It was all clear. The two coming from the right were the only people we'd seen on the road during dark in two nights.

The two continued on toward us, moving slowly but confidently. "Come on, you sons of bitches," I urged silently. I wanted them close, where we had a very good chance of dropping them. They came on, two men in black pajamas, carrying something in their hands.

"*Dai Uy,*" Lawrence whispered. "That's a shovel one is carrying."

"We got 'em, Ray. Let 'em start to dig before we do any-thing, then we go together. We'll take 'em both out at the same time. Keep breathin' easy. Don't get yourself excited. This is just another job. We don't want to get shaky from hyperventila-tion." You'd have thought I was as calm as a stone, but in fact, it was all I could do to keep from shaking like a leaf. Damn, it was exciting. The two VC were walking right into our zone of fire. Lawrence and I were about to kill the SOBs who had hurt Big Momma and many other Americans. They didn't have the faintest idea we were watching their every move. It was like two condemned men dancing before their executioners.

The road made a slight bend about a hundred meters right of the honey pot. Trucks had chewed up the edge there, and the two sappers had chosen that spot to lay their deadly surprise for the trucks they expected in the morning. They stopped, and one started to dig in the compacted soil of the roadway.

"Ray," I whispered. "it's about three hundred fifty meters from here. Set your sight and aim at the center of mass on the guy to the right. I'll take the one to the left. You got it?"

"Gotcha, *Dai Uy.* I'm ready when you are."

"Okay. I'm gonna count to three. We fire on three. Got it?"

"Roger."

"Ready. One . . . Two . . . Three. *Bam! Bam!* The two hunt-ing rifles went off within a gnat's whisker of simultaneity.

My target, which had been kneeling on the road, threw out his hands and fell face forward in the dirt. Ray's target was standing, and I saw him spin and fall like a dancer who'd lost his balance. The dark greenish figure started to get up, pushing away from the road like a man doing push-ups. His head was arched back, as if he was in great pain.

"Christ! You didn't get him clean. He's getting up. Hit him again, and do it right." I was nearly screaming in my excitement.

Quickly Lawrence jacked another round into the chamber of his rifle and took aim. The second shot hit the VC high in the back, because he jerked up, still supported by his arms, and pitched forward, face down and feet pointed our way.

"That got the bastard," Ray muttered.

I looked at the two silent and still forms. Neither moved. Finally, I scanned the area, and not seeing anyone, called Sergeant Garrett and told him of our success. "Stay in position until morning," I told him, "just in case some more show up. At daylight, come up to the road and catch a ride on the trucks. We'll meet you at the bodies."

"Roger. And way to go, *Dai Uy*."

"Roger, out."

I felt damned good. We'd made a solid hit on two VC mine layers caught in the act. That would be a good deterrent.

The rest of the night passed uneventfully, and as it grew light enough to see, we moved out of our hiding spot and toward the two dead VC.

As we drew closer, something about the bodies disturbed me. Suddenly, Ray gasped in choked voice. "My God, *Dai Uy*. They're women! Oh, God, what have I done?"

I moved to the one I had shot. The bullet had hit her right under her arm and passed through the frail body, killing her instantly. It was the old grandma-san who sold Cokes by the roadside. She must have been a plant of the Viet Cong, reporting on our movements. Ray was standing by his target. The long black hair was matted with dried blood. I rolled her over. It was the young granddaughter, the front of her chest blown away, flesh, blood, and muck all over the dirt where she had lain. Beside her lay a Soviet antitank mine, ready for planting. It would have blown a truck to smithereens, along with most anyone riding in it.

By that time Ray was over by the side of the road, puking his insides out. I fought the same urge myself. Nung, my Yard radio operator, was the calmest of the three of us. "VC dead. No more mines. Good." He nodded, and stood by the bodies, his dark brown face impassive, as if embarrassed by the reaction of the supposedly tough American warriors.

I went to where Ray was sitting, his head between his knees, fighting back tears and nausea. "Nung's right, Larry.

They were VC. They knew the score when they started this. It was their choice. We just did what had to be done."

"Oh, shit, Captain. I've bought Cokes from her a dozen times. I just can't shrug it off. She was an old woman, and the girl isn't sixteen yet."

"I know, but it's done. You can't beat yourself up over it. Remember what they did to Big Momma. Think of the men on our trucks she was trying to kill."

Lawrence looked at me with red-rimmed eyes. "I'll try, but it doesn't help much."

"I know, but accept it and shake it off. I see the trucks coming. Come on, we need to get these two wrapped up in poncho liners."

I reported in to the CO and Major Skelton as soon as we got back. Both were surprised to learn our minelayers' identities.

Donahue shook his head. "Shit, but all sort of crap's gonna hit the fan when the two of them are discovered. We'll have a dozen villagers in here demanding an investigation into the murder of two innocent women by American snipers."

"They won't be found, sir," I answered quietly. Both men looked at me.

"I brought the bodies back with me. I figured we could take them out in the bay and dump 'em. The sharks would take care of the rest, and we could deny ever having anything to do with their disappearance. It would leave a good message without subjecting us to local aggravation."

Lieutenant Colonel Donahue's eyes reflected his distaste with what I was proposing. "Jesus, Captain. Get out of here. I don't want to know anything about anything. Take care of the garbage detail, and keep your fuckin' mouth shut, you hear?"

"Yes, sir."

And I did and we did and they did and nobody ever did. Only the horrible memory of how they looked, lying there on the road, remains with me.

18

Truck Thumpers
or
Take a Life, Give a Life

The tragic night of the roadside kill transformed the once feisty Ray Lawrence. He became a much more solemn person, and began to get smashed at the O-club on a fairly regular basis. The killing of the two women weighed heavily on his mind. On duty he worked hard, doing his job to my satisfaction, but he was no more a virgin as far as the war went. None of the lighthearted fun and games now, just doing his job or drowning his memory in booze.

I tried to help him find comfort for his tormented conscience, telling him over and over that he had done the right thing, but he was slow to recover his composure. Worrying about him made it easier for me to live with what had happened. In convincing him it had been the right thing to do, I convinced myself. The picture of the two of them lying so still and crumpled on the dirt road stuck with me, but the sickening guilt went away, and I suppose that was all I could hope for.

We never heard much of anything about their disappearance from the local villagers. I'm sure questions were asked by someone, but with no physical evidence, and the sure knowledge that someone knew what the old gal was up to, the inquiries were minimal. For everyone else, the two simply were not by the side of the road anymore, and that was that. In the flux of the war, unexplained disappearances were not that uncommon.

After a couple of weeks, the memory became more tolerable, and the war went on. Men came and went, some died, and some lived to return home. B Company took all my work time training the new recruits. I amused myself at night counting the days until my rotation date. A late season typhoon hit the coast, preventing cross-border operations, and the VC stayed quiet, too busy keeping dry. Nothing happened except the camp almost washed away, and everyone's floor was flooded. The bright side was the high surf generated by the weather. The crashing waves were wonderful to play in, and just about everybody got in some intense bodysurfing.

As the rains slackened, B company went on alert as the re-action force for a month. I started watching the field reports coming in from the recon teams in the bush and decided if anything popped this time, I'd go. It would be my last, and after I returned, no matter what the reason, no more trips to the woods. I was getting damn close to my DEROS (date expected return from overseas). Having made the decision was a relief, and I slept a little better for it.

In the hope that a little action would help him deal with his guilt and remorse, I planned to take Lt. Ray Lawrence with me if we did insert. We received an insertion alert within a week.

Major Angle, our briefing officer, passed out some high-altitude infrared photographs of a spot in the jungle. Barely visible was a small cluster of huts outlined by the fires burning inside them.

"The air force sent these over this morning. They were made last night. Look at the circled spots. The small ones are the hot engines of wheeled vehicles. The bigger ones are hootches. The flyboys think it's a motor park, with some as-signed mechanics or guards living nearby in the hootches. This may be the road running up to the place."

I struggled to see what he was describing, but wasn't sure about it. I would have to take the photointerpretation boys' word for it. I passed the pictures around to the rest of my people as Major A continued.

"The bad weather has given the NVA a chance to push

truck traffic south, and there have been several possible sightings to the north of this location in the last forty-eight hours. I want to put a platoon of your troops in at dusk, somewhere about here, north of this park. You'll report any trucks that you spot coming down the road tonight, and sweep the village tomorrow morning. The air force will hit the place at first light tomorrow, and you can check the results. Pick up samples of what the trucks are carrying if you can, and of course, bring back any POWs you happen to come across. Study the map and be at the heliport at 1700 for pickup."

I was concerned about the weather and asked for a three-day forecast. "It's gonna be cloudy, and maybe some rain, but not heavy," the weather NCO from the S-3 shop said. "You'll be able to get in and out if you don't stay too long."

Lieutenant Lawrence, Sergeant Garrett, and myself spent the remainder of the day reviewing the mission and studying the map of the area, which was just southwest of Base Area 910. That's where I spent some time on the ground a couple of months earlier, looking for a suspected bulldozer making a road. I concluded the NVA must have finished the project.

"By God, I'd sure like to get some trucks, wouldn't you, *Dai Uy*?" Garrett was almost beaming at the thought.

"I don't know," I answered. "They might be chock-full of NVA, as mean as junkyard dogs. I wouldn't care too much for that with only thirty people to back me up."

"Naw," Garrett airily replied. "The NVA soldier walks to work. Trucks will have ammo and supplies, not troops inside."

"I sure hope you're right." I pointed at a spot about five klicks north of the suspected truck park. This looks like a good place to land. What do you think, Ray?"

"Looks fine to me, *Dai Uy*."

We picked a reasonable-looking LZ, made our plans, and headed back to the company area to get the men ready. Promptly at 1800 hours, only an hour late, we were on our way. The setting sun outlined the dark clouds above the western horizon in brilliant shades of red and gold. "Red sky at night, sailor's delight," I mumbled to myself as we leaped from the hovering choppers and headed into the bush. It didn't take long for the moisture-covered brush to soak us. Because of the higher altitudes in the mountains of eastern Laos, I knew it was going to be a long and uncomfortable night.

It got cooler, and we all grew more miserable as we thrashed our way in the direction of the unseen road. I was watching the point man in the fading light when he held up his hand and motioned me forward. There it was, a muddy one-laner, carved out of the hillside we were descending, and well hidden by the high trees overhead. Alongside the road was a footpath, and it showed evidence of heavy use, although there weren't any tracks since the last rain, which had probably been the night before.

I put the men in a linear ambush covering about two hundred meters of the road and moved out to check the area for myself. There were no fresh tracks on the road, but that didn't mean much. Certainly, it had been used in the recent past. All we could do was hope that some trucks would come by our ambush that night. I would allow the trucks to pass if there were more than three, and the air force could hit them at the truck park. If three or less, we would ambush them ourselves.

We were in an excellent spot for a hit. The road was cut along the side of a hill too steep for any escape except up or down the road. If we had to fight, they would have to come uphill, and I had the recent memory of the advantage that meant for a defender.

We settled in and tried to stay as dry as possible and warm, both feats impossible for even the best woodsmen among us. As high as we were, the temperature dropped into the low sixties at night. For someone just off the beach at Da Nang, that was cold. All we could do was wrap ourselves up in our ponchos and try to stay dry and warm.

Around 0200, we heard the sound of trucks approaching. Around the bend from the north came four vehicles, driving very slowly, with only a tiny beam of light emitting from heavily masked headlamps to illuminate the way. As they passed us by, I could see the driver and his shotgun rider, both straining to see the road through the dark, misty gloom. When they disappeared around the far curve, I called in the news to Prairie Fire Control. "Looks good for your raid tomorrow. Four juicy trucks just went by, headed for the truck park."

"Roger, Sneaky Six. We'll drop at 0600 tomorrow. Thanks. PF Control out."

I wiggled back into the relative comfort of my poncho, assuming the rest of the night would be quiet, and we'd head out at first light to sweep the bombed-out truck park. I was wrong again.

Around five, just before I gave the "Move out" command, we heard the sound of more trucks headed our way. I strained to see through the gray mist of the foggy, early-morning light. These trucks would never make the truck park before the air raid. I waited, debating what to do. I called Lawrence, with the first squad at the far front of my line of troops. "Ray, can you make out how many?"

"I think it's just four, *Dai Uy*. They must be trying to make it to the truck park before it gets daylight."

"Okay," I decided. "Sergeant Garrett will hit the lead truck with an M-72." That was the army's shoulder-fired antitank rocket. It would hammer the crap out of a thin-skinned vehicle like a truck. "As soon as he does, you take out the last truck. We'll have them trapped on the side of this hill, and maybe can get them all. You copy, Garrett?"

"Got it, *Dai Uy*. I'll take out the lead as soon as he gets even with me. Give 'em hell."

As I watched the lead truck go by, it started to rain. The enemy truck was a fairly new, Russian-made, 2½-ton cargo carrier, almost an exact copy of the 1944 Lend-Lease GMC trucks we sent to the Soviet Union by the thousands. The trip south hadn't been easy; the body was mud-spattered and scratched. The two men in the cab were both concentrating on the road as it was too light for headlights, yet still plenty difficult to see any distance. They never even looked our way.

The first truck rumbled past and then the second. It was just ahead of my location when the lead truck was hit by Garrett's rocket. The impact nearly obliterated the truck's passenger compartment, and the drivers were reduced to hamburger by the hot shrapnel. Lieutenant Lawrence's men blasted the last two trucks, shattering windshields and punching holes in the metal cabs with their rifle fire, but nobody seemed to be shooting at the second truck in line. It drove on, almost as if the driver was so shocked by the carnage going on that he froze.

Swiftly, I took quick aim with my little M-79 Thumper and fired the 40mm grenade at the rear of the truck. It flew inside the canvas-covered cargo area and *kerblam!* the whole truck disappeared in a mushroom of smoke and fire. My target had been filled with 82mm mortar ammunition and 122mm rocket warheads. The explosion ripped through the countryside, scattering dirt and truck for what seemed like miles. The concussion pushed me against the ground like a hard wind slaps paper against a brick wall. Unexploded rounds rained down around us, adding to the general hazard.

The truck was a mangled mass of smoking metal. Greasy black smoke fought upward against the falling rain. I had hoped that the rain would muffle the sound of our attack from the enemy down the road, but the noise of the truck exploding was so loud I was uncertain that could be possible. It was something to behold. We were lucky we were well protected by the trees around us. Shredded scrap from what once had been a truck was flung about everywhere. In the silence, I got to my knees and looked around. The first truck had rammed into the side of the hill, completely blocking the road to any further travel. The second truck was almost gone, the third truck was sitting where it had first been hit, and the last truck in line had run off the road and turned over on its side.

I signaled the men forward. A hasty look ensured that all the occupants of the destroyed vehicles were dead, and none of the trucks would ever carry supplies again. Unfortunately, none of the drivers carried a map showing where their final destination was or where they planned to lay over for the day. That would have been quite a coup to bring back to CCN.

The first truck contained medical supplies, the third was filled with small-arms ammo, and the last truck held spare truck parts, including several new tires and a complete truck engine lying among the jumble of items strewn around the cargo area. The second truck was completely destroyed but for some unexploded mortar rounds strewn about.

Grab a sample from each truck," I called to Lawrence. "Then booby-trap the works. I want to get out of here before anybody comes to investigate the sound of the explosion."

We put trip-wired explosives throughout the cargo of ammo and the truck parts. We used the five-gallon cans of gasoline for the medical supplies. The person who tried to unload anything would set off a bonfire of epic proportions. The booby traps would ensure that none of the supplies would ever be used against us as well as cause major hurts among any salvagers. We left the area satisfied it was a job well done.

A point to note: The trucks were Russian, the ammo was from East Germany, Czechoslovakia, and Hungary, and the medical supplies were Chinese and Swedish. The truck parts were from China, and the rockets were Russian. I wished the suppliers themselves had been driving the trucks instead of hapless conscripts from some village in North Vietnam.

We headed back into the woods and turned south toward the truck park, five or more miles away. As we made our way through the wet brush, the distant noise of the air strike rumbled through the rainy air. The ground shook as five-hundred-pound bombs impacted. The roaring thunder of the jets pulling up from a bomb run was music to our ears. We were in a good mood as we slipped and thrashed our way toward the air strike.

By the time we reached our destination, the planes were gone, and all was still. I looked through the trees at the small cluster of huts and the trucks we had seen the night before. The flyboys had done a good job. The four trucks were all smashed, smoking ruins, and most of the huts were flattened heaps of straw and wood.

We moved cautiously toward the huts, our rifles ready and senses alert. It was all quiet. We found six men, all quite dead, and obviously North Vietnamese in origin. The trucks were burned and shredded, but we didn't get too close. The air force had used CBUs (cluster bombs) to start their little show, scattering numerous little softball-size bomblets about the truck park. When the CBU releases its several hundred bomblets, some do not explode on first contact with the ground. They lie there as sensitive as baby rattlesnakes. The slightest movement could set one off.

The rest of the drivers and the NVA soldiers stationed at the truck park had cut out for parts unknown. I told Lieutenant Lawrence to make a quick search of the hootches, and we'd get out, too, before they brought someone back. While he did that, I called in our findings to Prairie Fire Control and alerted them that we would be calling for extraction as soon as we found a suitable place to make our LZ. The answer was music to my ears. "Roger, Sneaky Six. Good job. Prairie Fire Control standing by to vector in extraction choppers on your orders."

Lieutenant Lawrence came running up to me, excitement all over his face. He grabbed my arm, pulling me in the direction he wanted me to go. "Captain Nick, come quick. We found a woman hiding in a dugout behind that hootch over there." He pulled my arm to hurry me along. "Houmg talked to her. She's the wife of one of the dead men. He was a mechanic, and she came down to be with him. Captain, she's gonna have a baby."

"Probably why she didn't run with the others," I said. "That would have been a sight to see, wouldn't it? A pregnant

VC trying to outrun a jet laying five hundred pounds of hurt on her head."

"No, *Dai Uy*," Lawrence interrupted. "I mean she's having a baby right now. That's why she didn't run. We gotta help her."

We reached the only hut still standing. A young woman was lying on a filthy, cloth mattress, gasping as the contractions hit her. She was dirty, scared, and obviously just minutes away from delivering the little VC she'd been carrying for nine months. It flashed through my mind that she had no business there, the shape she was in. But then maybe she wasn't pregnant when she had arrived.

"Shit. What the hell can we do? We've got to get outta here. The NVA will have someone coming here *mach schnell* to see what happened."

"We just can't leave her, Captain. We can't."

Ray Lawrence was determined to repay fate for his action on the road, and I knew that, short of our physically carrying him away, he was going to help that enemy woman.

"All right, I'll see what we can do. Do you know anything about helpin' a woman have a baby?"

"Jeeze, Captain. I'm not even married." Lawrence's face grew white at the thought. "You got two kids, don't you?"

"Yeah, but I didn't deliver 'em. I just watched, and even then all I looked at was my wife's face, not what was going on down below."

"You can do it, *Dai Uy*. I know you can. What do you want me to do?"

Well, I'd seen enough movies in my time to know the answer to that one. "You get the men out in a defensive perimeter. Put lookouts up and down the road. Then boil me lots of water. I saw a couple of pots out there; the stream is behind the hootch. And send me Houmg. He's older, and probably has several kids of his own. Get to it, Ell-tee. We don't have all day."

Ray rushed out, eager to be helpful. I could hear him

shouting instructions to his soldiers. Houmg stepped through the doorway, clearly doleful about his special assignment. If I'd had left it up to him, he would have slit her throat and beat feet for the LZ. The Montagnards were very practical people.

I went to the side of the girl, who appeared to be barely out of her teens. She was painfully thin and her swollen stomach seemed ready to burst. Her navel was distended, her tummy was so big. Her eyes were red and teary. She was gulping air as fast as she could swallow. Her fear was almost palpable. Who could blame her? She was completely at our mercy. And, a good dose of hate was there, overriding all other emotions. She didn't want me there, but didn't have a clue as to how to get rid of me. I felt like telling her the feeling was mutual, but to what avail?

"Ask her if the water has broken," I instructed Houmg. He rattled off several questions in Vietnamese, faster than I could follow. The woman shook her head, but didn't say anything. Houmg grabbed her arm and asked again, shaking her hard, to emphasize his demands.

She mumbled something and then dissolved in tears at the agony of her contraction.

"She lose water when planes come, *Dai Uy.*"

"Okay, I'm gonna take a look at her. Make sure she holds still." I moved between her legs and pushed up the dirty smocklike gown she was wearing. Gulping, I looked at her genital area. I didn't see any sign of the baby's head yet. I looked up at the woman. Houmg had his big knife pressed against her throat, just daring her to kick me or something. Except for her panting, she was quiet.

One of the Yards brought in the first pot of warm water. It was far from boiling, but was all I had. I took the soap bar from my pack and washed my hands and then, using my handkerchief, washed her stomach and bottom.

I had just finished and looked up, when she let out a yell and some blood trickled from her vagina. I saw the first wet, curly, black hairs of the baby's head as it pushed through the little opening into its new world, like it or not. A world where the inhabitants spent their days fighting one another.

The woman took a couple of deep breaths, and I cupped my hands to catch the head. The next contraction did it. The little head, misshapen and as soft as putty, squirted out. The little face was covered in a white, chalky film. I struggled to keep my stomach down. The shoulders were next. The little body was sort of sideways as it exited the womb. With a squirt of blood and clear fluid, the baby popped into my hands.

I took the wet hankie and wiped his nose and eyes. The little rascal was a junior VC. I held him up by his heels and slapped his bottom. The result was a tiny scream of indignity and rage. Seeing the spot he and his mom were in, I couldn't blame him.

I laid the tiny body, still covered with the white mucus from the womb, on the belly of his mother and tied his umbilical cord with a piece of my bootlace. I cut his link with his mother with my Buck killing knife, whose blade was as sharp as any scalpel. That was the last thing the maker had intended for the steel blade. I remembered how the doctor had rubbed my wife's stomach after the baby came out. It was supposed to help expel the afterbirth. It worked, faster than I expected. The placenta glopped all over my thigh as it squished out. I took my poncho liner and wrapped the little squirt in it. My job done, I gave him to his mother.

She was about half conscious. Her body was drenched with sweat from the exhausting effort of giving birth to the little VC recruit. I wiped her face with the last of the water and looked at the face of my enemy. Her eyes met mine. She didn't look so dangerous and she was already starting to recover from her exertions. I wondered what she would think of the only American that she probably ever saw up close. He had killed her man and delivered their baby. How would the two actions stack up in her opinion of me? For an instant, I think I saw a slight smile in her eyes, but I may have been mistaken.

I gave her my best John Wayne. "Well, little lady. I've gotta git now. Your folks will be along soon. Good luck to you and little junior here." I got to my feet. "Come on, Houmg. Let's get the fuck outta here."

The old Yard gave me a half smile and headed out the door. I always wondered what he told his kids about the day he helped the crazy Americans kill and then birth a VC.

"What was it, Captain?" Lieutenant Lawrence was fairly jumping up and down in excitement just outside the door.

"A boy. Probably already being taught to hate us."

"I don't care," Ray announced. "I'm glad we helped. I feel real good inside right now."

I smiled at the young redhead. "That's swell. Now, what do you say we find someplace to land choppers? I want to get home to CCN and a hot shower."

The smile on his face would have charmed the socks off the most calloused cynic. "That's an affirmative, *Dai Uy*, affirm." Lawrence was on his way to recovery. Maybe in some mixed-up sort of way, we had evened the score for past offenses.

19

Say So Long to Sandy
or
Losing the High-Tech War

There are occurrences in a war which leave profound and permanent impressions on those who experience them. Every soldier experiences them. Some are good, some bad. Some are memories you treasure, and some become nightmares. One such experience had a very definite and life-changing effect on me. It involved me and Sgt. John "Sandy" Sanderson, one of the many young NCOs assigned to CCN as recon team members. Sandy had been in SVN about six months, running recon on Team Blacksnake as the One-one, or second in command, when I took command, and he went to work for me.

He was a fine young soldier, brave and dependable in the bush. When the leadership position on Recon Team Asp became available, I had no trouble agreeing with Sergeant Fischer's recommendation that the twenty-year-old soldier take command of the team. He worked hard, and his team was in first-class condition when they were certified as ready to go. I watched in approval as he led his team of soldiers during the train-up phase of its preparation for field operations. I grew increasingly fond of the young Tennessee soldier, even though I stayed as aloof as possible. The only son of an upstanding Memphis family, his gentle southern style and baby-face good looks made him an easy man to like. He went out of his way to get along with just about everyone.

Sandy had joined the army after two years of college. He had attended the army's instant NCO academy after basic training and then volunteered for Special Forces training. He was the top graduate of his class at the Phase I and Phase II Special Forces NCO courses at Fort Bragg. Of course, Sandy wasn't going to be a career soldier, but he was a damn good soldier just the same, the epitome of the American citizen soldier. I couldn't help but like him far too much.

CCN was doubly blessed by the caliber of the young men who filled its ranks. They were all double volunteers, for SF and then CCN. All were confident and proud of themselves. They may have had doubts about the way we were prosecuting the war, but they accepted their jobs and took gratification in doing them right. The SF units in Vietnam had no trouble with the drugs and blatant insubordination the rest of the army was cursed with by that time in the war. CCN officers could safely sleep at night and confidently go into the field with any of our men without fear of fragging (the deliberate killing of superiors by soldiers from the ranks).

When I considered the quality of the American NCOs we were privileged to command, and add to that the brave and loyal Montagnard strike troopers, I am convinced CCN had the best troops in South Vietnam. I seriously wondered why every officer in the U.S. Army didn't try to get into Command and Control North. I don't remember ever meeting a CCN enlisted man whom I didn't like and respect. I hope I left them with a similar impression.

The night before Sandy took his team into isolation for the first time as team leader, prior to insertion behind the lines, he stopped by my tiny orderly room and invited me to have a drink with him at the NCO club.

"Sure, if you want. I'd be happy to. How about 1930? I should be finished with my paperwork by then."

"That'll be fine, *Dai Uy*. I'll see you then." Sandy smiled and left me to the relentless paper pushing. I barely made the club by the agreed-upon time.

"Hi, Captain. What're you drinkin'?"

"Just beer, thanks. I've sort of taken the vow ever since the camp was overrun last August."

Sandy ordered for me and queried, "Would you like to go out on the patio? It's too nice a night to stay cooped up inside."

I had been behind my desk all day. The little covered patio looked out over Da Nang Bay and at night was as beautiful as any peaceful beach on earth. After the sun came up, it would be a much different story. The daytime view was less inspiring. Then, you saw the polluted gray waters, the smog over Da Nang city, and the numerous ships anchored haphazardly in the shelter of the semicircular bay. Standing solidly at either end of the bay, the two guardians, Monkey Mountain to the north and Marble Mountain to the south, loomed dark and somewhat forbidding.

We sat and sipped our beer, casually talking of inconsequential things for a time, enjoying the gentle swish of waves lapping against the sandy beach beyond the razorwire barricade. Before I realized it, Sandy was really opening up to me, telling me things I never knew of himself. I listened, not sure where this was all leading.

He paused and took a sip of his beer. "I've even got a little girl back home. Her name's Nancy Sue."

"You don't say. Your wife?" I didn't remember that from his personnel file.

"No, my daughter. Her mother and I were going together when I got her . . . well, you know. That was one of the reasons I joined up. I knew I wasn't ready for marriage yet. I sort of planned to make things right when I got home. It really hurt my folks, my knocking up Suzanne like I did."

Sandy flipped the cap off another beer. "I was wrong not to do the right thing, I know that now."

"That's all right. You can make it up when you get back." I was getting a mite uncomfortable with what was going on. It was a job for the chaplain, not me.

"That's why I'm talking with you, Captain. I don't expect to get home. I've made out a new will naming Nancy as my beneficiary. I wrote a letter to my daughter and my folks. I want to leave them with you to take care of for me if I don't get back from this mission. You make sure they get sent to them. Will you do that for me?"

"Hell, what are you talking about? Of course you'll get back. Don't even think otherwise."

Sandy looked out at the dark water. "No, it's not gonna happen. I've had a feeling for some time now that my string has run out. I'll not make it back from this one."

"Well, hell's bells, Sandy. I don't know what to say. You want off the roster for the mission?" I hoped I wasn't hearing that from this kid I liked so much.

"Negative, Captain, I don't want that. It wouldn't matter anyway. I'll go. I've got to. If I was here at camp, or in Saigon, or in the bush, the same thing will happen. If it's gonna happen, it's gonna happen. I'll go with my team. You just promise me you'll take care of this stuff for me if something does happen. You promise?"

"Sure, I will. But dammit, Sandy. Maybe you shouldn't go out if you feel that way. Shit fire, I don't know what to do."

"Don't sweat it, *Dai Uy*. I'll do my job. I just wanted to make sure you know what to do if something happens and I buy the farm."

I shook the hand he offered and spent a few more minutes with him, but I was damned uncomfortable. I tried to reassure him that he'd be okay, but he just nodded, as if humoring me, and stared at the dark water. I don't think he really heard a word I was saying.

Finally, I made my excuses and headed for Major Skelton's desk in the TOC. I respected the veteran officer and wanted his opinion.

"You think he's trying to crap out of the mission?" Major Skelton voiced what was the most logical explanation to Sandy's bizarre prophecy.

"I don't think so, sir. Sergeant Sanderson is a fine NCO. He seemed really sincere to me. I don't know what to think."

"Well, certainly, we can't let a man out of a job every time he gets a bad feeling. I've been scared, and so have you. All you can do is take his letters for him and give them back when he comes in. He'll feel like a fool then and won't pull a stunt like this again."

"I suppose so. I don't mind saying it was eerie, hearing him say it the way he did. Well, thanks, sir. I'd better get some rack time. See ya tomorrow." The major waved me out and returned to the stack of papers on his desk.

A couple of days later, Sandy took out his team, which was assigned the job of planting magnetic sensors along a new stretch of road another team had discovered. If the sensors were placed in the right location, any wheeled vehicles that drove past would set them off, alerting the airborne controllers in the Prairie Fire aircraft to call in an air strike. At least, that was supposed to be the plan. It was one of many high-tech schemes we tried to implement during our watch on the Ho Chi Minh trail.

Sandy's team found the road and placed the sensors along its edge, and then pulled back to its RON site. On the morning of the next day, the team was scheduled to be airlifted out. I went over to the TOC to listen to the extraction on the big radio. Several TOC members were already gathered around. "What's going on?"

One of the intell sergeants looked up at my interruption. "Team Asp is in trouble. They're receiving fire on the LZ. They've called for air support. The choppers are orbiting away from the LZ waiting for it to cool off." That meant the unarmed choppers were hoping the LZ wouldn't be hot before they returned for them.

We all waited anxiously, listening to Sanderson and the airborne controller discussing the requested air strike. After what seemed a long time, but wasn't, the fighter-bombers arrived. They dropped their bombs and agreed to a strafing run along the hillside where the recon team was waiting. The plan was for the air force to knock out the heavy sniper fire, allowing the choppers a chance at getting into the LZ.

The first plane made its initial strafing run, and I heard

Sandy give the corrections for the second plane. It was silent for a few seconds and then, *"Mother of God, pull up! Pull up!"* The airborne controller was going crazy over the airwaves.

"What's wrong?" Our radio operator queried.

The answer from the controller chilled my blood. "The second plane missed his target and strafed the hilltop instead. He strafed the ground where Asp was dug in with his guns on full stroke. Jesus, man, nobody could live through that."

The F-4 Phantom jet was armed with a 20mm Gatling gun as its main armament. The weapon was a deadly device, designed to bring bad hurt on men in the open. I had seen it in action just a few weeks earlier on the hilltop, back in July. I knew what it could do. The men in front of my position that terrible night had been blown to pieces. Just scraps where there had once been a living man. The 20mm shell exploded on impact with the ground, spraying hot shrapnel in all directions. When six thousand of them are coming down every minute, it puts a lot of hurt on anything in its way.

I listened as the extraction choppers carefully returned to the location of the unlucky recon team. The enemy fire was suppressed, and they encountered no resistance during the recovery of the team members. The pilot reported the bad news to those of us standing helplessly beside the radio in anguished anticipation. "Three KIA and three WIA." The entire team had become casualties.

"Roger," came the reply from Covey. "Take 'em direct to III MAF Evac Hospital. I'll try and get a report from the air force. Covey out."

I do believe we would have promptly lynched any air force jet jockey unfortunate enough to be around us at that moment, but in truth, it was just a bad break. After a careful investigation, the air force released an official report, which simply stated that the aim point was unclear, and it was an accident, and they were very sorry, etc., etc.

Meantime, I had three wounded Americans and three dead Yards to worry over. The team One-one had a bad hole in his leg, and Sandy, the team One-zero, was desperately injured, hit in the neck by a bit of shrapnel from an exploding shell. He was unconscious and barely alive.

Early the next morning I drove over to the evac hospital, which was only about a mile up the road. The team's One-one had already been medevacked to Japan, and Sandy had been taken to the hospital ship *Repose*, anchored in the middle of Da Nang harbor. The *Repose* was one of two fully equipped hospital ships serving off the coast of Vietnam. It was as well staffed and equipped as any modern hospital and much closer to the action. Only the very, very seriously injured soldiers ended up on it. It must have been a depressing assignment for the doctors and nurses assigned to the converted passenger liner; they received a relentless stream of mangled and dying young men. That would have been enough to make me go off the deep end.

I spoke with Lieutenant Colonel Donahue the next morning. "I'd like to go out to the *Repose* and see how Sergeant Sanderson's doing."

The old man was agreeable. "I don't suppose it will hurt. Take his mail and anything you think he might need. I'll tell Sergeant White to get the motorboat ready for you after lunch."

"Thanks, Colonel. I hope it'll boost Sandy's morale. He was feeling low before the mission even started."

First Sergeant Fischer and I pointed CCN's little motorboat toward the hospital ship immediately after lunch. The water was smooth and reasonably clear for a change. The hull of the big gray and white ship soon loomed over us. The massive red cross painted on its side was a great bull's-eye to any enemy submarine that might be in the waters. Fortunately, North Vietnam didn't have any submarines. They just had unending columns of brave young men to feed into our grinders.

I asked for Sergeant Sanderson as soon as we climbed on the main deck. A white-suited corpsman took us down into the bowels of the ship to a sick ward and turned us over to a navy nurse, who was boss of the floor. She was dressed in a starched white uniform, white hose, and soft-sole white shoes. Her light brown hair was sort of pinned under a nurses' cap, and except for the tired look on her face with dark circles under her soft brown eyes, she was darned attractive to a horny soldier like me. Thank goodness for angels like her; she had more important things on her mind. She tended the suffering.

"You can only stay a minute, Captain. The sergeant is badly wounded and needs his rest."

"How bad is it?"

"He has a severed spine. Right now, he's paralyzed from the chin down, with just a little feeling in his hands and arms. We'll know more after the swelling in his spine goes down."

"My God. That's awful. Will he get better?"

"Maybe." She smiled at us tiredly. "We'll have to hope so, won't we? Follow me."

She led Fischer and me to a bed at the far end of the ward. The occupant was almost hidden from view by tubes and wires and a portable iron lung noisily pumping air into the still patient. It was Sergeant Sanderson. He was silent and pale, looking weak and helpless in his medical contraption. "Just a minute," she firmly reminded us.

"Hi, Sandy. Glad to see you. How you feeling?" I tried to sound as upbeat as I could in those cheerless surroundings. The tile floor was some shade of blue, and just about everything else was navy gray. The swabbies must have stripped the market of gray paint. Everything they owned seemed to be the same dull shade of gray. The only bright color in the room was the white sheets and bandages covering the occupants of the gray, iron-frame beds. But the ship was cleaner than any place else I ever saw in South Vietnam, and it was cool, thanks to the air-conditioning. The ward was full, about twenty beds, each separated by a cloth screen pulled open to make the room seem less enclosed. The men were all silent, desperately wounded, and mostly dying, I suppose.

Sanderson's eyes opened at my greeting, and he smiled

weakly. His throat and upper chest were covered in bandages, and a tube was inserted in his mouth, so he couldn't answer. But he did blink a greeting in reply.

Fischer and I mumbled some platitudes about hurrying up and getting well. I didn't feel like I was doing much to raise his morale. Finally, we patted his arm and got the hell out of there.

"You'll take good care of our friend, please, Lieutenant Wright," I told the nurse, reading the nametag on her crisp, white uniform.

"We will," she assured us. "He's in a bad way. A lot will depend on how hard he fights to live the next few days." She stopped and took something out of her desk drawer. "You want to see what hit him?"

Into my hand she dropped a tiny sliver of metal, no bigger than a fingernail clipping. "This is what hit Sandy? This little thing?"

She nodded. "It cut his spine nearly in two, right at the third cervical vertebra. Almost seems impossible, doesn't it?"

I dropped the offending sliver of metal back on her desk. "Some of the men like to keep the stuff we take out of them. That's why I've kept it." She put it back in her drawer.

"Please, Lieutenant. Call me at CCN if I can be of any help." I passed her our phone number, and Fischer and I hurried outside. The cloying smell of ether and disinfectant was nauseating me. As we left, I peeked back at Sandy, lying so still in his gray-painted hospital bed. The chest pump wheezing, tubes in his arms and nose, the cardiograph blinking on the table beside him. The *blip, blip* of his heartbeat traced in the green phosphor of the cathode ray tube. *Blip, blip. Blip, blip.* The miracles of medicine working to keep the young soldier alive.

The high technology that had paralyzed him and then allowed him to be rescued from the jungle was now augmented by the high-tech medical equipment that was keeping his lungs pumping and his heart beating. The whole thing was a perfect example of our high-tech approach to that war. We fought, lived, and died by the machines, and our bodies took the pounding meted out so dispassionately by the objects of our creation.

The sun was a welcome sight after the depressing scene in the ward. As we headed back to our camp, I discussed Sandy's condition with Sergeant Fischer. "He'll have to fight off the infections that he'll come down with next," Fischer commented.

"What do you mean?"

"I've seen men paralyzed before. Their lungs and guts get infected real easy, since they're lying so still on their back all the time. Yep, he'll come down with something, you watch and see. That will be his next big hurdle."

The next few days were busy, and I had to put Sandy's plight at the back of my mind. I put off going back out to see him until the weekend. I was anticipating going Sunday afternoon, but got a call Saturday morning from Lieutenant Wright, on the *Repose*. "Sergeant Sanderson has a pneumonia infection in his lungs. He wants to see you. Can you come out today?"

"Sure. I'll be there right after lunch."

"No, come now. He's in bad shape. Don't wait, please."

I headed out on our motorboat. The water was choppy and restless, and the low, dark clouds in the eastern sky promised a storm before the night was over. I got another corpsman to guide me down to the ward. Lieutenant Wright was as crisp and clean as before. But her eyes looked even more tired if that was possible. "Go right in," she instructed me. "He's waiting for you."

I softly hurried over to the bed where my young sergeant lay. The iron lung was still pumping away and the cardiotrace was still blipping on the screen. "Hi, Sandy. How you feelin'?" Wow, was that an original greeting.

He had to whisper around the tube in his mouth, but I got his message. "Don't forget your promise."

I nodded. "Yeah, don't you worry. I'll send the letters and

handle everything. But you won't need me to. The people here tell me you're gonna be just fine. You've got to fight hard and lick this thing, is all."

Sandy whispered and I bent down until my ear was next to his mouth. It sounded as if he asked, "Can you stay with me?"

I nodded and squeezed his arm, hoping I was helping. "Sure, Sergeant. I'll stay with you a while. I've got all day. Let me bring you up to speed on what's happening back at camp."

I sat beside him and started telling him about the comings and goings at CCN. I couldn't tell if he was listening or even heard me, but it made me feel like I was doing something useful. Nurse Wright came in from time to time and looked or touched or gave him a shot of medicine through the tube dripping its contents into his arm.

In the next bed was a burn victim. He was Vietnamese. I didn't know if he was North or South and I didn't want to know. It didn't matter anyway. Two men, desperately hurt, and we were using every high-tech device available to keep them going. I could only pray the machines would do the job.

About five, Sandy's breathing grew markedly shallower. Lieutenant Wright was nervously beside him every few minutes, checking, fiddling, and injecting. Sandy's hand clenched, and I grabbed it with mine. His grip was weak, but I could feel it.

"Hang in there, soldier. You can beat this. Just hang on and fight." Anxiously, I looked for a sign. Did he hear me?

Sandy choked, and I felt a slight squeeze of his hand. I squeezed back, hard. The blipping monitor of his heartbeat went flat. A bell rang, and the nurse rushed to his side, followed shortly by a white-coated doctor. The doctor didn't even acknowledge my presence, he just pushed me out of the way and started to do whatever he did when his patients quit breathing. I stepped back and stumbled to the doorway, fighting the tears that threatened to overflow. I hadn't even had time to say so long before he was gone. White-hot rage coursed through me again, just like when Paul Potter was killed. Too many good kids were being wasted in that meat-grinder of a war.

The bell was silent, and the doctor was putting his stethoscope away. His shoulders sort of slumped, and he said something to Lieutenant Wright. She wrote something on Sandy's chart, and pulled the sheet over his head. Then, she walked around to the heart and lung machines. The line was flat and still. She flipped a couple of switches and shut down the lot of them. High-tech had failed Sandy, and all I could do was say, so long, as two husky corpsmen put his still form on a gurney and wheeled him down the sterile corridor.

"I'm sorry about your friend, Captain." The white-suited nurse was standing beside me. Her voice reflected the weariness and loss she felt. "He was terribly paralyzed. He would have never moved a muscle in his body below his chest for the rest of his life. Maybe it was better this way."

"Maybe, I don't know. All I know is that he had a lot to live for. Now his daughter will never know her father."

I stood on the deck of the USS *Repose*. I don't even know how I got there. I leaned against the railing and looked down at the water below. I fought to keep my guts from spewing out. Revelation washed over me in thunderous waves. Cause and effect are curious comrades. I'd seen worse, done worse, maybe even felt worse, but a tidal wave of comprehension flooded my brain. I finally admitted it to myself. We weren't going to win the war.

Like fog blown away by wind to reveal the sun, bright and shining, I knew. That was it for me. I wasn't going back there, no goddamned way, no siree. A little ol' back-assed country was gonna whip us, as sure as I was standing on a boat in the water. I would resign my commission rather than return again. I was the fifth generation of my family to wear the uniform of our country, and the first to lose, unless you counted my great-granddad on the Confederate side. My relief at the decision was so profound that I knew it was the right choice.

Slowly, I drove the motorboat back to CCN. The shock of losing Sandy and the realization of what I had decided made the trip seem long and slow. I wasn't happy with my vow, just satisfied that for me it was the right thing to do.

I didn't have much of a problem with the antiwar protesters, as long as they fought to influence the politicians to end the war. They made a choice, I made a choice. That was what America was all about. I didn't want them on my case because I chose to honor my oath of allegiance. I knew I'd bop the first one who insulted me when I returned. I had to fulfill my own sense of honor and could not worry about theirs. It was just that I had come to know the war was wrong for me. I couldn't be a part of its continuance any longer. My passion, which at first had been just as fiery in favor of the war as the anti's was against it, had been quenched in the hotter flames of fire and death. It cost too much to fight for no purpose, with no clear goals or vision as to what we wanted to accomplish, no understanding of the price being paid by those doing the dirty work. The butcher's bill was too dear.

Sergeant White helped me pull the boat up on the trailer we had made to haul it back and forth to the supply shed. "How's Sergeant Sanderson, *Dai Uy*?"

"He's dead. Died about thirty minutes ago, just like that." I snapped my fingers. "We lost a fine kid. The machines couldn't keep him alive. Just another high-tech failure in this goddamned high-tech war."

"That's too bad. He was a nice guy. Say, they're serving fresh ice cream at the mess hall tonight. We'd better get our ass in gear, or it'll be all gone before we get there."

20

Marble Mountain Graveyard
or
Time to Go Home

My long-awaited DEROS was getting so close I could almost reach out and touch it. Only two weeks and a day left in country. I decided to celebrate a little early, so on the first Monday in December I took all my company officers to see the Bob Hope show at the big outdoor amphitheater over at the Da Nang Air Base. It was quite a spectacle and gave me a chance to show off a little. I had met Bob and his wife, Delores, on my previous tour in 1966.

Bluffing one of the MPs into believing I was an old friend, I conned my way past the guards to the trailer the performers were using as a dressing room. Bob was real nice and friendly, even though I'm certain he really did not remember me at all, but his wife did.

Delores Hope was a sweet jewel of a person and as natural as spring rain. She acted as a hostess while Bob got ready and then introduced my officers to Bob. Then she arranged for us to sit right in front, right behind the wounded men in wheelchairs from the local hospitals. That was as close to the stage as anyone healthy could get. After the show, we got to talk with Ann-Margret, Rosey Grier, and some of the Golddiggers, a dance group of beautiful young women who performed on several of the popular TV shows back home. My guys were impressed with me! They thought I could do the impossible.

We returned to camp quite enchanted with the afternoon's entertainment, and I was now elevated to the highest level of esteem by my young officers. It meant as much to them that I had gotten them a handshake with a pretty girl as it would have if I had gotten them back from Indian country in one piece.

It was a good way to finish off my tour, alive, unhurt, and admired. Of the five captains I had met on the plane trip from America, over a year past, I was the only one still around. One was KIA, one badly hurt in a jeep accident, and the others medevacked out with combat wounds. All I had was a small scar in my back and an even smaller one on my calf to show for all of Charlie's effort to get me. I took Major Skelton to the club for a beer and got a tacit assurance that I wouldn't go back into the field unless it was the most dire of emergencies. I began to relax and coast home, so to speak. Once again, I was asking too much of Lady Luck. She had one more little hurdle for me to clear before I headed home across the pond to the land of the big PX.

Major Buelher, the S-1, or personnel staff officer, called me to his office and passed the word that a new captain was being assigned to command B Company the following week. I would take a couple of days to turn over the unit and get him broken in. Then I could sit around as a supernumerary until my orders to DEROS arrived. Just like my friend Paul Potter had been doing when I arrived so long ago.

The new officer transferred up from CCC (Command and Control Center), our sister unit to the south. They did their work in Cambodia, as we did in Laos and North Vietnam. He had extended to get a command assignment, but because CCC didn't have a slot available he came north to us. He appeared to be a top-notch officer, and I felt confident giving up B Company to him. He was shorter than me, but solid, and had plenty of self-confidence. He was a Citadel graduate and was ramrod straight about soldiering. He was already in shape for the demands of leadership and anxious to take charge. I was happy my company was getting such a good officer.

We started the cycle of inventorying company property and signing over the unit's accountable items from me to the new CO. I sold my jeep for three hundred dollars and some of the nifty toys that I had so painfully accumulated for three hundred more, so I had money for a first-class vacation when I got home. I gave away to my officers and NCOs what I didn't sell until all I had left was my rifle and the Buck knife I'd carried the entire time I was in country.

The day after, we had the change of command ceremony, and I surrendered my precious B Company to its new commander. Afterward, the CO called me in his office and pinned a couple of medals on me for my scrapbook. Then gave me a surprise I wasn't expecting.

"Nick, we're gonna put a hit on the VC in Marble Mountain. It goes tomorrow at 0800. A and B companies will be air-landed on top, and the troops will work their way down to the ground." The massive mountain, about four hundred meters to the south of our camp, was honeycombed with caves from the marble quarrying that had occurred there before the war. VC were in there all the time, and occasionally took a pot shot at us or the 3d Marine Amtrac Battalion on the far side. Fortunately, for the most part, they stayed quiet, and in return, so did we. When they got too aggressive, we would shoot at the side of the hill or mine the approaches to the place. That was usually enough to keep the occupants of the mountain quiet. There were rumors that the VC had a hospital, resupply storage, and even R & R barracks inside the place.

I never wanted to know bad enough to go find out if the rumors were true or not, and felt like saying so, when Colonel Donahue continued.

"The 3d Marine Amtrac Battalion will surround the base of the mountain and police up anybody that tries to get away. Since you're not tied up with anything, I want you to go over and be my liaison with the Gyrenes. It should be a piece of cake. We'll have four hundred men on the mountain and six hundred surrounding it."

I accepted his casual confidence in the coming operation and left him visualizing the coming glory the little battle would bring. He never got a chance to go over the border so the coming operation would probably be the only combat action he would have a chance to get in on his entire tour.

I'd looked at Marble Mountain many a long hour when I passed the hours as night shift OD (officer of the day). Ten times what we were putting on the mountain wouldn't be enough to cover the numerous cave and cutaway areas of the forbidding rock massif. The mission would probably be a first-class cluster fuck, in my opinion. Suppressing a shudder, I looked up at Marble Mountain as I walked back to my room. I knew I'd have another long and sleepless night in store for me.

I reported to the headquarters of the 3d Amtrac Marines the next morning at 0600 hours. All I had was a pistol, water, and a knife. My intention was to stay well back of the action and simply report by radio to Colonel Donahue what the Marines were up to. I didn't even check out a rifle, since I figured a pistol would be more than enough for what I was going to do. I took old Houmg with me to be my radio operator; the new B Company CO had the services of my old team of bodyguards and radio carriers. Houmg was armed, as always, with a well-used M-16 and his Montagnard knife.

As I drove around the dark mass of the mountain, I prayed the VC would let us come and go in peaceful ignorance. I was damned shaky about the whole scheme and grateful I didn't have to lead the men due to land on top in two hours. The first problem was the size of the chopper force; only five choppers were going to be lifting our troops to the top so it would require several hops to transport everyone there. The element of surprise would be long gone before any action against the enemy commenced.

They would have plenty of time to get ready for us. Any contact on the way down would be initiated by the VC. Just maybe, the VC would fade away and let us thrash around a while. We couldn't stay long, so they could hide out a bit, then walk back in and take over after we left. That's what I crossed my fingers would happen.

Houmg and I reported in to the Marine battalion HQ for briefing by their S-3. Their whole operation rested on the assumption that CCN's landing on top would cause some reaction by the VC inside the mountain. Then the Marines would react to the VC action. Otherwise, squads of men would have to be sent to search the numerous caves and corridors cut throughout the interior of the mountain.

"I don't know, Major," I noted to the Marine staff officer. "Those folks have been using that place for years. It'll be damn hairy, and we'll be at their mercy. At best, they'll just move out and let us blunder around chasing shadows. If they want to be contrary, they'll suck us in, then kick our butts."

The Marine briefing officer countered my objections. "We've covered that in our plans. Our men will have CS grenades and gas masks with them. If the VC hit us, the troops'll pop some tear gas and withdraw. Then we'll flood the area with long-lasting nausea gas. Charlie will be sorry he ever fucked with us, believe me." The confident Marine was too clean and well organized to be anything more than a professional staff office. That in itself was a red flag.

To tell the truth, I'd heard BS like that before, and mostly from the staff desk-warriors who never heard a round crack close by their ear. Charlie was smart, tough, and mean. I doubted whether a little tear gas was going to do him a trick. But, I'd learned the folly of arguing with a determined senior officer; that was like pounding my head against a rock, so I shut up and nodded my seeming acceptance of the current wisdom.

"Whatever you say, Major. I'll join one of your rifle companies during the operation. My orders are to pass on information from our people as they proceed down the mountain." I hurried out of the S-3 shop and fell in with one of the Marine units slowly trudging out of the compound and taking up positions along both sides of the dirt road. At the wave of their commander's hand, they started walking toward the dark mountain, which was just then becoming visible in the early morning light.

The Marine grunts were old hands at that sort of stuff and spoke little while staying ten yards apart as the unit snaked its way down the road. Most of the men carried M-16s, and all had two or three CS grenades hooked somewhere on their web gear. Neither Houmg nor I had brought gas masks since we never anticipated using them. If the Marines did start using the antiriot grenades, we would have to get away as fast as possible or accept the consequences.

We finally reached the base of the mountain and took up positions around the old marble quarry entrance, a cavelike opening many meters across and high. Several trucks could have driven inside the hill at the same time. I stayed well away from the opening and waited for the airborne phase of the operation to start. It was almost 0800, and according to the voice on the radio, the first load of troops was airborne.

I watched as an empty chopper flared off the top of the mountain and rolled right, heading back toward CCN. The first men were on the ground, far above me. I could imagine their anxiety as they waited for the arrival of their comrades. Then a second and a third, until all five choppers had lifted away and rolled overhead, returning to the CCN chopper pad for another load of human cargo. It took over an hour before I was informed that everyone was on the ground and the troops were starting down. So far, they had seen no sign of the enemy. I reported that to the Marine lieutenant colonel who was in charge down at the bottom of the hill. He nodded and returned to his radio, talking to one of the other company commanders among the three Marine units surrounding the base of the mountain. He seemed to be a more field-oriented Marine, with the steadiness of years of command behind him. In his fighting gear, with his helmet and sunglasses on, he was the picture of a fighting Marine officer.

Houmg and I settled down beside an old roadside shrine. It

gave us shade and some cover if any snipers were thinking of plinking away at us. For a couple of hours, it stayed quiet. The reports from the men coming down the hill were always the same: "Negative sign of enemy." I had hopes the men would make it all the way to the bottom without seeing any sign of the enemy.

Around 1000 hours, old Houmg, who was watching the hill while I listened to the radio, pointed up toward the hill. "*Dai Uy*, look."

Shading my eyes, I could see several men rappelling down a rocky slope about five hundred feet above me. They would stop partway down the face and, dangling from their tiny safety lines, poke at openings in the rocky face of the sheer bluff.

I was just about to say something about how exposed they must feel when shots rang out, and the men scooted on down their ropes, disappearing into the trees at the base of the sheer face. "Contact," the radio needlessly informed me. "A Company has been fired upon. There's a casualty. He's fallen off his rappel rope."

"Who was it?" I queried. I was grateful my old unit was on the far side of the mountain.

"Lieutenant Brice. He fell into a rocky crevasse, and his current location is unknown."

"Roger," I replied. "I'll see if we can send some men up to help you look for him." The firing above me had quieted. "Anything further on the contact?"

"Negative. They shot at us from some small openings in the face of the cliff. They must have pulled back. We don't see anything now."

I got on the radio and called the Marine command post. Quickly, I reported what had happened to the CCN troops. The Marine commander made no promise when I asked for men to go look for Brice. "As soon as we've swept the hill, I'll make some available." It was the best I could get from him, even though I wasn't sure that Brice was dead. Later, when we finally found him, it was clear he had been killed instantly, but at the time, I was plenty agitated at the Marine CO. I struggled to control the sharp retort that flashed to my tongue. He was obviously more concerned about his men and their mission than my man.

Rather than get myself into trouble, I slammed the phone into its cradle and stomped away, back to my little spot in the shade of the shrine. Everyone was tense and alert, but nothing more happened until some of our men came out of the trees at the bottom of the hill. I went over to Captain Woods, the A Company commander. I explained what the Marine colonel had said.

Woods was sweaty and tired, but didn't get upset. "That's okay. Sergeant Iverson was still on top of the cliff and saw him fall. He says he can find the spot. I'm sending a recovery team after him now."

"Any chance he's still alive?"

Woods shook his head. "I don't see how. He was right in front of the opening where the VC shot from, and he fell well over a hundred feet into rocks. Goddamned SOBs. Shot him without warning. It was plain murder."

I nodded sympathy, but wondered if Woods thought he'd ever be warned before the enemy opened up on him. This wasn't the Old West or anything, but I understood his feelings. We tended to put a different slant on things when we were the getters, rather than the givers. I went back to my radio. Houmg was signaling that somebody wanted to speak to me. It was the Marine colonel. He wanted to see Captain Woods over at his command position. Woods instructed the men who were going after Lieutenant Brice, and then headed down the road toward the Marine CP (command post).

I went over to the latest group of men to come down the mountain. One of the American sergeants was smoking a cigarette while he relaxed in the shade.

"How was it?" I asked.

He blew a heavy stream of smoke into the hot air. "Rugged.

There's ten thousand little holes all over the damned place. Charlie can come and go at will. We'll never be able to shut him outta here, no matter what we do. We'd have to take cement and cover the whole damn hill solid."

Woods came back from his meeting with the Marine. "The Marines are going to send men into the caves along the base. We're the reaction force if they get into trouble."

"Oh, shit. I knew they would. Those poor grunts are gonna get hammered now, you watch and see."

"Nick, I'm gonna go up and stay with my other two platoons. Do me a favor and take over Brice's platoon here, will you? You make the decision on what to do. I'll call you if we need you for anything." He took off at a trot, leaving me trying to frame a good reason why I couldn't comply with his request.

I watched while numerous heavily armed Marines carefully entered the big hole that was the main opening into Marble Mountain. They moved deeper into the cave, while I brought my platoon up to the entrance and deployed them where they could fire into the huge opening. Then we waited. . . .

It didn't take long for Mr. Charles to react to the uninvited incursion into his stronghold. Echoing throughout the cavernous mountain was the sharp cracking of rifles. The high-pitched *crack* from the M-16 and the deeper *ker-pow* of the AK-47s. Fumes of tear gas stung my eyes, and through their white clouds stumbled the ghostlike silhouettes of men running out of the opening. The VC had done just what I feared. They had waited until the Marines got deep inside, and then opened up on them from hidden nooks and crannies. It was a miracle that most of the men involved got out alive. The tear gas had done what the Marines had hoped. It had given the pinned-down Marine grunts inside a chance to get up and run like hell for the exit and safety.

The Marine captain in charge of the search teams came up to me. "I have a couple of men down inside. I want your folks to cover me while I go after them. My guys are still fighting off the effects of the tear gas."

I had talked with the Marine officer earlier that morning. He was a good guy, and I wanted to help him if I could. "Okay, but we'll have to wait until the CS clears. My men don't have masks." The captain, named Guenther, nodded. He was a fine-looking fellow, as opposed to most Marines, who were usually ugly brutes, at best. At least, compared to us handsome army types. With his tall, well-built frame and dark moustache, à la Clark Gable, he was probably a real lady killer.

Captain Guenther continued. "I've got men KIA in a couple of different passages. The worst one is where I'm headed. I could use your help if you want to come along." He stared at me with the hard question evident in his eyes: "If you have the balls for it, soldier."

Now, I wasn't going to let any Marine outdo me, so of course I agreed. Bad mistake. Wouldn't I ever learn?

In a few minutes, the gas fumes cleared, and we carefully eased our way back into the cave. The lingering smell of the CS gas made our eyes water and our noses sting and run, but not to the point of quitting. Guenther sent one of his lieutenants and some of his men one way and turned down a different dark opening, with me, Houmg, and a couple of Marines right behind him. The rest of my platoon was spread around the inside of the big cave, to cover us as we came out.

Just as we turned a corner, I turned and looked back. The bright opening of the cave beckoned to me. I think I was as scared as I have ever been. A cave is no place to be when bad guys want to shoot at you. The tunnel darkened in a hurry. Guenther turned on his flashlight and we followed its round glow deeper into the bowels of the mountain.

Guenther whispered to me. "My man's right up here. He's dead, I'm pretty sure. Be real quiet. The VC are all over the place."

Well, he sure didn't have to tell me to be quiet. The only

sound I was making was the panicked wheeze of my breath as I tried to fill my lungs with the acrid air. It was utterly silent and pitch black. The menacing gloom of our surroundings pressed down upon me like the mountain itself. The tunnel narrowed. We were forced to crawl on our hands and knees.

Suddenly, by the light from the Marine's flashlight, I saw that the passage in front of us opened up again, and lying there was the still form of the dead Marine. I was third in line, and as the first two stepped out of the constricted passage, the VC opened fire. They were shooting down at us from positions in a big cavern that opened out beyond the tunnel. The flashlight was immediately extinguished, and all we saw was what we could see by the bright muzzle flashes from the rifles. There was quite a bit of light, as everybody seemed to be firing as fast as they could. The total effect was pure chaos. Later, I had a hard time dancing at a disco, the effects of the lights were so similar to what was happening in that cave.

Crawling as fast as I could, I headed for the opening of the tunnel. I didn't have any cover where I was. Bullets screamed around me as the hot lead ricocheted off the rocky surfaces, and the occasional tracer left its fiery red or green glow around the circuit. I don't mind saying I was really terrified by then, but the worst was yet to come.

I had almost reached the exit of the crawl space when I felt a hairy, prickly movement all over my back and head. I'd brushed the top of the tunnel, and it was covered with cave spiders, similar to hairy, oversize daddy longlegs. Several had fallen on me and were running around, doing a very good job of scaring the living hell out of me. I had to clench my teeth to keep from screaming like a madman. I was so terrified, I disregarded the whizzing bullets and jumped up in the tunnel opening into the cavern so I could brush and shake the terrifying creatures off of me.

Of course, the bad guys spotted me in the flashes and turned their guns my way. The splattering of bullets against the wall at my back alerted me to my hazard, and I dove for the cover of a small boulder, about twelve inches high, that I saw out of the corner of my eye. It was all that stood between me and the zipping bullets of the VC. More than one hit it, and bounced away, screaming in frustration at the miss. I was so scared, I couldn't fire back. I just lay there shaking, trying to get control of my terrified body and force it flatter against the rock floor of the cave.

About the time I calmed down enough to breathe without wheezing, the VC pulled back. They didn't want to fight it out to the finish, just convince us to leave them alone. I certainly was convinced. As the firing stopped, Captain Guenther rushed over to his KIA and started pulling the body toward the opening to the tunnel. Houmg turned on his flashlight and shined it upward, toward where the VC had fired at us. That was a very courageous thing to do if they were still there. They were gone, thank goodness, and the reflected light gave us enough vision to get out of there. I had recovered my functions enough to help, so I grabbed hold of the dead man's web gear and together, Captain Guenther and I dragged the limp body back the way we came. I was *very* careful not to touch the top of the tunnel with any part of my body. One go-round with the hairy spiders was enough for me.

To my profound relief, we retreated without any further trouble and soon were outside the cave, watching the other recovery party emerge, carrying a very badly wounded Marine with them. I had a bad case of the shakes and put my hands in my pockets to hide the tremors from the dusty Marine officer beside me. He seemed to take the chaos and terror in stride, increasing my admiration for him.

"Thanks, Nick. That was a close one."

"Yeah," I answered. "I thought for a minute there that we were in our graveyard." I picked up a slab of marble rock and handed it to Houmg. "Hang onto this. I'm gonna have it made into a tombstone." And I did just that. I still have the marble. I had a desk nameplate carved on it by one of the many marble workers that lived around the area. It is in my office.

The CCN search team finally found the body of Lieutenant Brice, and we wrapped up the operation. I doubt if we hurt any of the enemy, but we never knew. The Marines burned a load of long-lasting nausea gas in the opening of the cave complex, and we got the hell out of there. I don't think it made much difference to Charlie. He would just use another entrance until the effects wore off.

I shook hands and said good-bye to Dan Guenther, my brave Marine comrade in the darkness of Marble Mountain. Imagine my surprise and delight when twenty years later, in a checkout line of a store, my brother ran into him. In the course of their conversation, Dan related the story I am telling now and that I had told my brother. We had a great re-union the next spring when I went out to Denver. It generated many memories that had been long forgotten.

That was my last trip out of CCN with guns on. My DEROS day arrived. I made my good-byes and headed off to Cam Ranh Bay to catch a flight home to America. I suffered through the bureaucratic jumble of forms and paperwork, and, finally, it was my turn to go.

I stood outside the receiving room watching the big Pan Am 707 glide in for its landing. The rest of my fellow passengers waited inside the air-conditioned building, but I wanted to savor the sounds, smell, and sight of Vietnam just one more time. I watched the new arrivals filing off the plane, their time in country just the opposite of mine. I thought about the tour I'd just completed. A swirling mixture of emotions fought for dominance.

Pride. I had done what few other men will ever do. Once, when I was young and lean and a mean fighting machine, I had taken men into Indian country, and brought them back. When the bullets cracked past their faces, their eyes turned to me for guidance. I experienced a powerful, almost godlike feeling. They lived or died according to my decisions. I pray I made the right ones, and mostly, I think I did.

Sorrow. I tasted the bitter dregs of regret. The loss of those I had grown to love as only men thrust into the jaws of death can love another man. I flogged myself with guilt. I had lived when so many better men had not. Why was that? Who decided the final roll of the dice? What cosmic force caused them to crap out and not me?

Anger. I felt the blood rush of anger. Anger that we were wasting our time, our money, our sweat, and most important, our blood in a futile conflict that our leaders didn't have the will to win nor the guts to retreat from.

Anticipation. I glowed with an aura of anticipation. I would see my loved ones soon. Could I ever tell them what it was like? Would I ever want to? Mostly, I just wanted the familiar warmth of loved ones surrounding me, scouring away the filth of war from my brain with their TLC. It would help me to be whole again.

Weariness. I was tired. I was worn physically and mentally. War does that to you. You wear down like a cheap windup clock. The emotions dull, and life goes into remote control.

I swallowed against the throat-tightening choke of sadness. A phase of my life was over. I had never felt more alive than when I put it all on the line and stayed whole. I knew I would never come this way again. I knew I would leave the army rather than return to a war nobody back home cared enough about to finish. Which is exactly what I did when they tried to send me back a year later.

I had come to that place proud, confident, sure of my priorities and commitments. I came there trusting in the commands of those appointed over me by virtue of elected office or military rank. I doubted that I would ever again be able to trust so completely someone merely because he was "in power." I would never again ask what I could do for my country without asking why should I? I was returning a far different person and knew my feelings and attitudes had been dramatically changed by my experiences. For better or worse would have to be determined. But forever different.

The door opened, and the men inside started filing out, anxious to get on the "Big Bird Back to the Land of the Free." It was time to load up. I walked under the arch that proclaimed from this side, FAREWELL TO VIETNAM. My head was high. I was only crying on the inside.